Women in Arab society

Women in Arab society

Work patterns and gender relations in Egypt,
Jordan and Sudan

Seteney Shami, Lucine Taminian, Soheir A. Morsy,
Zeinab B. El Bakri, El-Wathig M. Kameir

BERG / UNESCO

First published in 1990 by
Berg Publishers Limited
Editorial Offices:
165 Taber Avenue, Providence, R.I. 02906, USA
150 Cowley Road, Oxford OX4 1JJ, UK
Westermühlstraße 26, 8000 München 5, FRG

and

the United Nations Educational, Scientific and Cultural Organization
7 Place de Fontenoy
75700 Paris, France

Library of Congress Cataloging-in-Publication Data

Women, work and social position in Arab society : case studies from
Egypt, Jordan, and Sudan/Unesco.
  p.   cm.
Includes bibliographical references.
ISBN 0-85496-724-9
  1. Rural women—Employment—Arab countries—Case studies.
2. Rural women—Employment—Egypt—Case studies. 3. Women in
agriculture—Egypt—Case studies. 4. Rural women—Employment-
Jordan—Case studies. 5. Women in agriculture—Jordan—Case
studies. 6. Rural women—Employment—Sudan—Case studies. 7. Women
in agriculture—Sudan—Case studies. I. Unesco.
HD6206.W67   1990   90-39662
305,43' 00962—dc20   CIP

British Library Cataloguing in Publication Data

Women in Arab Society: work patterns and gender relations in Egypt, Jordan
and the Sudan.
1.   Arab countries. Women. Social conditions
305.4209174927
ISBN 0-85496-724-9
     92-3-102655-0   Unesco

Jointly distributed by Berg Publishers and Unesco throughout the world except
for the United Kingdom where Berg has exclusive sales rights.

Printed in Great Britain by
Billing & Sons Ltd, Worcester

Contents

v

Contents

Appendix: Report of the Unesco Regional Working Group on Women's Participation in Public Life in the Arab States Region, organized in co-operation with the Institute of Archaeology and Anthropology, University of Yarmouk (Irbid, Jordan, 13 to 16 December 1986)

vi

List of maps and tables

Maps

Tables

Preface

The impetus for the studies in this book on Jordan, Egypt and Sudan arose from the recommendations of the Unesco Regional Working Group on Women's Participation in Public Life in the Arab States Region organized in co-operation with the Institute of Archaeology and Anthropology, Yarmouk University in Irbid, Jordan, from 13 to 16 December 1986. One of the proposals of this meeting was that Unesco sponsor a cross-cultural research project on the effect of social and economic changes on patterns of women's work and on value systems concerning women's social position, taking into account *inter alia* the impact of the oil economy on the region and on individual countries therein. The Irbid meeting and the follow-up studies presented in this book form part of the activities undertaken by Unesco's Division of Human Rights and Peace, Sector of Social and Human Sciences, in the area of social science research on questions concerning the advancement of women and their participation in economic, scientific and political life. This book is witness to Unesco's continuing co-operation and commitment to working with scholars of different regions in the study of gender relations and of constraints to women's equality in the social and economic life of their societies.

Based on fieldwork, the studies bring to light variations in the forms and types of women's work in a rural and urban context. Gender-based discrimination continues to exist in rural areas and may be accentuated by social and economic changes. Rural peasant women still lack basic rights of access to land and credit, control over the fruits of their labour, the opportunity to benefit from new mechanical instruments of production and the occasion to participate fully in community and public life. In urban areas, although there may be relatively speaking more social and economic services and opportunities, in most cases women still remain disadvantaged compared to men.

However, the picture painted of women is not one of powerless beings. The studies show that women are actively involved in multiple productive and reproductive roles, including managing the subsistence food production of their societies. It is in fact their active role in subsistence agriculture that allows for the release of men into commercial crop production and salaried labour in urban centres of the home country or abroad in other countries of the region. These women, engaged in subsistence family production and seasonal farm labour, as well as the urban women in the squatter community of Amman (Jordan) and in Saganna Town, Khartoum (Sudan) show resourcefulness and demonstrate courage in working out daily and longer-term survival strategies for their families, kin and communities.

Through this book we are able to gain further understanding of the views of these women on their situation and on changes affecting them and their families. It is only when gender relations can be understood from the ground and from the social actors concerned themselves that we have any hope of understanding the complexity of social realities and the impact of change. From such a basis, it may be possible to assess realistically the types of support and positive changes which may be useful to specific communities.

The case-studies in this book, prepared by eminent women scholars of the region, provide a new contribution to social science theory and empirical investigation on the dynamics of gender relations in Arab society. The book will be of interest to policy-makers, the scientific community, universities, women's associations and non-governmental organizations, both regional and international.

It should be noted that the opinions expressed in the studies presented are those of the authors, and do not necessarily reflect the views of Unesco.

Note on contributors

Dr Seteney Shami is an anthropologist and heads the Anthropology Department at the Institute of Archaeology and Anthropology, Yarmouk University in Irbid, Jordan. Her research interests include urban anthropology, ethnicity and Middle Eastern ethnography. She has conducted research among the Circassians in Jordan, focusing on the social history of the community, with a special interest in leadership patterns. She has also conducted a field study on two squatter areas in Amman, with a focus on community organization, household structure and child care. An emerging interest is on settlement patterns in the Middle East and especially the development of social groups in urban centres in an historical perspective. Dr Shami was the national organizer for the Unesco Regional Working Group on Women's Participation in Public Life in the Arab States Region (Irbid, Jordan, 13 to 16 December 1986) convened in co-operation with the Institute of Archaeology and Anthropology, Yarmouk University.

Her recent works include: 'Studying Your Own Society: The Complexities of a Shared Culture', in Sorayya Al-Torki and Camilia El-Solh (eds), *Studying your Own Society: Arab Women in the Field*, Syracuse, NY: Syracuse University Press, 1988; 'Anthropology in Arab Universities', in *Current Anthropology*, Vol. 30, No. 5, Dec. 1989: 649–54; and 'Settlement and Resettlement at UMM Qeis: Spatial Organization and Social Dynamics in a Village in North Jordan', in Jean-Paul Bourdies and Nezar Al Sayyad (eds), *Dwellings, Settlements and Tradition*, New York: University Press of America, 1989.

Ms Lucine Taminian completed an MA in anthropology at the Institute of Archaeology and Anthropology, Yarmouk University in 1988. Her main research interests are social history, study of rural societies with emphasis on land use, forms of labour and female labour participation. For two years (September 1984 to September 1986) she worked as a research assistant for the Amman Urban Upgrading Health and Population Assessment project, directed by Dr Seteney Shami and Dr Leila Bisharat. More recently she participated in a study group on 'land fragmentation and socio-economic classification of clients in the lower Zarga catchment area' commissioned by the Ministry of Agriculture. She is author of the chapter 'House Types and their Socio-Economic Implications: A Case Study of a

Village in the Foothills' in Martha Mundy (ed.) *Settlement Patterns and Social Structure in the Jordan Valley*, Irbid: Publications of the Institute of Archaeology and Anthropology, Yarmouk University (forthcoming).

Dr Soheir A. Morsy is an anthropologist specializing in the study of health systems. She has taught at Michigan State University and the American University in Cairo. Dr Morsy has spent the academic year 1989/90 as Visiting Professor in the Department of Anthropology, University of California. Her research and teaching interests include women's studies. She was recently invited to join the Editorial Board of *The Women and International Development Annual*. Her most recent works include 'Field Work in my Egyptian Homeland: Towards the Demise of Anthropology's Distinctive Other Hegemonic Tradition' in Soraya Al-Torki and Camilia El-Solh (eds), *Studying Your Own Society: Arab Women in the Field*, Syracuse, NY: Syracuse University Press, 1988, and 'The Internationalization of Egyptian Labour: A Note on Social Consequences' in Richard Moench (ed.), *The Sadat Decade in Historical Perspective*, Syracuse, NY: Syracuse University Press (forthcoming). She is currently working on a chapter on 'Political Economy in Medical Anthropology', in Carolyn Sargeant and Thomas Johnson (eds), *Theory and Method in Medical Anthropology*, Westport, Conn: Greenwood Press, in press.

Dr Zeinab Bashir El Bakri and **Dr El-Wathig Kameir** are sociologists and lecturers at the Department of Anthropology and Sociology, University of Khartoum in Sudan. Their research interests range from sociology of urbanization, industrialization and migration to sociological theory and gender issues. They have co-authored a number of studies including 'The Political Participation of Women in Sudan', in *The International Social Science Journal*, Volume XXV, No. 4, 1983, and 'The State of Women's Studies in Sudan', in *Review of African Political Economy*, No. 27, 1984.

Dr El Bakri has been active in developing women's studies in Sudan. She recently initiated a programme of short duration courses on women and development for planners at the University of Khartoum. She is a member of the Association of African Women for Research and Development and sits on the editorial board of the *Sudan Journal of Development Reseach*. The forthcoming book *Third World Women's Struggles*, London: Gower Press includes a chapter by her entitled 'The Sudanese Women's Movement Post-April 1985'.

Introduction

Seteney Shami

At the close of the United Nations' Decade for Women it was concluded that the main obstacles still hindering the advancement of women were firstly tradition, and then the lack of financial resources and political will (Hijab, 1988). Does the work of anthropologists, practitioners of the discipline most concerned with questions of tradition, support this conclusion? The three studies presented in this volume are concerned with examining the position of women in specific contexts, both rural and urban, in three Arab countries: Jordan, Egypt and Sudan. The varieties of experience presented and the changes documented by these studies show that generalizations are not easily reached and that, even within a region affected by common forces and conditions, women's social position and patterns of work vary according to locality, group and class.

The studies show clearly the complexity of factors which help to determine the position of women and assess the impact of regional economic trends and national policies upon women's work and participation in various aspects of social and political life. They avoid schematic model-building and focus instead upon interrelations. Societal values and gender ideologies are shown to play a significant role which should not be under-estimated, but they are articulated differently in concordance with other factors. It becomes clear that the concept of tradition cannot be utilized or applied simplistically. There has to be a clear conceptualization of what this concept comprises: a multiplicity of social values and expectations, but likewise a particular division of labour and strategies for survival within a constantly changing context.

Approached in this way, the study of women constitutes a valid topic not only due to its intrinsic value and interest, but also as a key to understanding economic, cultural and social patterns and formations. The changing position of women within a certain social group or structure can be a sensitive indicator of changes, some quite subtle, in different aspects of society and community.

I. The family and the household

For too long, the approach to women's work in the Arab world has been rigidly quantitative and simplistic in its formulations of what constitutes an 'economic contribution'. The view of women, or men for that matter, as individual actors making decisions that maximize their positions must be replaced by a focus on those units which organize and share in the responsibility of production and reproduction. This is especially true where economic insecurity and institutional instability reinforce the need to diffuse economic risks through group solidarity. These units may vary by place and time, but as the studies in this volume show, the family and the household always play a determining role in terms of decision-making as well as economic organization. The study of the strategies pursued by these units brings to light the complexity of the attempt to place discrete and quantifiable boundaries on women's work and economic roles.

Tracing the changes in the strategies pursued by the household, in which women play an important part both as perpetuators and victims of such strategies, shows clearly the differential impact upon the household of general patterns in the larger economy. One important finding of the three studies is that, especially in rural areas, some 'traditional' patterns and relationships are in fact reinforced by 'modern' forces of labour migration and the intensification of market-oriented production. Therefore the study of women's work – whether urban or rural – must consider their labour in the family and the household as well as their input into sectors of the economy accessible to them. These two spheres may overlap, especially (although not exclusively) in rural areas, where family farms, share-cropping, or even wage labour may involve the whole family, or various members of the household and kin group. The analysis of agrarian transformation in the three studies shows that the modernization and capitalization of agriculture does not eliminate small landholdings and family farms, but may in fact lead to their perpetuation. Therefore the labour of women continues to be determined, both in its nature and scope, by the requirements of family and household. Similarly in urban areas, different members of the same kin group, whether residing in one household or several, may pool their resources and engage in common economic enterprises.

Women's entry into the formal labour force, therefore, can only be understood in relation to the nature of their labour in the domestic group. The decreasing economic importance of that labour to the family, relative to labour outside the family, will facilitate their entry into the formal labour market. The reverse is also true, so that when outside employment does not give returns commensurate with the economic cost resulting from the loss of women's labour to the family, their entry into the labour market will be blocked.

The focus on the family/household, as Rassam (1984a) points out, helps clarify the decision-making process involved in women's participation in the formal labour force, as well as the impact of this participation on their role in the family. On the one hand, women's work is conditioned by the general situation affecting women in society (job opportunities, laws, traditions, past history, education); on the other hand, it is part of the strategies adopted by families and households for coping with the particular economic conditions of their class. This necessarily implies that the study of women's work must take into account, in each community studied, the structure of the family, the domestic group, the kin group and the nature of economic relations within these groups.

The three studies show a common factor in the strategies employed by families in the communities studied, in spite of differing conditions and constraints. This is the attempt to diffuse economic risk through the participation of family members in wide-ranging and varied economic activities involving different sectors of the economy. While men and boys are often in a position to receive the benefits of education and to take advantage of the economically more remunerative activities, women tend to enter the informal sector or become the backbone of subsistence agriculture. In other words, women perform those activities that ensure family survival while men pursue avenues which may lead to family mobility. In some cases, however, where rapid changes in society seem to offer the opportunity for mobility, women do participate in the formal labour market and become a further means of investment and accumulation for the family.

It is clear that women's participation in the labour force cannot be conceived in terms of simple questions and measures of 'increase' and 'decrease'. Rather, women's relationship to the formal labour market is one of constant negotiation conditioned by relative advantage and disadvantage. In the informal sphere and in subsistence activities, however, women are universally active and essential.

II. Women's roles and development

While the investigation of women's economic roles and the relative importance of these roles remains a question of empirical accuracy and conceptual clarity, the assessment of the implications of women's work for their general well-being and 'advancement' is a difficult question, both from the theoretical and moral points of view. It is in this respect perhaps that the investigation of social values and cultural prescriptions becomes essential. An understanding is required of the various components (social, political, economic, ideological and legal) that make up women's role and status. In this way women's roles are not treated as a 'unitary construct' (Quinn, 1977: 182) and simplistic assumptions about changes in these roles due to single factors are avoided, as is the assumption that women's participation in the labour force leads automatically to 'emancipation' (Rassam, 1984a).

Many studies have shown that development favours men and that with the modernization of traditional economies, women are often marginalized in the non-competitive sectors (Quinn, 1977), where conditions of production may worsen and exploitation increase (Keddie, 1979). Alternatively, women may participate in the modernized sector, but only within very limited spheres or 'women's professions' (Quinn, 1977: 185). While these two phenomena are apparent in every society, which of the two processes occurs appears to be a result of a complex combination of rural and urban differences mixed with class factors. As Rassam (1984) points out, the former process often appears to be the fate of poorer urban and rural women, while the latter is open only to those who attain a certain level of education or occupational skill. Such educational and occupational opportunities, in an inequitable society, are often made available only to the privileged classes. However, where the class structure of society is undergoing rapid change, unexpected permutations may occur.

In addition, planned development affects both the class situation of women and their specific roles at the local level, especially those development projects which lead to the restructuring of the local economy and have an impact on the existing forms of labour. In the case of development projects aimed specifically at women, the impact is often ambiguous since development planners may have certain conceptions of the role of women and incorporate these assumptions into their projects. Studies are increasingly conducted to assess the actual situation and needs of the target population. However, projects are often designed, and specific programmes

xvi

implemented, on the basis of the inaccurate premise that women's traditional role in society was not productive and that it is only with 'modernization' that women have begun to take an active role in the society and economy.

The three studies in this volume show that the changes in the economic activities performed by women do not necessarily lead to 'empowerment'. In fact in the rural areas, activities now performed by women which used to be carried out by men, are devalued and considered 'feminine' and hence inferior. Within the family and the kin group, the new roles of women certainly lead to changes in attitude and possible increases in decision-making and authority. However, these changes are never unambiguous and their long-term effects are yet to be seen. In some cases, rather than acquiring new authority, women have lost their earlier ideological and material support structure, which has not yet been replaced.

III. Methodological considerations

The translation of the above considerations and analytical approach into an appropriate research methodology is not a simple matter. The concepts of work, participation and economic contribution must be clarified and treated systematically. Careful definitions are especially important in statistical studies and censuses, as Zurayk (1985) shows in her discussions of how to capture the complex and often ambiguous nature of women's work. As the case-studies show clearly, economic participation and contribution cannot be measured in terms of the hours of labour performed by a woman or by the wages that she earns. While women's hours carrying out specialized and organized work may in fact be increasing in certain sectors and under certain conditions, this does not necessarily mean that women are determining the terms of their participation in the labour market any more than before, or that they are controlling the returns of their labour.

Local-level studies and the thorough investigation of women's work, whether in the formal labour force or not, readily show that national-level surveys often fail to capture the intricacies of women's economic contribution. This, in fact, may apply to men's work as well, and raises a methodological problem related to social class. In the poorer classes, both men and women, within families, have to resort to complicated strategies in order to survive. The questionnaires used in many of the existing studies often seem to have been designed with an ideal type of industrial society in mind, and assume that a person has only one occupation, and a household has only one head and one source of income. Such studies fail to capture the reality of the situation.

These biases may be exacerbated, in the case of studies on women, by the assumption on the part of the designers of questionnaires and the interviewers that women do not contribute to the economy. Questions have to be phrased carefully and in conformity with local concepts and dialects since the people themselves may not apply the term 'work' to economic activities that are conducted within the household or within the family enterprise.

The totality of women's participation in the labour force can only be grasped through complementary data at different levels of abstraction, ranging from national-level surveys to in-depth surveys and anthropological studies. In the case of the Arab world, gaps in the available literature make certain types of analysis difficult. In spite of some welcome contributions to the literature on women in Arab society (Hijab, 1988), studies that locate the experience of women within the regional economic and social structures are not available. The picture of women's work in Arab society is therefore incomplete and vague in its details. It is hoped that the three studies presented in this volume, with their clear indications of differences and similarities between the experience of women in three settings, may present a contribution to furthering our understanding of those factors which are leading to the radical restructuring of women's position in Arab society.

References

HIJAB, NADIA, *Womenpower: the Arab Debate on Women at Work*, Cambridge: Cambridge University Press, 1988

KEDDIE, NIKKI, 'Problems in the Study of Middle Eastern Women', *International Journal of Middle Eastern Studies*, 10, 1979: 225–40

QUINN, NAOMI, 'Anthropological Studies on Women's Status', *Annual Review of Anthropology*, 6, 1977: 181–225

RASSAM, AMAL, 'Introduction: Arab Women: The Status of Research in the Social Sciences and the Status of Women', in Unesco (ed.), *Social Science Research and Women in the Arab World*, London, Dover, NH and Paris: Unesco and Frances Pinter, 1984: 1–13

——, 'Towards a Theoretical Framework for the Study of Women in the Arab World', in Unesco (ed.), *Social Science Research and Women in the Arab World*, London, Dover, NH and Paris: Unesco and Frances Pinter, 1984a: 122–38

ZURAYK, HUDA, 'Women's Economic Participation' in F. Shorter, and H. Zurayk (eds), *Population Factors in Development Planning in the Middle East*, New York and Cairo: The Population Council, 1985: 3–58

1

Women's participation in the Jordanian labour force: A comparison of urban and rural patterns

Seteney Shami and Lucine Taminian

I. Introductory remarks

This study aims to examine the changing patterns of women's participation in the labour force in Jordan. An investigation of these patterns shows definite shifts over time, especially during the past decade or so when the fluctuations in the national economy have been intense. Changes in the regional oil economy, as well as the increase in planned development on the national level, have had a significant impact upon the structure and nature of women's work. An understanding of the ensuing patterns, as well as an assessment of their implications for women's social roles and expectations, requires research and analysis in different areas. In this way, the differential impact of national and regional economic trends on the local level can be clarified.

The bulk of the data presented in this study concerns women in the lowest socio-economic strata of Jordanian society: urban squatters, and rural landless and small landholding peasants. These

We should like to thank all those who made this study possible. Firstly, our gratitude goes to the people in the areas studied for their hospitality and patience. Secondly, a number of institutions extended their facilities and resources, among them the Institute of Archaeology and Anthropology at Yarmouk University, the Urban Development Department and the Jordan Valley Authority. Finally, we thank Sana Kawar for her assistance with the tables in the urban study, Farha Ghannam for her general support and map-drawing, and Shukri Shami for his help in computer graphics and technical advice.

Funding for the field research was provided by grants from Unesco's Division of Human Rights and Peace, Sector of Social and Human Sciences, and from IDRC, Canada.

data are analysed in the context of general trends in Jordan as a whole, in so far as this can be elicited from the available studies and national-level surveys. The study will therefore evaluate the existing literature and analyse the situation of women within social groups that are often disregarded, or least represented, in statistical surveys. Through this comparative approach and the examination of data at different levels the study will explore indications of structural changes rather than simply document temporary shifts in the situation of women in Jordanian society.

A. Women's work in Jordan

It would seem from available data that women's participation in the Jordanian labour force has been increasing in recent decades, reaching 12 per cent in the early 1980s (Masri and Abu Jaber, 1983), or possibly 16.9 per cent (Mujahid, 1985). Some point out that this is higher than in most Arab countries (Owen, 1983). Nevertheless, the female labour force reveals a 'top-heavy' distribution, since those not engaged in agriculture are mostly employed in the services sector with a very small percentage in manufacturing (Mujahid, 1985). This trend has intensified in the past two decades and 65 per cent of working women are now in government employment, of whom 50 per cent are teachers and 15 per cent work in banks (Khasawneh, 1986).

As for the manufacturing sector, one study of female factory workers in Amman shows that this sector attracts young, single women of low education (The Jordanian Institute for Social Services, 1978). Of the sample of 293 women, 51.9 per cent were below the age of 20 and 87.7 per cent were single. A total of 17 per cent were illiterate and 39 per cent had only elementary education. Furthermore, 76.5 per cent were engaged in manual work and poorly paid.

The assessment of women's participation in the agricultural sector is particularly problematic because of the differing definitions of employment and the contradictions between the various studies available (Mujahid, 1985). This makes it difficult to generalize about increasing or decreasing participation in this sector. Mujahid (1985) estimates that 70 per cent of the total female labour force is in agriculture and constitutes 33 per cent of all labour, taking into account both paid and unpaid labour. Of these, only 2.6 per cent are paid and permanent workers, 17.5 per cent are paid and non-permanent, and 79.8 per cent are unpaid.

As for future trends, statistics on education continue to show clear differentiation between men and women both as regards level of educational attainment as well as choices of field of study and training (Masri and Abu Jaber, 1983). This indicates that women's participation in the labour force will continue to be circumscribed by the limits of the education and training made available to them.

The position of women in Jordan is greatly affected by the migration of men to the oil-rich, labour-importing countries, both because of their absence and because of the effect of the remittances sent home (Basson, 1984, 1985). This out-migration has increased significantly since 1973 due to the extremely limited job opportunities within Jordan (Birks and Sinclair, 1980). Migration has been sustained by, and in turn has led to, a rapid increase in educational attainment among the population.

The migration of qualified workers has also resulted in rapid occupational mobility within the country (Birks and Sinclair, 1980). This indicates that migration is affected by, and is itself affecting, the class configuration in Jordan. Not only is the situation of women as a group changing, but so is their class situation as well, as opportunities and access to resources fluctuate, new expectations emerge, and new norms arise that govern behaviour and roles. These fluctuations can result in both increases and decreases in women's participation.

The absence of men should lead to women filling the ensuing gap at home, as Masri and Abu Jaber (1983) point out. Although this seems to have occurred in some Arab countries, such as Yemen (Rassam, 1984a), in Jordan the situation is complicated by replacement migration (Birks and Sinclair, 1980). This, in Jordan, means large numbers of Egyptian and Asian workers, estimated in 1980 at 80,000 (Findlay and Samha, 1985), taking up the vacancies created by absent Jordanian males. This not only impedes the entry of women into vacancies in the labour force, but may in fact displace them from those spheres where they have had high levels of participation in the past. This is a phenomenon that manifests itself clearly in the agricultural sector, but also occurs in urban areas where domestic services are increasingly performed by non-Jordanians.

In the public sector, however, the general policy of the state was to reduce dependency on non-Jordanian labour by providing a better environment for women's employment through legislation and planning (Hijab, 1988). This led to a substantial increase in women's participation in the formal labour force (Masri and Abu Jaber, 1983). The policy of 'integrating women into the development process' and increasing their participation in the labour force was first stated in the National Development Plan of 1975–80. This was to be achieved by promoting female education, organizing special training programmes for women, and establishing child care centres. The policy was also expressed during several conferences and seminars on women, organized by different governmental and non-governmental institutions and in co-operation with UN agencies (see Annotated Bibliography).

Although there are no studies on the relationship between the increase in women's participation and the recruitment of non-Jordanians in the different sectors of the economy, some data are available as an indicator of general policy in the public sector. In 1985, 32.7 per cent of government employees were females and only 6.1 per cent were non-Jordanians (Khasawneh, 1986). Moreover, non-Jordanian labour is usually employed both in the private and public sectors for manual work, and does not therefore compete with women, who are concentrated in clerical and secretarial jobs.

In addition to labour migration, planned development also affects both the class and the particular situation of women. Rural and urban societies have both been greatly transformed by the development projects of international and local agencies. Planned development is a phenomenon also associated with the recent boom, since oil wealth enables states to commit large amounts of resources to such projects. Some development projects aim at improving the results of out-migration, especially those, such as the Jordan Valley Development project, which seek to attract people to employment in agriculture. There are no analyses of the overall impact of planned development on the situation of women in Jordan. The few existing studies aim either at assessing the specific needs of the women targeted, such as education and vocational training (Shuraydeh and Sabbagh, 1985), or evaluating the socio-economic conditions of women recruited into specific income-generating projects without determining the effects of the project under consideration (Harb, 1983; Princess Rahma Development Centre, 1980). Though such projects should pave the way for more female participation, and sometimes do, the effects are complex and varied as the case-studies below will illustrate.

B. The case-studies

Two case-studies will explore the changing patterns of women's work in two very different parts of Jordan. The comparison of these two areas will clarify some of the methodological points raised above, and will indicate the over-simplification common in generalizations about women and their conditions in Jordan. Not only do urban and rural women labour in very different contexts, but national and regional economic changes and development processes also affect them differently.

The common denominator in the two case-studies is the fact that the communities involved represent some of the lowest socio-economic groups in Jordan, and that they have been the target of ambitious development projects funded by national and inter-national agencies. In both case-studies, the historical background and evolution of the community under study will be described, as well as the impact of the development projects. The changing patterns of women's work will be explored, followed by life-histories of selected women in the community. These accounts will illustrate some of the patterns discussed and add the experiential component without which the picture remains abstract and incom-plete.

Throughout, it must be kept in mind that some aspects of the socio-economic conditions studied have undergone considerable transformation as a result of recent economic changes in Jordan. The roots of rapid economic regression could already be discerned in 1984, but its full impact was yet to be felt. Under these new circumstances, return migration and rising unemployment may expel women from the formal labour force. However, the rise in the cost of living may once again compel women to enter spheres of employment that were perceived as unattractive at the time of the research. A comparative study of the same, or similar, commu-nities would further the understanding of the factors determining the conditions and characteristics of women's work.

The rural case-study focuses on an area in the southern Jordan Valley situated on the eastern shore of the Dead Sea (see Map 1.1). There are two villages in this area, al-Mazra'a and al-Haditha, which overlap and which were both affected by irrigation projects of the Jordan Valley Authority (the agency responsible for all aspects of development in the area). Fieldwork in the region was conducted for five months, from June to October 1987, and during January and February 1988. The data collected included the oral history of the area, the changing economic structure and patterns of agriculture in the community (with a special focus on land owner-ship), and the present organization of land-use and agricultural production. Throughout, the focus was on women and their changing conditions.[1]

---

1. This fieldwork was conducted by Lucine Taminian as part of the research for her MA thesis. For a full account, see Taminian (1988). The research was partly

Map 1.1 Ghor al-Mazra'a/al-Haditha and its surroundings

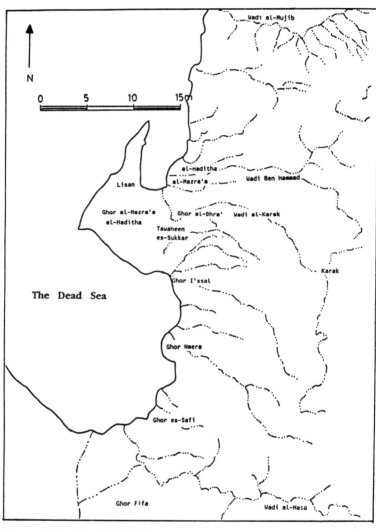

Source: Jordan Maps 1:250,000

funded by a Unesco grant to Dr Seteney Shami and Ms Lucine Taminian for the study of 'Women in the Jordanian Labour Force'.

Since the lands of the two villages overlap, discussion of land ownership and land-use applies to the two villages, whereas the discussion of population and farming activities refers to the village of al-Mazra'a only.

6

The Jordan Valley is one of the most important agricultural areas in the country, due to its fertility and the availability of water for irrigation from the Yarmouk tributary of the Jordan River and winter springs. Although the Valley as a whole has been the target of many surveys and studies, there is a dearth of detailed information on the specific conditions of the peasantry. Irrigation is constantly being expanded, and many resources have been mobilized to develop agriculture in the area, making it an excellent site for studying women's role in agricultural labour and the impact of the modernization of technology on female participation in the labour force.

The urban case-study focuses on two squatter areas located close to the city centre of Amman (see Map 1.2). The eighteen-month anthropological study was conducted from August 1984 until February 1986 and was part of wider research aimed at assessing the impact of a World Bank funded project to upgrade five squatter areas of Amman.[2] The data are extensive: in-depth anthropological data from two of the areas; a detailed baseline survey, conducted in 1981, of the five areas including physical and environmental conditions, household structure and composition, and a health survey of a sample group; and a follow-up survey, conducted in 1985, in four areas assessing changes in the above. In addition, there are the reports of the consulting agencies and individuals involved in various aspects of the project.

The anthropological component of the study focused on household and community structure and the impact of development on both. The effect of women's work on their position and authority in the family was studied, as well as its impact on the domestic economy. Comparative data were collected, since the study was conducted in one site which had been upgraded and another which, although initially surveyed, had been passed over for upgrading. The data collected via the upgrading project add an important dimension to existing information on Amman. Most studies of the city have centred on the problems caused by its rapid expansion. This is certainly a significant phenomenon, since current estimates show that more than 60 per cent of the population of the East Bank

2. This fieldwork was conducted by Seteney Shami and Lucine Taminian as a field assistant. The study formed part of a larger project entitled 'The Amman Follow-Up Health and Population Assessment Project' co-directed by Dr Leila Bisharat (UNICEF) and Dr Seteney Shami (Yarmouk University). The anthropological part of the study was funded by IDRC (Canada) and the assistance of the Urban Development Department (Municipality of Amman) is gratefully acknowledged.

Map 1.2 Location of five squatter areas in Amman

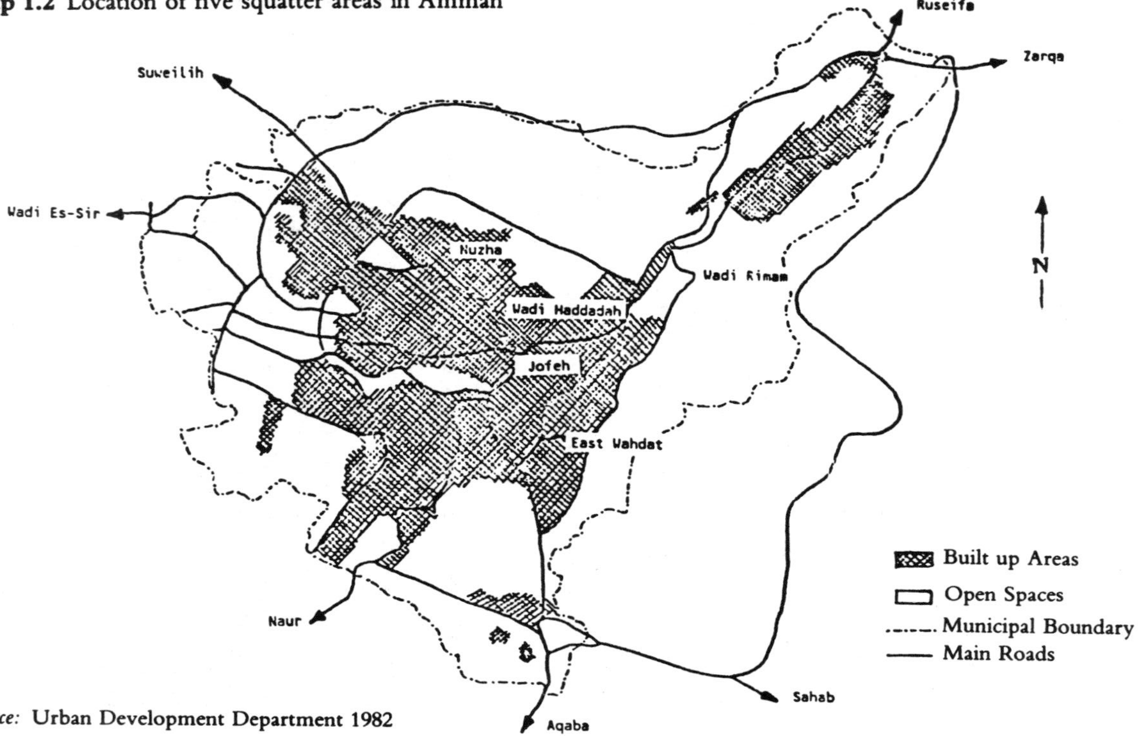

N

Built up Areas
Open Spaces
Municipal Boundary
Main Roads

Zarqa
Ruseifa
Sahab
Aqaba
Naur
Suweilih
Wadi Es-Sir
Wadi Kinam
Wadi Haddadah
Jofeh
East Wahdet
Nuzha

Source: Urban Development Department 1982

live within a radius of 30 km of the city centre (Zagha, 1987). Government directorates were set up to study the characteristics of urban growth and to plan for its future. Most research on Amman has therefore taken place within this context and consequently focuses on such issues as transport, housing and health. Studies of the last two issues do provide some information on women, but since squatter and refugee areas constitute about 25 per cent of households in Amman (Madanat, 1987) the study of such areas and communities illustrates the conditions under which a substantial portion of the population live. Squatter areas represent typical conditions for the urban poor, with the added factor of insecure tenure.

The two case-studies will help clarify the factors determining the conditions of women's work and affecting their entry into the formal labour force. Most existing studies on women in Jordan explore only certain isolated aspects of women's work, and were prepared in the context of specific development projects or as policy statements. Women's work is related in an intimate and complex fashion to national and regional economic trends and policies, and this relation needs to be explored more fully. While this is beyond the scope of the present study, the survey of the current literature and national level surveys and statistical studies (see Annotated Bibliography) may help identify existing gaps and indicate where efforts need to be concentrated.

II. Rural case-study: The southern Jordan Valley

Ghor[3] al-Mazra'a/al-Haditha forms part of the southern Jordan Valley and lies between 400 and 370 m below sea level (see Map 1.1). It comprises around 16,000 *dunums*[4] which are irrigated and included in the Southern Ghor Irrigation Project. Part of this land is highly saline due to its proximity to the Dead Sea, and thus not cultivable without reclamation. The area is irrigated by the waters of three sources: Ain es-Sikkeen, Wadi Ben Hammad and Seil al-Karak. Before the construction of the irrigation project, the waters of Ain es-Sikkeen and Wadi Ben Hammad had been used only to irrigate the lands of Ghor al-Mazra'a/al-Haditha. Seil

---

3. The Jordan rift valley is known as the Ghor. Sections of it are named after villages or their inhabitants. Ghor al-Mazra'a/al-Haditha refers to the land adjacent to the two villages: al-Mazra'a and al-Haditha.
4. A *dunum* is a measure of land equalling 1,000 m^2.

al-Karak had been used to irrigate both this area and the land extending on both sides of Wadi al-Karak, which is 16 km. long. With the introduction in the 1930s of irrigated vegetable farming in the foothills, the amount of water from Seil al-Karak decreased gradually and, by the early 1970s, its waters stopped reaching Ghor al-Mazra'a/al-Haditha. Consequently, the lands that had been irrigated by these waters were not cultivated again until the irrigation project was completed in the winter of 1987/88.

The availability of water resources in Ghor al-Mazra'a/al-Haditha is one of the factors that enabled the formation of a stable agricultural society which has lasted for hundreds of years. The Ottoman records from the late sixteenth century indicate that Ghor al-Mazra'a was inhabited by fourteen families (kin groups) and produced around 2,100 sacks of wheat, 1,200 sacks of barley and 1,000 sacks of corn yearly. The fourteen families together owned 200 goats and 800 buffalo (Hutteroth and Abdulfattah, 1977: 162).

The travel literature reports that Ghor al-Mazra'a/al-Haditha produced all the cereals and livestock it needed, and exchanged surplus production for its other needs. Burckhardt, for example, who visited the area in the 1820s, describes the extensive fields of cereals, corn and tobacco in the area and mentions that the merchants of Karak frequently came to al-Mazra'a to buy tobacco. The importance of the area at that time was due to its location on the route of trade caravans carrying cereals, wool and dairy products from Karak to Hebron and Jerusalem and bringing back clothing, tea and coffee. Burckhardt says that the village of al-Mazra'a was inhabited by around 300 families living under the protection of, and paying tribute to, the Sheikh of Karak (Burckhardt, 1822: 388–91).

Lynch, who visited the area in 1842, corroborates Burckhardt's observations. He also mentions that, besides cereals, corn and tobacco, the people of Ghor al-Mazra'a planted indigo, which was a most valuable crop and marketed in Jerusalem, Hebron and Gaza. Plants were irrigated by spring waters running through mud canals (Lynch, 1849: 342–5). It seems that the prevailing mode of production was agro-pastoral and, in addition to farming, the inhabitants of the area kept large herds which they grazed on the surrounding hills.

As the region was incorporated into the world market in the late nineteenth century, the increase in commercial activity led to an increased demand for agricultural products, especially the cereals produced in the plains of Hauran and Balqa in the north and Karak in the south. The merchants of Nablus and Jerusalem carried these products to the coastal cities of Palestine for export. Because of its location in the far north-east of the projecting Lisan area (see Map 1.1) and because of the abundance of salt on the nearby shores, the village of al-Mazra'a then became a collection point both for salt and the cereals produced in the Karak area. The goods were carried by boat from the eastern shore to the western shore of the Dead Sea, and then transported to the Mediterranean seaports. This attracted merchants to the area and by the 1930s they managed gradually to take over ownership of the fertile irrigated lands and to turn many of the previous landowning peasants into share-croppers cultivating the land for them. These merchants did not invest their money in agriculture, because of the low profit rates compared to commercial investment, but they did encourage a transformation to vegetable production.

The mechanization of agriculture began in the 1950s, when the demand for vegetables increased in the neighbouring Arab markets. Tractors were used in al-Mazra'a for the first time in 1953 when one of the capitalist farmers bought one and used it for ploughing his land and others' lands for hire. Farmers began to use fertilizers and improved seeds and seedlings to raise the productivity of the land and shorten the growing period. Although investment in agriculture increased after 1950 and techniques of production improved, irrigation techniques did not change and the traditional method of open-canal irrigation continued until the Jordan Valley Authority carried out the southern Ghor Irrigation Project in the early 1980s as a part of its development plan.

A. Social groups in Ghor al-Mazra'a/al-Haditha

In the past, the *hamula* was the main social unit in Ghor al-Mazra'a/al-Haditha. The word refers to what may be loosely termed a 'tribe' – a patrilineal kin-group composed of several descent groups. According to the inhabitants of the area, *hamula* refers not only to the number of families with kinship relations, but also includes the families that joined the *hamula* in certain periods. The word *iltifaf* ('winding around' or 'intertwining') is used to refer to the process of joining the *hamula* by gradual incorporation and, as time passes, becoming fully part of it and meeting the same obligations in case of blood feuds. This process was mainly based on labour: the family joining would work for a *hamula* which was in need of additional labour, and in return it would receive protection and land. The new family would intermarry, become part of the *hamula*, and be considered as a branch of the kin-group.

Land was the material basis of the *hamula*. The people of the area

11

relate that at an unspecified time, the land was distributed among the *hamulas* that had participated in the takeover battle against the al-Shatti *hamula* which once cultivated the area. The participating *hamulas* were al-Nawaysheh, al-Ajaleen, al-Awneh, al-Dgheimat and al-Khanazreh. The land was distributed according to the codes or 'laws' of tribal distribution, but each of the first three *hamulas* received an extra share because of their major role in the battle, and within each *hamula* the sheiks (chiefs) were awarded the major share. Each family in the *hamula* was then awarded its share of tribal land.

Social differentiation between *hamulas*, and between the sheik of the *hamula* and its other members, continued until the middle of this century to be based, but not exclusively, on ownership of land and livestock. The religious status of the *hamula* sheik was also a means of gaining a bigger share of land. The al-Ajaleen and al-Awneh, for example, were awarded more land because their sheiks were dervishes and Sufi followers.

With the cadastral surveys and the registration of privately owned land in the 1930s, the *hamula* lost its material basis, but has remained a social unit within which families exchange aid, especially in times of emergency. The residential unit has become the basic social unit and the *hamula* has been transformed into a socio-political organization through which people solve serious disputes and enter municipal elections. Land ownership is no longer the sole material basis of social differentiation between families and households, as education and employment have begun to play an equally important role.

According to the 1987 records of the Malaria Department, of the 4,335 inhabitants of al-Mazra'a village 3,723 live in 451 houses, and 612 in 70 goat-hair tents. The records show that during the past fifteen years the population has been unstable. It has decreased in some years and increased in others, because some families working as share-croppers move from one year, or even one season to another, depending on where they can find work. A family may cultivate its own land, or work on another's land as a share-cropper. Some family members, especially the males, may have other jobs, and family farms depend to a large extent upon the work of women and children while the males seek work in the public or the private sector. A small number of men are regular wage labourers, while seasonal wage labour is confined to unmarried women and widows.

The typical village family tries to find additional sources of income in order not to depend completely on farming. Men leave farming to women and children and seek other employment, preferably in or near al-Mazra'a, in order to be able to assist in agriculture when needed, while at the same time supplementing the family income. If the family is large, then one of the sons may join the army or the civil service if he has twelve or nine years of education, or he may work as a wage labourer in the private sector. The young people prefer the army to the civil service for the privileges which the army provides for the family, such as free medical care, cheap goods from the Military Consumer Corporation, housing loans, and in order to get an early pension. Military pensions require only fifteen years of service, as opposed to thirty years in the civil service. After retiring from the army, they try to find other employment or set up small private enterprises.

The survey of al-Mazra'a showed 556 people working in the public and private sectors (Table 1.1), with 58.8 per cent of the non-agricultural workforce in the civil service and the army. The majority of these are in the army (38.8 per cent). The ninety-seven state employees hold jobs that do not require special education or training, most of them working as messengers or watchmen in state establishments in Karak or al-Mazra'a.

There is also a small number of teachers constituting 2.5 per cent of the non-agricultural labour force. This is the lowest percentage, due to the small number of university and community college graduates in the village. There are seven university graduates, four university students (all of them male) and fifteen community college graduates (four of them female). The very small number of women working outside the agricultural sector is worth noting: eight in the civil service and two teachers. Farming depends to a great extent upon women's work, which limits their educational opportunities. Families do not encourage girls to complete their studies as they are needed for housework or farming, and because work opportunities for women are lacking in al-Mazra'a. Many girls never attend school, and most of those who do leave after the first six or nine years. Between three and six girls complete the secondary education annually.

Table 1.1 also shows the Arab Potash Company to be the second major employer after the army, employing ninety-nine people. Of these, fifty are untenured, with a salary of 90 JD per month[5] and no fringe benefits; forty-nine are tenured, enjoying benefits such as social security, health insurance and two extra months' salary per year. They are either specially trained technicians or truck drivers.

---

5. At the time of the research one Jordanian Dinar (JD) equalled approximately US$3.

Table 1.1 Non-agricultural labour force by sector and sex in al-Mazra'a

Count Row % Col %	State Sector			Private Sector		Labourers		Others		Row Total
	Army	State agencies Employees	Teachers	Potash company	Other companies	Construction labourers	Day labourers	Drivers	Grocery owners	
Male	216	89	12	99	30	15	36	32	17	546
	39.6	16.3	2.2	18.1	5.5	2.7	6.6	5.9	3.1	98.2
	100	94.7	85.7	100	100	100	100	100	100	
Female		8	2							10
		80	20							1.8
		8.3	14.3							
Column Total	216	97	14	99	30	15	36	32	17	556
	38.9	17.4	2.5	17.8	5.4	2.7	6.5	5.8	3.1	100

Source: Field Data and Potash Company Records 1987.

In addition to those working in the public and private sectors, there are fifty-one day labourers who work irregularly. The number of construction workers is small, as families carry out all non-skilled construction work themselves and leave the rest to skilled labourers from Karak. A number of companies also execute major projects in the area and employ dozens of day labourers. These are not included in the table for want of accurate figures. Furthermore, a common family enterprise owns and runs small groceries, the work often being carried out by women and children.

The above-mentioned figures demonstrate the low level of education in the community. Not until the end of the 1970s did schools in al-Mazra'a teach beyond the compulsory stage, that is, the first nine years of school. After this, students who wished to complete their education had to go to Karak. The village people say this made continuing education difficult. The daily trip from al-Mazra'a to Karak and back, the winter clothes needed for Karak's cold winters, and other expenses laid a heavy burden on the family. Some also claim that influential people from Karak prevented too many people from al-Mazra'a joining the army or working in the public sector in order to keep them working for absentee landlords.

B. Development projects

The Jordan Valley development projects first began in the north and then expanded to include the central and southern parts of the Valley. In the early 1960s the East Ghor Canal Project irrigated a major part of the northern Valley. The canal substantially changed agricultural production, as vegetables, fruit trees and banana plantations replaced cereal production. Development projects were halted by the 1967 Arab–Israeli war and its aftermath, but they were reactivated in the Comprehensive Development Plan for the years 1975–82. In the light of this plan, the Jordan Valley Authority was established to supervise development projects.

Following the construction of the East Ghor Canal, a series of temporary laws were promulgated, most significantly in 1962, 1968, and 1973, according to which the land was redistributed among previous landowners and new applicants. Minimum landholding was stipulated at 40 *dunums* and the maximum at 200 *dunums*. Priority for land usufruct was to go first to the farmer who owned and cultivated the land; second, to the full-time farmer who did not own the land; third, to the landowner from outside the Jordan Valley (Khouri, 1981). These laws were later re-issued as the

Jordan Valley Development Law No. 19 of 1988, according to which landownership was confined to the Jordan Valley Authority (JVA) and only the farmer entitled to land usufruct. This meant that he had no right to sell his land, but that his children were entitled to inherit it, in which case they were considered partners in the land. According to the same law, selling and buying was allowed among partners, but at the land value prevailing prior to the implementation of the development project. Moreover, it entitled the JVA to confiscate the land if the farmer failed to meet his obligations.

In the early 1980s the development project expanded to include the southern Jordan Valley, which extends from the north of the Dead Sea to the south of Ghor es-Safi. The project included the construction of retaining walls to prevent soil erosion, irrigation canals and water purification stations as well as desalinization processors. There were 47,000 *dunums* of land included in the project. Landholdings were divided into 30 *dunum* units and distributed according to the same laws applied in the northern Jordan Valley. However, due to the small size of the landholdings of the local farmers in southern Ghor, permission was granted for units to be shared by between two and four farmers. Thus the minimum holding in this area is 7.5 *dunums* and not 30 *dunums* as in other parts of the Valley.

The drip irrigation project connected every unit of land to underground irrigation canals and at the corner of each is a box containing a pump, a water meter and a pressure gauge. Beside this box is a barrel with a filter, in which fertilizers and water are mixed. Each unit owner is obliged to construct a drip irrigation system to a standard design. The Jordan Valley Authority provides loans of 3,000 JD at an interest rate of 7 per cent repayable within six years after production, to enable farmers to cover the high costs of irrigation.

The project also included building schools, medical centres, and housing for teachers and employees from outside the Valley. Residential areas were established and divided into 200–300 m^2 units distributed among the families. Beneficiaries were granted loans of 2,500 JD for each unit at an interest rate of 5 per cent on condition that the house be completed within two years.

Loans granted by the Jordan Valley Authority and other credit institutions have made the farmer dependent upon them. Improving the means of production has raised productivity, but has also raised the cost of production. No study of the project areas in the Jordan Valley is yet available to determine whether profits cover costs. It is, however, noteworthy that the increase in production in the early 1970s coincided with the expansion of external markets and increased demand for vegetables and citrus fruits in the markets of the Arabian Gulf. But the latter markets have been closed to Jordanian produce since the early 1980s, and the lack of alternative outlets has led to lower prices, sometimes falling below the cost of production. Small producers have suffered losses as a result. Large-scale producers probably did not suffer similarly, due to their greater ability to control the market. Farmers of al-Mazra'a/al-Haditha believe that their conditions will worsen when their accumulated loans become due, and some of them are afraid that the JVA will confiscate their lands if they fail to pay.

The project also has an impact on labour requirements and land ownership. It has led to an increase in arable land area to include even the saline lands, in addition to intensifying agriculture through year-long cultivation. It has become possible to produce all kinds of vegetables in different seasons, and this naturally requires production programming so that cultivation of different labour-intensive crops is not taking place simultaneously. Although drip irrigation has reduced the daily working hours necessary for weeding and watering, those during the peak season will remain unchanged until planting and harvesting are mechanized. In the past, the open mud canals needed constant cleaning and supervision during irrigation hours to prevent obstruction, a time-consuming and exhausting process. With drip irrigation the farmer can programme irrigation hours to suit his own schedule.

The land distribution that followed the implementation of the project changed the previous structure of land ownership. As the minimum landholding was stipulated at 7.5 *dunums*, it followed that small landowners owning less than that, and who made up 60 per cent of all local owners in the late 1960s, lost their holdings. The number of local landowners decreased from 628, or 92 per cent of total landowners in the 1960s, to 321, or 78.7 per cent in 1987.

Whereas land distribution has led to the destruction of tiny holdings, known as *shikaras*, it has preserved and perpetuated smallholdings (7.5 *dunums* or more), since the selling and buying of land is forbidden except between partners in a unit. These small-holdings are mostly owned by local farmers and run as family farms, and would probably have disappeared had small farmers been free to sell their land. As for large landholdings exceeding 200 *dunums*, the extra land above the maximum landholding allowed was registered by the landowners in the names of various members of their families and are still run as family holdings. The majority of these are owned by non-local farmers who depend on the work of share-croppers and wage labourers. Thus the development project has perpetuated some family farms, while at the same time generating a demand for wage labour through the substantial changes it has brought about.

C. Women and agricultural labour

Women's role in agriculture is defined by their relation to the land, which has always been men's property. Women's participation in agricultural production is limited to the demands made on their labour, which differs according to forms of land use and the sexual division of labour therein. The decision concerning their participation in production depends on the structure of their household and its source of income.

In the early 1930s, land ownership in Ghor al-Mazra'a/al-Haditha was privatized and made subject to legislation which gave women the right to inherit land. Before that, land was a *hamula* property and possession was limited to male members. Land was thus first registered as men's property, and in spite of the right to land inheritance even today few local women own land and the size of their holdings is very limited. Of the total number of landowners in the late 1960s, thirty-six or 5.3 per cent were women who owned 171 *dunums* or 1.5 per cent of the total land area, the average size of their holding being 4.75 *dunums*. In 1987 the number had increased to forty-nine women or 12 per cent of landowners, possessing 542.5 *dunums*, or 6.3 per cent of the total, the average size of their holding having increased to 11 *dunums* (see Table 1.2).

In addition to these local women landowners, there are absentee women landowners. They are small in number but own considerable property. In the 1960s three of the five large landowners were women. Two were their fathers' sole heirs, and one undertook the reclamation of state property in return for ownership. In 1987 the number of absentee women landowners had reached thirty, owning 1,372.5 *dunums*, or 15.9 per cent of the total land area. Whatever the size of their landholdings, absentee women landowners do not manage the land themselves but either lease it or authorize one of their family members or relatives to manage it for a share of the profits.

The small number of women landowners in al-Mazra'a compared to men (see Table 1.3) is due to the prevailing traditions in the area, which in turn are based on men's control of land. According to these traditions, women should not inherit land even though

Table 1.2 Female landowners in Ghor al-Mazra'a/al-Haditha

	Number of owners*		Area owned** (dunums)		Average size of holdings (dunums)	
	Local	Absentee	Local	Absentee	Local	Absentee
1965	36 5.30%	5 0.70%	171 1.50%	1,213 11%	4.75	242.6
1987	49 12%	30 7.40%	542.5 6.30%	1,372.5 15.90%	11	45.75

* Total landowners = 680 in 1965 and 408 in 1987.
** Total area = 10,993 dunums in 1965 and 8,647 *dunums* in 1987.

Source: The Jordan Valley Authority and Department of Land and Surveys, 1987.

Table 1.3 Male and female landowners 1965/1987 in Ghor al-Mazra'a/al-Haditha

	Number of owners*		Area owned (*dunums*)		Average holdings (*dunums*)	
	Male	Female	Male	Female	Male	Female
1965	639	41	9,609	1,384	15.1	33.7
	94%	6%	87.50%	12.50%		
1987	321	79	6,732	1,915	20.4	24.2
	80.60%	19.40%	77.80%	22.20%		

Source: The Jordan Valley Authority and Department of Land and Surveys, 1987.

the law gives them this right, for a woman is not responsible for her own living. Someone else bears this responsibility, normally her father or brother if she is single, or her husband if she is married. Besides, if she takes her inheritance, after her death 'the land goes to a stranger', that is, her husband or her children, who may belong to another kin-group.

Women know that they have the right to inherit, but they give up this right because, as one woman says: 'I do not want my brothers to get angry with me.' Brothers are traditionally the main resort of their sisters, as is illustrated, for example, by the girl who blamed her widowed mother for not remarrying and bearing a son – a brother – 'to help us face the difficulties of life', or the woman who threatened her husband, who intended to divorce her, with her brothers: 'I have five brothers and their houses are open to welcome me.' (She did not mention her father's house.) Consequently, women prefer to give up their share of inheritance to their brothers. Women are, on the other hand, traditionally allowed to inherit their husband's land, because a widow has lost the man responsible for seeing to her needs. Besides, by inheriting her husband's land, it does not 'go to a stranger' but is kept for his family – his sons. Hence most women landowners in al-Mazra'a are either widows or have no brothers. A few have also inherited their father's land. This explains the increase in the number of women landowners in the late 1980s and may be due to the increasing contribution of women to agricultural labour, especially on the family farm.

Local traditions governing women's right to landownership did not apply to *shikaras*. Even if *shikaras* were owned by men, they remained under women's control in the sense that women farmed them and controlled the products. *Shikara* production was mainly for household consumption, and women's control over it was consistent with their responsibility as mothers and wives.

D. Forms of land use and the changing patterns of women's work

At present land-use in Ghor al-Mazra'a/al-Haditha takes three forms: the family farm, share-cropping and wage labour. The family farm is the prevailing form of land-use, comprising 77.1 per cent of all the holdings and covering 36 per cent of the whole area. These farms are owned by 172 local farmers, eleven of them women. Eighteen of the holdings are worked by share-croppers, two of whom are women. These share-croppers also employ family labour in cultivating their holdings, which is the prevailing form of labour in Ghor al-Mazra'a/al-Haditha. It is employed in 85.2 per cent of the holdings which cover 46 per cent of the cultivated area (see Table 1.4).

Exclusive wage labour occurs on 6.7 per cent of holdings, or 19 per cent of the total area, belonging to capitalist farmers from Karak. Some non-local capitalist farmers prefer to lease part of their holdings to share-croppers, while employing wage labourers on another part, so that should prices fall the share-cropper bears part of the loss. Local capitalist farmers whose owned and rented holdings are too large for their families to cultivate then lease part to share-croppers. Farms using mixed forms of labour, that is wage and family labour, amount to 8.1 per cent of all holdings and cover 35 per cent of the whole area.

1. The family farm   A family farm is where the farmer cultivates land that he owns using his and his family's labour. Family farms differ according to their size, family labour available and capital. A farmer who owns 30 *dunums* of irrigated land may not be able to cultivate it all if his family is small or consists mostly of children, even if he owns the capital. The same is true of a farmer who has enough family labour but insufficient capital. In each case the farmer may rent out part or all of his holding. A farmer with a small holding but a large family and adequate capital may rent more land if family labourers fail to get employment outside the family farm.

The division of labour on the family farm is based on sex and age, but has changed, however, according to type of production and the development of the means of production. When agro-pastoral production prevailed, most agricultural work involved in cereal cultivation (e.g. ploughing and harvesting) was the responsibility of men, while livestock herding was the women's and children's job. The division was not rigid, as women did carry out some agricultural activities: gathering the wheat crop in bundles, carrying them to the threshing floor, shovelling the threshed wheat and packing and storing the crop. Men may also have herded livestock, especially in spring when grazing took the flocks outside the Ghor.

The participation of women in agricultural activities increased with the transformation to vegetable production in the 1930s. Women participated in almost all aspects of production except irrigation, marketing and supervision of the production process, and continued to control the entire production process in small holdings, *shikaras*, where production was for family consumption.

Table 1.4 Land holdings by owner's sex and type of labour in Ghor al-Mazra'a/al-Haditha

Count Row % Col. %	Family labour Number	Area	Wage labour Number	Area	Mixed labour Number	Area	Row Total Number	Area
Male	177 84.3 93.1	3,472.5 44.8 95.4	15 7.1 100	1,507.5 19.5 100	18 8.6 100	2,770 35.7 100	210 94.2	7,750 97.9
Female	13 100 6.9	167.5 100 4.6					13 5.8	167.5 2.1
Column Total	190 85.2	3,640 46	15 6.7	1,507.5 19	18 8.1	2,770 35	223 100	7,917.5 100

Source: Field Data 1987.

The use of modern irrigation techniques greatly reduced the burden of agricultural work both on men and women. Drip irrigation relieved men of the task of opening, closing and cleaning the mud canals. The use of mulch together with drip irrigation minimized the growth of weeds and relieved the women of weeding. Moreover, these improvements made it possible for women to control the production process, including irrigation, which was formerly believed to be too difficult.

The extent of women's participation in the family farm depends on its size and the amount of family labour, as well as outside employment opportunities for males. Where the size of the holding is appropriate to the size of family and outside employment is not available, women's contribution is confined to intensive seasonal labour, while men do all the daily work. When men are working off the farm, women are left in charge of all production processes except marketing, which remains the men's responsibility. The same applies on family farms owned by widows, who run their farms but still depend on a male relative or a neighbouring farmer to market their production. Where there is excess female labour, women work as seasonal wage labourers on other farms.

2. Share-cropping The transformation to commodity production eventually led to the appearance of share-cropping, in which a large landowner uses the family labour of a landless farmer in return for a share of production which varies according to the farmer's contribution. If his contribution is confined to labour only, his share of the production ranges between 25 per cent and 30 per cent of the harvest. If he contributes capital as well, he is considered a full partner, and has the right to participate in organizing the production process as well as earning an extra share.

The trend towards share-cropping was reinforced by the change to vegetable production in the 1930s, especially since this was not accompanied by an improvement in means of production. The cultivation of one *dunum* of vegetables required many more working hours than a *dunum* of cereal, with a consequent increase in the number of share-croppers working in large landholdings. As most of these belonged to merchants from the Karak area, the supervision of the production process was entrusted to small farmers from Karak in return for a share of production. Farm overseers who made enough capital became capitalist farmers in turn, and rented land from the absentee landlord, at first in kind and later in cash.

At present the share-cropping production process involves two parties: the capitalist farmer who supplies the capital and organizes and supervises the production process; and the share-cropper who offers his and his family's labour for 30 per cent of the product. If indebted to the capitalist farmer, he gets only 25 per cent of the harvest.

To avoid debt, a share-cropper tries to find additional sources of income and some family members seek employment outside. As in the case of the family farm, the possibility of outside employment depends to a great extent on the structure and size of the family and the employment opportunities available. However, the share-cropper is limited by the terms set by the capitalist farmer. With-drawing labourers from the family reduces its size and lessens the family's chance of being employed by capitalist farmers, who prefer large families with a number of adult females.

The division of labour on a share-cropping farm, and the extent of women's participation, are similar to those on a family farm. Women may contract with a capitalist farmer as independent share-croppers only if the farmer is a relative. Female share-croppers are either married or widowed (but not necessarily heads of their households) and the size of the holding they cultivate is usually small. Women may share-crop to secure extra income and a steady supply of vegetables for the family, since the farmer who is a relative, unlike the 'stranger', does not object to their taking their daily ration of vegetables from the farm or even to their offering 'vegetable presents' to a sick relative. They may also secure an extra source of income by planting vegetables not produced on the farm on field borders for family consumption and to be distributed to relatives and sold to neighbours. In return, women must give extra help to their kin farmer in the peak season, in addition to their regular work as part of the share-cropping arrangement.

3. Wage labour Wage labour first appeared in Ghor al-Mazra'a/ al-Haditha with the beginning of fruit tree plantations in the late 1930s to which it remained confined, while share-cropping prevailed on land planted with vegetables. With the introduction of mechaniz-ation and the use of modern irrigation in the late 1980s, wage labour began to replace share-cropping, but only to a degree: the fluctuations of vegetable prices resulting from the closure of re-gional markets to Jordanian produce made investment in agricul-ture very risky.

However, the withdrawal of many labourers from agriculture and the consequent reduction in the size of available families has made share-cropping an undesirable option compared to wage labour. In addition, share-cropping is a contract to which the two parties are committed till production is completed, as its termination by either party would impede the production process. Thus, no matter how unsatisfied either may be with working conditions, they do not terminate the contract. Wage labour, on the other hand, does not imply such a contract, and employment can consequently be terminated by either of the parties at any time without impeding production.

In large landholdings where farming demands regular daily labour as well as intensive labour during peak seasons, wage labour takes three different forms: permanent monthly, permanent daily and seasonal. The first depends mainly on Egyptian male labourers, the second on local male labourers and the third on local female labourers. In the first, capitalist farmers prefer Egyptian to local labourers since the former have no social obligations whatsoever and are willing to work day and night, when necessary, for 50 JD per month. Local labourers are reluctant to accept these terms, considering their work for a capitalist farmer as temporary while awaiting a switch to share-cropping or employment in non-agricultural sectors.

Female labourers are employed only during the intensive labour season, because the terms of female labour set by the local community make males better candidates than females. According to social norms, women should not work on a 'stranger's' farm beyond the assigned working hours, even if they are paid for the extra time, and should work in groups of two or more. These conditions are not appropriate to the working conditions on large farms, where permanent wage labourers are employed.

Widows and unmarried women constitute the female wage labour force, as married women are restricted to family labour. Single women prefer wage labour to unpaid work for the family since they can keep some of their wages for themselves; but the decision is not theirs: they are expected to contribute to the family income by working on the family farm while males work outside. However, single women do not consider themselves obliged to work on the family farm if the farm is controlled by a married brother who only partially contributes to the family income.

Given all these changes, farmers in Ghor al-Mazra'a/al-Haditha believe that the introduction of modern irrigation technology has led to the feminization of agriculture, and that men, therefore, must seek employment in the non-agricultural sector. Despite this, men still maintain the right to supervise production generally believing that women are not capable of dealing with irrigation, using insecticides and chemical fertilizers, and marketing.

Open canal irrigation had always been dealt with by men because, it is said, opening, closing and cleaning the mud canals required 'strong backs' and occasional night work. Even though modern technology has made irrigation an easy task requiring nothing more than turning on valves and watching the flow of water in the pipes, men still retain this responsibility that symbolizes their control over the production process and the product. Women are entrusted with the task of fertilizing the soil with manure but not with chemical fertilizers, since the latter involves the use of the metric system, believed to be beyond the understanding of women accustomed to traditional measures. For the same reason women do not prepare insecticides for spraying, and only spray when a hand-pulled and not a back-carried pump is used.

In spite of this, women generally carry out what they believe to be 'male tasks' when they have to, but the majority of farming women being illiterate, they are hesitant to get involved in marketing, as this requires dealing with different marketing agents and bills. Thus, in farming households headed by females, the women controlling the production process usually seek the help of a male relative or neighbouring farmer for the marketing. This does not mean that women have no experience of marketing, since they manage 'house to house marketing' in a direct relationship between producer and consumer where the products were originally produced for local consumption. When women had control over animal and *shikara* produce, in agro-pastoral production prior to the implementation of the project, they used to sell these products, as well as wild herbs, to the households in Karak.

Women's working patterns have changed with the switch from cereal to vegetable production and since the implementation of the development project. Their participation in family labour has increased and they now participate in seasonal wage labour, but the change has not given them control of the whole production process on the family farm. Men still retain control, and even in female-headed households, where the husband is absent and most of the farming activities are carried out by women, the husband still makes the decisions about farming whenever he is present, thus ensuring that he does not lose control over production and can take over if he leaves his job. Hence the saying: 'labour is for women, the product is for men' who control the product not only through their ownership of land, but through the belief that they 'own' their wives as well. As one man put it simply: 'The women are mine, therefore the tomato is mine.'

The new law of land distribution which defines the minimum landholding as 7.5 *dunums* has destroyed the *shikaras* which were cultivated by women as house gardens, the product of which was for domestic consumption with any surplus being given away to relatives or neighbours in return for favours. Today, women control only the produce of their backdoor gardens and the few goats they are allowed to keep near the house. These are kept not only for their products but also to be slaughtered on special occasions such as the birth of a boy, a son's wedding or the roofing of a newly built house. The following life history illustrates the changes in women's work throughout their lives.

E. Life-history: Sa'diyah

Sa'diyah is a twenty-four-year-old widow. She is slim and lively. When she smiles her eyes twinkle and so does her golden tooth. When she talks about her two children and her late husband, her eyes cloud over with tears. 'She is a reliable worker', says her employer: she works hard and urges the other women to do likewise and not waste time in play. The women accept her admonitions and go back to work. Sa'diyah participates in conversation about work, marriage and the future. She also sings: sad songs about death and farewell, happy ones about love and the beloved. She smiles warmly at the flirtation taking place between two workers nearby. She understands it and expresses sympathy but refuses to let their love impede their work. It is true that she is not a *waqqaf*, an overseer, in charge of supervision, but her conscience does not permit her to accept laziness. She believes in earning a *halal* living, an honest one. To her, this means that the work must be commensurate with the pay (eight working hours for 2 JD).

Sa'diyah was born in al-Mazra'a, but does not know the date.

> Before marriage, they took me to the Shari'a judge for an 'age-estimation certificate'. I remember that I was about thirteen years old at the time, but, upon the request of my parents, the judge issued a certificate saying that I was sixteen so that my marriage would be legal. My parents are peasants, my father is from al-Mazra'a and my mother from es-Safi. They met on a farm in es-Safi, where they both used to work, my father as a share-cropper and my mother as a day labourer.

Sa'diyah is the third child of a family with eight children, five boys and three girls. The boys were sent to school but the girls worked on the farm from childhood. The first two children, Sabri and Raja, completed middle high-school and then started to help the family in farming. Sa'diyah was the eldest of the girls and therefore bore the greatest share of responsibility for work, starting at seven. She learned to carry loads on her head. She used to carry a tin of water for a kilometre from the spring to their tent, gather firewood and carry it twice as far, all the way from the Dhra' area to the Muthalath area in al-Mazra'a where her family lived. She learned how to gather tomatoes and other vegetables. At the age of nine she began to herd the family's livestock, taking the flocks to graze in the thick *heesha* bushes near the Dead Sea, where Sabri gave her a hand after school.

Sa'diyah preferred herding to gathering tomatoes and herbs. While herding she had to be cautious and watch the flock so it would not wander on to neighbouring farms. She would sit under a tree overlooking the area, watching her flock. She was not afraid of spending most of her time alone in an isolated area, far away from the village, for, she says, the Ghor is safe and all its inhabitants are either relatives or neighbours.

Sa'diyah's herding duties did not last long, for she had to start earning some money and leave herding to her younger sister Aisha. She started working as a day labourer from seven o'clock in the morning until five in the afternoon for 30 piastres per day.[6] She was eleven years old, and gave her wages to her father after keeping a few piastres for herself to buy some sweets. Although she worked the same hours as a grown woman, she was only paid a quarter of their salary. Still, she was satisfied. As the work was seasonal and irregular, she also worked with the family on the farm. Two years later she married. It was considered shameful for a married woman to work as a day labourer, and as her husband was working as a share-cropper in 'Issal and Dhra', she started working with him.

Her late husband was her paternal aunt's son who, in spite of knowing that Sa'diyah was engaged to her paternal uncle's son, asked for her hand. A dispute ensued between the two but her uncle, strangely enough, put an end to it by advising Sa'diyah's father to marry her to her aunt's son because his own son was a drunkard and did not work. Of course Sa'diyah was not consulted.

Sa'diyah spent the first year of marriage with her husband's family in the 'Issal area where they worked. After marriage, her husband worked in farming on his own account. They moved to

6. One piastre = .01 JD

the Dhra' area after they left his parent's house. Although Sa'diyah did not get pregnant, they did not consult a physician. After two years she had a miscarriage in the sixth month of pregnancy and felt ill and weak. Immediately after she became pregnant again and gave birth to Ismail. Two years later, Mohammed was born.

Sa'diyah's husband's farm was 30 *dunums* and they mostly worked it alone. During the harvest season, they would ask their relatives for help and would do the same for them in return. Sometimes they employed three or four women for two or three days. The burden of work was on Sa'diyah because her husband suffered from heart trouble and frequently paid visits to the doctor, who advised him not to exert himself. During her six years of marriage she never stopped working on the farm, except for once when she had a miscarriage and lay in bed for five days until she stopped bleeding, and after the delivery of each of her two children, Ismail and Mohammed, when she stayed in bed for a week. Afterwards, she would take her baby to the farm where she would breast-feed him, and leave him under the doum tree while she went back to work. Sometimes she would leave him with her mother when the latter was not working.

Sa'diyah did not know of her husband's illness when she married him. The symptoms appeared two years later, when he felt constantly tired and sometimes fainted. The physician in Karak told him that it was his heart. After her husband's death, Sa'diyah left Dhra' to live with her parents in al-Mazra'a because she felt so sad and had lost her spirit for work. Then her son Mohammed fell sick with an infection and diarrhoea. She believes that the child fell ill because he suckled *khree'* milk, or 'horror milk', poisoned because of the immense sorrow she felt for her husband. As she could not afford medical treatment, she decided to work temporarily to earn the money needed. After Mohammed recovered, she began working as a day labourer whenever she received an offer. Today, five years later, she still does not consider working as a share-cropper, for her children are young and she needs money to meet their needs, and because 'working as a share-cropper requires a family to give a hand', she says.

As Sa'diyah is a serious, active and skilled worker, a large number of farmers ask her to work for them. She works only for those people who treat working women well and pay them their wages on time. Although Sa'diyah works longer than most other women in the Ghor, her total working time is only two or three months per year. During her five years of work, she has only been able to save 350 JD, from which she spent 50 JD on the marriage of her brother, Raja. This money does not all come from her work, for she also receives 25 JD per month in assistance from the Welfare Department.

With the rest of her savings, Sa'diyah decided to build a small house. She received 280 m² from the Jordan Valley Authority, because she is a widow with children. She is now worried about the construction costs. The money she had saved covered only the cost of the foundations and the posts. She bought cement blocks from a landowner who agreed to be paid in instalments, as did the builder; but she has to pay 50 JD per month, which she cannot afford. Even if she worked thirty days per month, which never happens, she would earn only 60 JD, leaving her with only ten dinars to cover living expenses. Welfare assistance is irregular and sometimes two or three months pass between payments.

Sa'diyah stays awake at night thinking of ways to obtain the money she needs. Sometimes she considers borrowing from the man for whom she now works, but she worries that in that case she will have to work for him for free the next month. Her parents do not have the money, for they are in debt as a result of Raja's marriage. Raja is unemployed and his whole family is dependent on his father and one of his sisters, Aisha, who is a wage-labourer. Sa'diyah's mother and youngest sister tend the flocks and do the housework, and Sabri works in the Potash Company for 90 JD, an amount that hardly covers the expenses of his own family of eight.

Money is not Sa'diyah's only problem: she also has to follow every step of the construction process. She finishes work in the fields at four o'clock and immediately goes to the hill where her new house is situated. She walks the twenty kilometres, sometimes being lucky and getting a ride in a passing truck. There she waters the concrete, carries bricks and does everything to save money. If she asked her young brothers to help her, she would have to give them some money and buy them some sweets, which she cannot afford.

She returns home at six o'clock, washes herself, feeds her two children and goes to bed early. A twelve-hour working day leaves her exhausted, in her words, 'a corpse'. She wakes at midnight and cannot go back to sleep for thinking about her new house and the future of her children. In spite of the trouble involved in building the house, she says that she will not give up; she is determined to secure a home for her children, aware that if she does not do it now, before they grow up and expenses grow with them, she will never be able to do it at all.

Sa'diyah wants to ensure a 'reasonable life' for her children and enable them to spend their time studying. She is aware that success in school requires comfortable living conditions, an 'independent' house and a steady income. She is constantly trying to get a regular job as school janitor or a worker in the Tomato Paste Factory in es-Safi. She has applied many times, but has never received an answer, although one of the senior officials of the es-Safi factory has promised to employ her. She would leave her children with her mother, as she does now, and go to the factory only two kilometres away every day. She would not object to working as a housemaid, for it is just like any other job, better than day labour and providing a steady income, but she cannot, because she would have to live away from her children.

Sa'diyah realizes that with her current income she will not be able to complete the house for years. She says that she will build the walls, for the time being, and the ceiling will follow later. Anyhow, she says, she would not be able to live in the house until Ismail was twelve. If she moved now she would feel lonely, for her children are still young. For the present she lives in a small room next to her parents. This is a good arrangement, for she can be sure her children are safe while she is working. The children also eat their meals with the family, but Sa'diyah does not allow all the members of the family to control them. Only her parents, her uncle, and occasionally her brother Sabri are allowed to do so, for they contribute financially to their care and therefore have the right to give advice.

Sa'diyah rejects the idea of getting married again. She says that she would never take such a risk, afraid that remarriage would be at her children's expense. She would not be happy if her second husband refused to look after them, and would not want to leave them with her mother or her mother-in-law.

Sa'diyah loves her work, and enjoys the companionship of other women. She boasts that although she does not have any training in farming, she can do whatever is asked of her. She operated the irrigation system at the nursery where she worked for five weeks. She can sow tomato seeds in plates, plant tomato seedlings and other vegetables, and harvest them, but she does not know which fertilizers and insecticides each kind needs. She decides whether a plant is healthy or not according to how it looks, but she does not know how to treat sick plants. She does only what is required; the other matters are the business of the *waqqaf* (the overseer) who is in charge of all the day labourers, men and women.

Sa'diyah has no ambition to become a *waqqaf*. She thinks that it is a man's job because he has to be the last to leave and the first to arrive. In the morning, he divides them into groups and gives them their instructions. Sa'diyah does not mind with whom she works, for she has a good relationship with all the workers, but she does like to work with women who work hard. Usually the women try to pressure a lazy co-worker. This sometimes causes trouble, but they often solve their problems themselves, without involving the *waqqaf*. But he has his own ways of knowing the ones who are not working hard and dismisses them.

Sa'diyah has many friends, and when the *waqqaf* needs more workers she tells him of them, because she knows that they are hardworking. Otherwise she would lose face with the *waqqaf*. 'Anyhow', she says, 'I do not make any deals with the women, I leave it to the *waqqaf*, so that if he refuses to pay them, I shall not be blamed.'

She usually has no time to go visiting, but when one of the girls gets married, she participates in the wedding celebrations and presents her with the *nuqut*, the money given to the bride by relatives and friends.

Sa'diyah is quite aware of the fact that women take on more work in the fields than men. She and her two sisters are still working: Sa'diyah and Aisha as farmworkers, and Balqees, with her mother, takes care of the family's livestock. Her youngest brothers are still in school.

Sa'diyah is also aware that since she depends on her parents to take care of her sons while she is working, she is expected to contribute to the family in times of crisis. When Raja got married to his first wife, she gave him 50 JD to pay the bride-price and when he married his second wife, she sold her golden ring to cover the expenses. She realizes that once she can live independently of her family, she will be able to use all her earnings for the welfare of her children.

Sa'diyah regrets not having gone to school and blames her parents for this, but she also knows that it was due to circumstances. She hopes she will someday have the opportunity to learn to read and write. If she found somebody who would teach her, she says: 'I would learn fast, because I have a clean mind.' Since she herself was not sent to school, she is determined to send her children. She talks to Ismail about the necessity of education and he promises her that he will study hard and become a schoolteacher. Sa'diyah laughs as she talks about her dream of her own son becoming a schoolteacher rid of the toil of farmwork.

III. Urban case study: Squatter areas in Amman

The history of squatter settlements in Amman forms an integral part of the transformation of the city as a result of regional political events and economic trends. The major turning-point in the evolution of contemporary Amman came in 1928 when it was officially designated as the capital of Transjordan. At that time, Amman was one of the many agricultural settlements established in the late nineteenth century by Circassian immigrants to the Ottoman Empire.[7] As a result of its new status, the town immediately began to expand, attracting merchants, bureaucrats and rural migrants. New residential areas began to form along the hillsides surrounding the narrow valley that had originally comprised the whole of Amman.

In 1948 Amman received an influx of Palestinian refugees fleeing the war that followed the establishment of the state of Israel, as did most of the cities and towns of the region. The government and charitable organizations turned schools, mosques and public land into temporary shelter areas for these people. When it became clear, after the fighting subsided, that the refugees were not going to be allowed to return to Palestine, camps were set up by UNRWA (the United Nations Relief Works Agency) and large tracts of land were leased at the periphery of the city, the boundaries of the camps demarcated, and within them plots of regular size established. Each family qualified for a plot and, in time, shacks began to replace the tents and temporary shelters. The distribution of aid, food and medical treatment was systematized and schools opened. This is the present situation in Jordan, with the addition of camps established to house the refugees of the 1967 war and the ensuing Israeli occupation of the West Bank and the Gaza Strip.[8]

The squatter areas were formed in a parallel process, since the squatters were also Palestinian refugees. However, they had either come too late to be included in a refugee camp, were crowded out of a camp due to lack of space, or were placed in a camp that was far from work opportunities and from their relatives and co-villagers.

---

7. The Circassians are one of the groups who immigrated from the Caucasus to various parts of the Ottoman Empire in the late nineteenth century. They settled in agricultural areas in central Anatolia and greater Syria. For more details see Karpat (1972), Lewis (1987) and Shami (1982).
8. The status of refugee camps will probably be affected by Jordan's recent decision to sever legal and administrative relations with the West Bank as of July 1988. The exact impact of this decision on refugee camps and their inhabitants in the East Bank is as yet unclear.

They therefore built shacks on whatever vacant land was available adjacent to the refugee camps. There were two incentives to build next to a camp. First, there were relatives nearby upon whom they could depend for support. Second, as refugees they were eligible for UNRWA aid even if they did not live in a camp, and by living close by they would have access to UNRWA facilities, especially schools and clinics.

The squatter areas expanded after the 1967 war. As the refugees from the West Bank and Gaza Strip arrived, they also looked for family and kin from whom they had been separated since 1948 and many settled in the squatter areas for that reason. As the city of Amman expanded, both the refugee camps and the squatter areas became encapsulated in the midst of residential neighbourhoods and, at present, many of them are near the city centre. In more recent years they have also begun to attract poor rural migrants and non-Jordanian migrant workers, but the majority of inhabitants remain Palestinian refugees. Due to lack of space, newcomers are not able to build houses but instead rent or buy them from the original squatters.

Although these areas are squatter settlements in the strict sense that people have built houses on land without legal access, they constitute a special category. As refugees rather than rural migrants, the squatters pose a different set of problems for landowners and government. As squatters elsewhere, they are seen as illegal, unsanitary and unregulated populations (Karpat, 1976; Lobo, 1982; Lomnitz, 1977; Mangin, 1967), but they are not easily dislodged by usual legal measures and mass expulsion enforced by police and bulldozers (Gulick, 1967; Mangin, 1967), which would have serious political consequences. In a very real sense, then, there is little insecurity of tenure in these areas since the squatters are fully aware that, as a group, they cannot easily be evicted. Even legal procedures by landowners against individual households have not met with much success, since the courts are unwilling to authorize forcible eviction.

Although the materials from which the houses in the squatter areas are built may be flimsy, the general living conditions are not necessarily worse than in other poor neighbourhoods. This is especially true of the areas that were formed in 1948, which have become fully integrated into the city and have obtained access to basic services. Areas formed in 1967 show considerably worse environmental conditions.

A basic characteristic of all these squatter areas is the inequality of living conditions. That is, while one squatter household may create quite a comfortable and sanitary environment, its immediate neighbour may not. Since basic necessities are not ensured by public authorities, it is up to private and individual initiative to obtain the necessary amenities, and not all households have the resources or the know-how to do this. This leads to a high degree of dependency between neighbours while at the same time being a major source of conflict. If one household obtains access to piped water, then its neighbours will buy their water from them, which leads to constant argument over how much water was taken, how much is owed and so on. The same applies to electricity. Conflict sometimes arises over the overflowing open drain of one household, when its neighbour is connected to mains sewage.

These conflicts mainly take place among women, for it is they who watch one another and attempt to curb littering at community expense. The worst situations arise when conditions have gone beyond the control of the inhabitants, such as when sewage from other areas flows in open ditches due to municipal neglect, or when garbage dumping sites become a nuisance. In these areas, people try within their means to ensure minimum safety, such as using filled barrels to barricade the houses from the sewage flow, but they can do little else to better their environment. Naturally these are the locations where upgrading projects have had the most effective and beneficial impact.

A. Social groups in the squatter areas

Squatter areas have certain specific characteristics due to their particular historical development, especially regarding population composition and housing quality. Yet they cannot be considered as marginal areas, or their inhabitants as marginal populations. Studies of squatter areas in other parts of the world show that squatter populations, far from being marginal to the economy of their society, are an integral part of it precisely because they hold badly paid, intermittent and multiple occupations, thus constituting a cheap and malleable labour source (Lomnitz, 1977; Perlman, 1976; and Velez-Ibanez, 1983). In the Jordanian situation, in fact, the squatter population cannot be distinguished in any major way from the overall urban poor population, either in terms of occupation or income level. Furthermore, their arrival had an immediate impact on the country's economy by providing cheap labour. Currently people are employed in small workshops, in the construction industry, in low-level government employment, or are self-employed as small shop-owners, pedlars and taxi-cab drivers (UDD, 1981, 1985). In addition, most families have at least one member working in the Arabian Gulf states.

The two areas we studied were neither marginal, nor 'deviant', in the social sense. They represent fairly stable communities with little in- and out-migration (UDD, 1981). Family and household size and composition are typical of the urban poor in the country as a whole. Although squatter areas may give the impression of being bounded universes due to their physical characteristics, in fact their inhabitants' social networks stretch far beyond their boundaries. Relationships are mostly based on kinship, linking squatters to people living in adjacent neighbourhoods, in the refugee camps and beyond. Within the squatter areas the network of relationships is also determined primarily by kinship as well as by physical proximity or neighbourliness. The most important social unit is the household, followed by the wider kin-group. These units ensure the survival of the individual and the perpetuation of the group, through sharing of resources and buffering the constraints and burdens of life in the underclass.

There are different kinds of household, each representing family adaptation to particular circumstances. Most squatters (69.7 per cent) live in simple family households (SFH) which comprise a married couple or a single parent with or without children, while 10.2 per cent are extended family households (EFH), and 8.8 per cent are multiple family households (MFH). Another 11.3 per cent live in other types of family households, for example brothers living together. The former include a married couple, children and parent(s) or sibling(s) of the father and occasionally of the mother. The latter combines SFHs or EFHs, usually when a son continues to reside in his parent's household after marriage and the birth of his children.

A somewhat different type of unit is the multiple household dwelling (MHD). This unit comprises a number of families (which may be simple or extended), related to each other in different ways and living together under one roof. Since these families have their own income and maintain distinct budgets, they constitute separate households which exercise minimal resource sharing beyond that of the dwelling itself.[9] Although the structured survey of squatter

9. The terms distinguishing different types of household are used here according to the definitions by Laslett (1978). However, we prefer the term 'multiple household dwelling' to his 'houseful' to emphasize the fact that the components represent households and not other types of units or individuals. Also the term 'dwelling' here is not used according to Laslett's definition but refers to a structure surrounded by a perimeter wall, which makes it parallel to his term

areas did not attempt specifically to check on this kind of unit, it did record the number of households in each plot. The results show that 16 per cent of households share the same plot with another household, and 7 per cent with two other households (UJDD, 1985). It seems reasonable to assume that most of these are what we term MHD, while those with more than three households to a plot (8 per cent) are apartment-type dwellings.

Multiple factors enter into the process of household formation and the final structure of each household is decided by a combination of economic, cultural, moral and individual considerations. At the risk of over-simplification, one could say that extended family households and multiple household dwellings are generally the outcome of cultural norms that exclude the possibility of single people residing alone, especially women, the young and the very old. Multiple family households, on the other hand, are primarily the result of economic factors, where the new conjugal unit does not have the resources to set up an independent household and where the stem household benefits likewise from the continued presence of an additional earner, as long as his earnings outweigh the additional cost of wife and children.

It may seem surprising, given the emphasis in Middle Eastern literature on patriarchy, that people of all generations rarely spoke of the married son staying with his parents as part of his filial duty, but rather as the result of economic need. While there were debates over the relationship of mother-in-law and daughter-in-law, and people took sides over who was mistreating whom, all recognized that conflict was unavoidable and that the solution lay in separating the two households. On the other hand, when a widow lived alone instead of with her son, even if close by, this was always denounced on moral grounds, and the idea of sisters being left alone was inconceivable. Besides limited female participation in the labour force, this is an additional explanation for the low number of female-headed households in these areas, only 12 per cent in the 1985 survey (Bisharat and Zagha, 1986). Even if a mother or a sister are financially independent, and head their own household, they generally reside with their next-of-kin. This situation is conducive to what we have termed multiple household dwellings, and is often not recorded in surveys as a female-headed household because an older male in the dwelling is assumed, or said to hold this rank.

'premises'. Finally in our definition of the term 'family', we place as much emphasis on descent as on marriage. Thus, contrary to Laslett's definition, we consider that a household composed of brothers and sisters constitutes a family.

These tendencies, in addition to the demographic structure of the population in terms of sex and age (Zurayk and Shorter, 1988), may explain the statistical distribution of the types of household in these areas. The simple family household emerges as the statistical, and, we believe, the social norm. Whether this is the result of new social and cultural realities, or an historical feature of the urban Middle East, is a question to be answered by future research. It should be emphasized, however, that whatever the form of household, social and authority relations are not bounded by the walls of a dwelling, and patriarchy does not cease with the division of households. In most cases the married son tries to reside as close as possible to his stem family. It is not the splitting of the household that is perceived as a loss, but rather when a family leaves the neighbourhood altogether and thus weakens or severs the links of reciprocity expected of close kin.

This typology of households should not give an impression of stability over time within any given household. For any individual, the immediate social environment is constantly changing. The typical flow of the household cycle in these areas may be summarized as shown in the diagram.

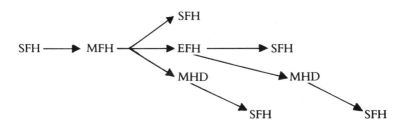

The most common pattern is of an SFH turning into an MFH through the marriage of one of the sons. The household may then become an EFH through the death of one of the parents, and eventually an SFH, through the death of the other parent and the separation of siblings. Some of the married sons will split off at marriage or, more commonly, a few years after marriage, and form an SFH, which then goes through a similar cycle.

These cycles may occur over very short periods of time. For example, a second son may get married within an MFH, increasing the number of families within the household. Then both married sons may leave and form an MHD by themselves, while the original household becomes an SFH. A separated daughter and her children may move in for several months and then go back to her husband's household. Therefore the designation of a household as a particular type, and even a particular size, may only be true for a short period of time. The average size of household in the squatter areas is seven (Bisharat and Zagha, 1986), which is also the national urban average (Zurayk and Shorter, 1988), but the study of any household over a period of time would certainly show great and sudden changes in size and composition.

Furthermore, as Zurayk and Shorter (1988) point out, these cycles are greatly affected by labour migration, which actually subverts the 'normal' cycle by, for example, taking the married son away perhaps at the very time he would normally have split off from the stem family, and prolonging the stay of his wife and children with the stem family. This type of household is still an MFH, but the absence of the son changes the nature of relations within the household, especially authority relations.

Running these large and changing households on a small amount of money is a time-consuming and difficult affair, and one on which women expend most of their energy. In order to manage, women of different households have to rely upon each other for help in housework, shopping and child care, for aid in financial emergencies, and for information. Households that reciprocate daily in such matters may be said to form 'mutual aid units'. Although such units are generally based on kinship, yet they are formed selectively: not all households related by kinship will form one unit. Rather, from all the possible combinations one or two units will emerge. Units tend generally to be formed between sisters-in-law, that is, between husband's sister and brother's wife (Shami and Taminian, 1985).

There are other ways in which the wider kin-group co-operates economically, as will be discussed below. Kinship relations are used to compel various members to co-operate in economic enterprises and to help one another in major emergencies. Some kin-groups even build up formal associations in order to ensure such co-operation. However, in terms of the daily survival of households in squatter areas, the mutual aid units formed and maintained by women are the main, and the most crucial, institution.

B. Development projects

The Urban Development Department (UDD) is the government agency in charge of development projects in the squatter areas of Amman. This department was established in 1980 with the task of developing and implementing urban upgrading projects in squatter areas as well as sites and services projects for the low-income population of Amman. It was the first agency in Jordan geared specifically to provide housing to low-income groups. Before this the Housing Corporation and the National Housing Bank provided loans, but their terms excluded those with an income of less than 200 JD per month and those who did not own land as collateral (Halcrow Fox and Associates, 1979). The UDD therefore aimed precisely to reach this income level, which otherwise had no access to credit.

The first set of projects, funded by the World Bank, involved the five squatter areas of Amman from which the data for this case-study are drawn. The project is particularly rich in documentation, both in terms of project progress reports as well as analyses of data from research activities, which constituted an important part of the project from the very beginning. The following account draws heavily upon all these documents (see Bibliography), as well as our own participant-observation research in both upgraded and non-upgraded sites.

The tasks set before the UDD were as follows:

> The mandate of the UDD, while emphasizing physical implementation of improvements, contains parallel action in a number of critical areas of social and economic development. This mandate includes:
>   1. upgrading in specified locations to improve and extend dwellings, raise the standards of water supply, sanitation, social amenities and access;
>   2. complementary programs in such areas as health education, environmental maintenance, literacy, vocational training and small business development to enable the beneficiaries, particularly the wives and children, to enjoy better health and prospects. (Bisharat and Zagha, 1986: 7)

The UDD project was multifaceted, its impact has been wide-ranging and it has affected many aspects of life in the squatter areas. After identifying the five project sites, all households were first registered as potential project participants. At the same time, a comprehensive base-line study was conducted, including a physical survey of the sites, a socio-economic survey and a health survey. Area and plot plans were prepared and care was taken to avoid major changes in the size and location of plots and, as soon as possible, the demolition of existing structures. Two of the sites studied were eliminated from the upgrading project because a highway was planned through large parts of these areas, but a portion of one of these was upgraded later.

The project defined the minimum plot holding as 50 m². Any smaller plots were either combined with an adjoining plot or added to planned public spaces. The displaced residents were given compensation and the choice of moving to one of the UDD housing projects elsewhere. Basic services were provided for every plot, the footpaths and alleys were stabilized and paved, and open spaces provided for recreation. In addition, community centres, health clinics and schools were built at each site according to needs identified by the initial feasibility study. Shops and workshops were also built and space allocated for building more commercial outlets. Loans were made available to raise capital for small business enterprises, and plans made for community centres to provide support through vocational training, with special emphasis on increasing women's participation in the labour force. This aspect of the project was called the 'economic stimulation' of the community (Halcrow Fox and Associates, 1979: xv).

In return for these services, the inhabitants were asked to pay a fixed sum for each square metre of land, to cover the cost of the land and the services. Upon payment, the land would become their private property. Loans at 8.5 per cent interest were made available through the Housing Bank for this purpose. Additional loans were also made available for building or expanding the houses, with the proviso that the UDD should approve the proposed construction plan and supervise the building process to make sure that it met municipal codes. The implementation of these plans obliged the UDD to have field personnel, including engineers and community workers, in constant contact with the inhabitants of the project sites in order to assess the situation of each household.

The UDD is now a Department within the Ministry of Municipal and Rural Affairs and has entered an expanded phase of operations involving low-income housing projects both within Amman and in other cities and towns. Although the upgrading project has been completed as originally planned, the UDD is still very much involved in the upgraded areas. Its main emphasis and most of its funds were allocated to legalizing tenure and providing physical improvements and infrastructure. After building the community and training centres, however, continued involvement of UDD project staff was seen to be necessary and additional funds and grants were obtained to enable them to organize activities in these centres.

In this way, the role of the UDD has gone beyond initial physical upgrading and has extended to social work and community development. The UDD has helped establish social committees and associations and organize community activities. It has organized training programmes and lectures for women, and established day-care centres. In this way, it has played an active role in restructuring community relations, including, at times, the creation of new community leadership. For the inhabitants of the project areas, the UDD has become their arbitrator in property and other problems, as well as their mediator with other government agencies and financial institutions.

The project has had a major impact on social relations within the squatter areas. As mentioned above, the upgraded areas did not originally constitute communities in the social sense, especially because the boundaries of the upgrading project were determined by the boundaries of municipally-owned land and/or by the UDD's success in buying the land from its owners at an affordable price. A community could be defined as the inhabitants of a self-delineated area within which the people interact intensively and on a daily basis, with which they identify, and to which they ascribe distinctive characteristics. According to this definition we found several communities within each project area and others which stretched beyond them. The upgrading process itself, however, led to the creation of a community by making the people of the upgraded area feel they belonged to a bounded location affected by common forces.

Long-standing relations between neighbours have been affected by the project. In cases where upgrading involved the removal of houses and the merging of plots, friction occurred between neighbours over who should buy out the other's plot. When one household took out a building loan and added a second storey, this violated the privacy of adjoining houses. Inequalities between neighbours also became physically visible. Those who were able to pool their resources and take advantage of loans built new houses, while their neighbours remained in their old ones.

These are not major inequalities in the overall class structure of the area. However, in a small community, any visible signs of inequality create tensions. Some families were able to convince relatives to extend resources for the building of a house, which became an attractive proposition once legal tenure seemed assured. Others were not as successful. It was therefore quite unpredictable who would be able to build a new house and who would not. There was not necessarily any correlation between those who were known to be 'rich' before the project and those who suddenly appeared to be so afterwards. Furthermore, a number of households who could not afford to pay for their plot had no choice but to leave the upgrading site. The 1985 survey shows that the percentage of households in this position reached 17 per cent, or 259 out of a total of 1,445 originally registered in the 1981 survey. Since this left vacant plots, the opportunity was given to better-off households from other parts of the city to move in and 139 households did so. This may, to a large extent, explain the rise in average income level in these areas from 80 JD per month in 1981 to 120 JD per month in 1985 (Bisharat and Zagha, 1986). It may also indicate that households were seeking new ways of increasing their income in order to meet loan obligations.

In addition to the impact of the project on community relations as a whole, households were affected individually. The project defined the family, composed of a married couple and children, as the basic social unit that could qualify as a beneficiary of the project. This was partly due to an attempt to decrease crowding in the area by improving the household's ability to add rooms to their house as well as encouraging members of the family to separate and form new dwelling units (Bisharat, n.d.). This created a strong impetus for MFHs to split up into their component families so that each would qualify for a plot. Some families even resorted to quickly marrying off their young sons so as to qualify for another plot. The new family could either move to a plot vacated by another family within the project area, move to another project area, or have priority in qualifying for a housing unit in one of the UDD's low-income housing projects.

However, the division of an MFH assumes that each component family has the resources to live independently after paying project costs. The 1985 survey shows that only sixty-five households (4 per cent) had split into two households since 1981 (Bisharat and Zagha, 1986). Although some may have done so in order to qualify for a new plot, many would have split as a natural part of the household cycle. It is reasonable to assume that many households would not have had the resources to split and more families within households may have found it necessary to stay together to generate the new level of income now necessary for survival in the upgraded area.

The project also led to increased dependence upon wider kin-networks. Families and households called upon their relatives for loans to help them meet the expenses of the project and repayments of housing and business loans. Although the resources obtained from relatives were eventually to be repaid, interest was out of the question and no time limit was set on repayment. It was tacitly understood that such an investment by relatives would be advantageous, since it would result in access to property, with possibilities for future income (e.g. by renting the property). How the wider kin group would specifically benefit from this ownership, however, remained vague. It was implied that redistribution and generalized reciprocity within the kin-group would eventually compensate for this burden placed on kin-ties, but in general the duty of kin to rally together in such a situation was stated in moral rather than contractual terms.

It is clear that the economic situation of squatter households underwent considerable change due to the project, though it is not clear whether the project actually led to greater economic insecurity than before. As mentioned above, the income of these households mostly derives from work in the service sector, the construction industry and low-level government employment. The first two categories are especially susceptible to fluctuations in the economy and were greatly affected by the recent economic recession in the region. As for government salaries, they rarely match the rising cost of living and most employees tend either to have another job or at least a secondary source of income. For example, some have a share in small enterprises with relatives, such as buying a pick-up truck to hire out for transport or for selling fruit and vegetables.

The monthly instalments on bank-loans imposed a considerable burden upon the household economy and to a large degree this burden had to be borne by the women, because of the structure of relations within the household, and especially the distribution of power and authority.

The authority to make decisions in the household is divided between men and women. The recognized head of the household is the father, as long as he is still working and in good health. The working sons, especially those who are married, also have a measure of authority. However, the domain of men in general lies outside the house, determining the general contours of the life of the household: income, place of residence, relationship with other heads of households within the kinship-group. Within these constraints, the women make the intricate decisions: how the income is spent, living conditions and daily interaction with kinfolk.

As regards the UDD project, it was the men who took the decisions concerning entry into the project and borrowing, and it was up to the women to re-define the situation within the household to fit in with the new conditions. The usual practice in the squatter areas is for men to turn over their entire wages and earnings to their wives or mothers, keeping a small amount of 'cigarette money' for themselves. This money is an indication of a woman's authority in the household and the measure of her control over it. It also means that it is up to the woman to make the money last the month and to provide for food, other necessities and emergencies. If the income is not sufficient on a regular basis, women resort to a variety of activities in order to generate the extra income needed, such as sewing, embroidery, making sweets and other foodstuffs to be peddled by children in the street, and so on. Women may even engage in light construction work, such as plastering, if the family is building an extension or making improvements to their house. They also carry sacks of cement and sand to save the cost of hiring a labourer. In addition, all women form and maintain networks with other women to enable them to raise money in emergencies, such as illness.

It is noteworthy that in the UDD project areas, it was largely the women who followed up on payment schedules with the bureaucracy, including trying to obtain extra time and flexibility on payments. One woman, whose husband works as a janitor in a government office, described her monthly budget as follows:

> My husband gives me all his wages. The first thing I do is pay the UDD instalment. Then I buy the household's monthly supplies of sugar, tea, rice and flour. Then I pay the water and electricity bills. What is left, I divide by the days of the month. This month we had more expenses because I had the baby at the hospital and because of the *al-Fitr* feast. So, in addition to my husband's salary, I spent the *nuqut* I got for the feast and for the baby, and also had to borrow 10 JD from my mother.

Clearly the UDD project has had an important impact upon the lives of women in the squatter areas. Women's work and economic strategies are crucial to the survival of the household and are constantly adapted to the changing context. The particular adaptation of squatter women to their changing circumstances shows the impact of the local, national and regional economy as well as the particular impact of the development project.

C. *Changing patterns of women's work*

Two things must be borne in mind when examining patterns of women's work in the squatter areas. First, the class position of the squatters, and second, their refugee status. The class position means that the household, rather than the individual, is the main economic unit. Decisions made by men or women can only be understood in relation to the structure and particular circumstances of the households to which they belong. This fact is central to the analysis of the participation of squatter women in the labour force.

The fact that the squatters are a refugee population means that patterns of labour, as well as all other aspects of life in the communities of origin, were disrupted due to the violent and abrupt displacement of the population. Furthermore, for the majority of the refugee families, an unsettled and insecure period followed their initial displacement. For some this lasted as long as six or seven years, before they finally settled with any degree of permanence. In addition, of course, much of the population are twice-refugees, having lived in camps on the West Bank and the Gaza Strip before being displaced again.

This much disrupted life-situation means that the older inhabitants of these areas, both men and women, have had to adjust to many different sets of conditions. Almost all the squatters, with very rare exceptions, are refugees from rural areas of Palestine, and have had to adapt to an unfamiliar urban environment in Amman, itself undergoing considerable change. One should not expect any kind of linear pattern or consistency to the occupational histories of the squatter population, as skills valuable in one setting may have proved to be of little use in another. In addition, achieving certain levels of education and acquiring skills was much harder for the refugee generation than for following generations. Furthermore refugees from the Gaza area had a special status as they were not granted Jordanian citizenship and hence could not be regular employees but were limited to certain kinds of work.

The 1985 survey of the squatter areas showed that working women numbered 202, or 7.8 per cent, out of a total of 2,590 women above the age of fifteen. If, however, students were excluded from the total number of women, then the percentage increased to 10 per cent. The main occupations of these women were, in descending order, janitors and maids, skilled clerical workers and teachers, and seamstresses. Less prevalent was employment as nurses and midwives, sellers and pedlars and unskilled clerical workers. In addition there were two cooks and only one factory worker. The employment of these women was equally divided between the public sector (35.8 per cent) and the private sector (35.3 per cent), while 26.8 per cent worked on their own account. The remaining 2 per cent worked as apprentices or for a family enterprise. A large number of working women were forced to support themselves and their households. Table 1.5 shows that the highest percentages of working women are among those divorced (33.3 per cent) and separated (31.8 per cent), with widowed women coming next (17.6 per cent). Furthermore, Table 1.6 shows

Table 1.5 Percentage of working women by marital status in five squatter areas in Amman

Marital status	Total women	Working women	% Working women
Married	1,298	56	4.3
Single	1,030	92	8.9
Divorced	30	10	33.3
Widowed	210	37	17.6
Separated	22	7	31.8
Total	2,590	202	7.8

Source: 1985 Survey Data by Urban Development Department of five squatter areas in Amman.

that only 41.4 per cent of working women receive monthly wages with full benefits. The rest, other than the self-employed, are paid on a daily basis or are on commission. This indicates that the majority of working women do not enjoy high job security and it must consequently be assumed that their employment fluctuates and that they may withdraw from the labour force from time to time.

The survey was careful to cover both full- and part-time work and to account for work performed at home. We can therefore assume that Table 1.7 is a highly accurate representation of the employment status of squatter women, although as discussed above, 'housewives' and 'students' also engage in economic activities of importance to the household.

In order better to understand the patterns of women's work and the changes that have occurred, it is useful to look at occupations by age-group. This analysis emphasizes both the constant adaptation of women's participation in the labour force and the changes that occur over a woman's lifetime. Finally, it suggests that participation in the labour force may not, in fact, simply be increasing but rather changing its character. Table 1.8 shows the percentage of working women by age-group both before and after students have been excluded from the sample, and Table 1.9 shows their specific occupations. It is clear that the lowest participation rate concerns the middle cohort, between 35 and 44, especially taking into account that 25 per cent of the 55+ women reported themselves too old to work. While it may be expected that the younger generation, with more access to education, may be entering the labour force in greater numbers, it is interesting to trace why women above the age of 45 work even more than the youngest cohorts.

The two older cohorts represent the refugee population and are those most affected by displacement. These women, who are now

Table 1.6 Women's occupation by type of wages earned in five squatter areas in Amman

	Monthly/Monthly	Daily/Monthly	Daily/Weekly	Commission	Profits	Row Total
Factory worker		1				1 0.5
Health worker	11	1		2		14 7.1
Skilled employee	46	7				53 26.8
Unskilled employee	4	6				10 5
Seamstress	6	13	7	20	3	49 24.7
Cook		2				2 1
Janitor	15	26	14			55 27.8
Seller					14	14 7.1
Column Total	82 41.4	56 28.3	21 10.6	22 11.1	17 8.6	198* 100

*This does not include 4 cases where the occupation was not reported.

Monthly/Monthly: Paid on a monthly basis with benefits.
Daily/Monthly: Paid on a daily basis at the end of a month, no benefits.
Daily/Weekly: Paid on a daily or weekly basis.
Commission: Irregular, according to the job.
Profits: Takes home any income above and beyond the costs of running the enterprise.
Source: 1985 Survey Data.

Table 1.7 Employment status by age-group of women in five squatter areas in Amman

Count / Row % / Col. %	Full-time	Part-time	Seasonal	Student	Housewife	Other	Row Total
15–24	64	5	1	570	528	7	1,175
	5.5	0.4	0.1	48.5	44.9	0.6	45.4
	39.3	13.5	50	99	29.3	100	
25–34	35	8	1	3	381		428
	8.2	1.9	0.2	0.7	89		16.5
	21.5	21.6	50	0.5	21.1		
35–44	18	8		3	314		343
	5.2	2.3		0.9	91.6		13.3
	11	21.6		0.5	17.4		
45–54	34	10			291		335
	10.1	3			86.9		12.9
	20.8	27			16.1		
55+	12	6			291		309
	3.9	2			94.1		11.9
	7.4	16.3			16.1		
Column Total	163	37	2	576	1,805	7	2,590
	6.3	1.4	0.1	22.2	69.7	0.3	100

Housewife : Includes girls not in school and other women not married to the head of household.
Other : e.g. Prisoner or person without passport not allowed to work.
Source: 1985 Survey Data.

Table 1.8 Percentage of working women by age-group in five squatter areas in Amman

Age group	Total women	Working women	% Working women	Adjusted % *
15–24	1,175	70	5.9	11.6
25–34	428	44	10.3	10.3
35–44	343	26	7.6	7.6
45–54	335	44	13.1	13.1
55+	309	18	5.8	5.8
Total	2,590	202	7.8	10

* Adjusted %: Percentage of working women among total women, excluding students.
Source: 1985 Survey Data.

Table 1.9 Women's occupation by age-group in five squatter areas in Amman

Count / Row % / Col. %	Factory worker	Health worker	Skilled employee	Unskilled employee	Seamstress	Cook	Janitor	Seller	Row Total
15–24	1	7	32	9	18		1		68
	1.5	10.3	47	13.2	26.5		1.5		34.4
	100	50	60.3	90	36.7		1.8		
25–34		5	18	1	11		5	2	42
		11.9	42.8	2.4	26.2		11.9	4.8	21.2
		35.7	34	10	22.5		9.1	14.3	
35–44			1		7	1	16	1	26
			3.8		26.9	3.8	61.6	3.8	13.1
			1.9		14.3	50	29.1	7.1	
45–54			2		10	1	23	7	44
			4.5		22.7	2.3	52.3	15.9	22.2
			3.8		20.4	50	41.8	50	
55+		1			3		10	4	18
		5.5			16.7		55.6	22.2	9.1
		7.1			6.1		18.2	28.6	
Column Total	1	14	53	10	49	2	55	14	198*
	0.5	7.1	26.8	5	24.7	1	27.8	7.1	100

* This does not include 4 cases where the occupation was not reported.
Source: 1985 Survey Data.

over 45 years of age, started their economically productive lives in a
rural setting. One would expect that their economic participation at
that time did not differ much from other rural women in the
region, apart from local variations in agriculture. Their educational
attainment is very low and Table 1.10 shows that only 1 per cent
completed primary school.

After displacement and resettlement in Amman, most of these
women began working outside the home, generally as domestic
servants or janitors in public and private institutions. Their economic contribution to the households during those early years was
critical, since it took men longer to find work and to obtain the
necessary skills for the new urban environment. Women also
worked in agriculture. Many of the squatter areas were on the
periphery of the city, on agricultural land slowly being consumed
by the urban sprawl. They cultivated small vegetable plots as
share-croppers or tended livestock, activities in which the men did
not participate. The need for space to keep animals was one of the
explanations given for not living in a refugee camp. Lastly, some
women worked as midwives and healers.

In later years, with more employment opportunities for men due
to general economic growth in the country and the region, as well
as the new opportunities for labour migration, there was a general
rise in the standard of living. This led to a reassessment of the need
for women to continue working outside the home. In most cases,
they stopped working as domestic servants. Those who worked in
the public sector tended to continue, for the associated benefits of
pensions and medical insurance. In addition, those who had dependent households for some reason (such as the death of the husband)
also continued to work. The 1985 survey shows that 12 per cent of
households in the squatter areas were headed by women. Of these,
89 per cent were above the age of 41, and 88 per cent widowed or
divorced. Their households were the most disadvantaged, two-
thirds of them having an income of less than 100 JD per month and
more than one-third with an income of less than 50 JD per month
(Bisharat and Zagha, 1986). This indicates that the returns from the
type of employment available are low, in fact lower than that
available to men of the same age group and educational attainment
(Bisharat and Zagha, 1986). Table 1.11 shows that divorced,
widowed and separated women are mostly employed as janitors
or seamstresses or engage in selling and peddling foodstuffs, all of
which are badly paid.

The women who did not have to support the household, therefore, withdrew from work outside the home. Many still contrib-

Table 1.10 Primary school education by age-group, males and females in five squatter areas in Amman

Age in 1985	Date of entry into primary school *	% Completed primary school Males	Females
15–24	1967–1976	89.5	82
25–34	1957–1966	77	56.5
35–44	1947–1956	56	19.5
45–49	1942–1946	34	1

* Assumes that all were eligible to enter primary school at six years old.

Source: Adapted from Bisharat and Zagha, 1986 p. 61.

Table 1.11 Women's occupation by marital status in five squatter areas in Amman

	Factory worker	Health worker	Skilled employee	Unskilled employee	Seamstress	Cook	Janitor	Seller	Row Total
Married		2	13	2	10	2	19	6	54 27.3
Single	1	10	38	8	27		6	1	91 46
Divorced					2		7	1	10 5
Widowed		2	1		7		20	6	36 18.2
Separated			1		3		3		7 3.5
Column total	1 0.5	14 7.1	53 26.8	10 5	49 24.7	2 1	55 27.8	14 7.1	198* 100

* This does not include 4 cases where the occupation was not reported.
Source: 1985 Survey Data.

uted to the household income through home industries such as sewing or embroidery, or making sweets and other foods peddled by children in the streets. Some opened small shops inside their houses to serve the neighbourhood. Midwives and healers continued their activities, but perhaps on a smaller scale and within the immediate neighbourhood. By this time, this cohort of women had grown-up children who could take over some of the economic burden of the household. Table 1.9 shows that these two cohorts were mainly engaged in janitorial work, sewing and selling, apart from two health workers, who were in fact midwives, and one cook.

The second cohort of women, in the 35–44 age-group, were born during or immediately following the 1948 refugee displacement. They began work at a time when the family was generally settled and women's work outside the home was becoming less crucial. Some may, as young girls, have assisted their mother and some may have gone into domestic service. Most abandoned these activities upon marriage and, if anything, engaged in home industries, such as sewing and embroidery. The main situation that would have impelled a woman of this age-group to work outside the home would have been the death or disability of their husband, or divorce. Women of this cohort represent 11 per cent of all female-headed households in the squatter areas (Bisharat and Zagha, 1986). An important factor that further discouraged this generation of women from entering the formal labour market was their limited access to education. Many had only three or four years' schooling, and the only employment available to them was the same low-paid jobs their mothers had. Thus 61.6 per cent of the working women in this age-group are janitors and maids (Table 1.9). The low numbers of working women in this cohort show that the economic returns are not commensurate with the losses resulting from their absence. Furthermore, the seven seamstresses (26 per cent) work from their homes.

The low level of educational attainment in this group is due to the inability to educate all children, males being favoured over their sisters. Table 1.10 shows that only 19.5 per cent of women in the 35–44 age-group finished primary school as compared to 56 per cent of males. In addition, the mothers of these girls were working outside the home, which further prevented the daughters, especially the older ones, from going to school. They substituted for their mother at home, doing the housework and taking care of their younger siblings. This pattern of the daughter substituting for the mother is still widespread today, even when the mothers do not have outside employment (Shami, 1985).

The third cohort, between the ages of 25 and 34, has similar experience to the previous group. This is especially true of refugees of the 1967 war. The difference, however, is that certain trends appear, which later become more evident. School attendance is higher for this group and the gap between girls and boys decreases. Of these girls, 56.5 per cent completed primary school as compared to 77 per cent of boys (Table 1.10). The importance of this is that when the oil boom of the mid-1970s increased the opportunities for female white-collar workers, a number of this cohort was finishing high school, the first substantial number of women in the squatter areas to obtain higher education and training. Although their numbers were low, they set a precedent for the following genera-tion. They represent 21.2 per cent of all working women (Table 1.9) and the percentage of working women in this cohort is 9.8 per cent of their age-group (Table 1.8).

Most of these women work as teachers and secretaries, and a few as nurses. UNRWA institutions which provided free training, and UNRWA schools and offices which hired these women, played a crucial role in furthering this trend. Some women (26.2 per cent) also trained in commercial sewing which enabled them to work in sewing workshops or to work from home on a wider scale than before. The frequent weddings in or around the community, each one entailing four or five dresses for the bride in addition to her trousseau and the needs of the family, keep many seamstresses busy. It is interesting to note the sharp decline in the numbers working as maids and janitors, showing clearly that while those with education and training may work outside the home, those without largely remain at home.

The pattern that emerges is one of a drop in participation of the current older generation of married women (those over thirty-five) in the labour market, while a new generation is entering into very different spheres of employment in the formal labour force. Table 1.8 shows that the youngest cohort, those aged 15–24 today, with increasing access to higher levels of education, are going out into the labour market more than their mothers (aged 35–44), but not more than their grandmothers. They are also concentrated in employment which requires a fairly high level of education or training. Quite a number of seamstresses are also included in this group although again they are working from home.

The 1985 survey shows that the trend is definitely towards increased education. It reveals that 52 per cent of girls under the age of twenty finish high school and 34 per cent of twenty-year-olds are still studying, which indicates that they are obtaining further education or training which will enable them to enter the formal labour force (Bisharat and Zagha, 1986), mostly in secretarial work and teaching. Only one woman of this age-group works as a domestic servant and most maids are older women who are heads of households or women from the most destitute households. Domestic work in Jordan is now mostly carried out by Asian maids.[10]

Access to higher education suggests an increase in choices for women, as well as freedom from manual work. However, for unmarried educated women now entering the labour force, the future may not necessarily be better than for previous generations. Their increased earning capacity may subject them to exploitation rather than emancipation. To make sense out of the emerging patterns, one has to abandon the view of women as individuals making career decisions and look at the household as the main economic and decision-making unit.

The household in the squatter areas still does not have the resources to educate all the children and males are still given preference. However, with the recent economic changes and the increasing opportunities for women to work in the rapidly expanding public sector, work for women may be easier to obtain in certain spheres than for men. The expanding bureaucracy and educational system has created a demand for teachers, clerical workers and typists. The rapid increase in two-year community colleges in Jordan is evidence of this transformation.

In the squatter areas father, mother and daughter were often heard discussing plans for her education. Not all girls can enter teacher training college since this requires good grades, but all can enter secretarial school, nursing school and certain technical courses. The various options are vigorously debated in the household, but not all the daughters in the household are given the same opportunities or encouragement to continue their education. The structure of the household, and the age distribution of the children, determines which girls finish high school, continue their education and enter the labour force, and which ones do not.

The general pattern is that the older male is given the opportunity for high-school education first, but if he is not performing well and if he has younger brothers, then pressure may be applied on him to drop out of school and start working at around the age of fourteen or

---

10. The devaluation of the Jordanian Dinar in November 1988 and the tripling of work permit fees will certainly lead to a reduction of Asian and other foreign workers in the country and may create a renewed demand for local women as maids.

fifteen. Most of these jobs are as apprentices in garages and other workshops. A similar pattern holds for the older daughters. They may be pulled out of school at the age of fourteen or so to help their mother at home (Shami, 1985). Thus the percentage of girls attending school begins dropping rapidly after the age of fourteen in the squatter areas (Bisharat and Zagha, 1986). Since fifteen is the minimum legal age for marriage, the drop-out rate is also related to this.

When the financial situation of the family is improved by a working son, and the needs of the mother for a helper in the house are satisfied, younger children are encouraged to perform well in their studies. This applies whether the next in line is a girl or a boy. In cases where both a boy and a girl are in this category at the same time, the emphasis is clearly placed on the boy, although the girl may also take the required examinations and talk about further education.

Educating these children may drain the resources of the family and so once again, the children next in line may be deprived of education. By this time, the oldest boy and girl may be in the process of getting married. Hence new workers are needed both outside the home, to increase the household income, and inside the home, to cope with the increasing amount of work. There is therefore an 'exchange pattern' between the siblings with the situation of each age-group determining that of their younger siblings. This variability in access to education and employment for girls likewise explains the variety of opinions expressed on whether 'in general' girls should or should not, do or do not, study and work. In fact, the household aspires to strike a balance between income-generating members at a given moment and those being prepared for and expected to generate income in the future.

A working daughter is expected to contribute to the household like her working brothers and possibly even more so, as boys are always assumed to be saving up for marriage and for the bride-price. Different norms and expectations apply to working girls, and especially educated ones, and their sisters. The former have much more freedom of movement and dress very differently in more 'modern' clothes. They also express opinions and ideas more freely, even contradicting their parents at times.

There is also less emphasis on marriage for these young women. Some of them expressed forceful opinions concerning their obligations to their parents before they could 'think of themselves'. These obligations often centred around buying land and contributing towards building them a house. There were several cases of women teachers working in Saudi Arabia or the Gulf States for several years and having their fathers living with them, unemployed but acting as the *mahram*, or the male guardian required for every woman by law in Saudi Arabia. After a few years and having gathered a small amount of capital, the two come back and invest in a house or a small business enterprise in the name of the father. Such women often remain unmarried, working for their families, and rarely getting any property or future security in return.

While parents may be reluctant to lose working daughters, they are in great demand as marriage partners. Many continue to work after marriage, but it is difficult to generalize or to predict future trends because most women currently in this category are still newly married. The question of what would happen to a working mother after the birth of children was always raised by the in-laws. Working women were not expected to have less children. There were also several cases in which such women went with their husbands to work in the Gulf States and sometimes the children were left with their grandparents.

The work of a woman affects her status and authority within her husband's household substantially. As mentioned above, men and women in the household make decisions in different domains, a matter rarely as simple as most discussions of 'patriarchy' make it seem. Authority within the women's domain usually falls to the oldest woman, the mother or the mother-in-law, unless she is too old or inactive, but other women in the household also have some share in this authority. The older unmarried daughters eventually share in their mother's authority vis-à-vis the other children and even vis-à-vis the father/husband (Shami, 1985).

A woman gains status and authority in the household, and in her husband's kin-group in general, through a number of factors. First is the financial resources she controls, then the number of children she has, and finally the quality of her relationship with her husband. A woman's financial resources consist of her earnings if she works; her portion of the bride-price, mostly in the form of gold jewellery; money presented to her by her own family, and especially her brothers, on special occasions; and the spending money given to her by her husband. A young wife, with the help of her own family, often uses her resources to help her husband buy or rent a dwelling separate from his parents thus gaining some measure of independence from her in-laws.

A working woman therefore controls resources that enable her to gain authority within the household as well as a degree of independence from her husband's family. For the new generation of working women this is an important consideration. In addition

to economic necessity, it may motivate them to continue employment outside the home after marriage. On the other hand, most
institutions offer no child-care facilities and a working mother is
made increasingly dependent upon her in-laws, or occasionally
upon her own family, for help with her children. This may deter
women from continuing to work after marriage or after the birth of
more than two or three children. It is usually at this stage that the
couple expects to set up an independent household.

D. Life-history: Muna

Muna is thirty years old and supports herself and her two younger
brothers by working as a typist in an institution which pays well.
She and her family came as refugees from Gaza in 1967. Muna's
father always encouraged her to study and to do well in school,
sitting with her every night and helping with her lessons. He
wanted her to get good grades so that she could go to college. But
in her last year of high school, her mother became ill with cancer
and Muna had to care for her and take over the household. As a
result, her grades went down and she did not do well in the
high-school matriculation exam. Since her exam results did not
allow her to go to college, she went to a secretarial training centre
instead, graduating at the top of her class. She still had difficulty
finding a job since, as a refugee from Gaza, she did not have
Jordanian citizenship. Eventually she was able to secure her present
job and has been working there for the past nine years.

Muna's parents are now both dead, and she lives in a four-room
concrete house with her two younger brothers and one older
married brother, his wife and four children. Muna also has a
younger sister who recently got married. It is clear that Muna and
her younger brothers form one household, while her married
brother and his family form another, even though they share the
house and use parts of it jointly. One large central room, the
rooftop and the toilet are used by all members of the house.
However, the married brother, Kareem, and his family have one
room for their private use, and a small three-walled space on the
roof which they use as their kitchen. Muna has her own room and
kitchen and the two younger brothers have their own room where
they also entertain guests.

There is a complex relationship between the two households.
Muna cooks for herself and her brothers, while her sister-in-law
cooks for her husband and children. On Fridays, Muna's day off,
she cooks for both households. This seems to be in return for the

sister-in-law doing most of the housework, including the washing for the whole house. Food is bought and kept separately. Muna is a good seamstress and makes most of her own dresses. She also sews for her younger sister, her sister's sister-in-law and her cousin's daughter-in-law. But she does not sew for her brother's children or for her sister-in-law. Although relationships appear cordial, tensions do exist. Muna's sister-in-law criticizes her for her way of life, and complains that Muna is always 'pretending' to be tired when she comes home from work and does not help in the house. Kareem is also sometimes irritated, or at least feels compelled to appear so, that Muna does not bother to inform him of her decisions. Once Muna had not even told him of her plans to go to Gaza on a visit with one of her cousins.

Muna was not yet born when the family first became refugees in 1947 and left their original village on the northern coast of Palestine and went to Gaza. Her elder brother was one year old. They consider Gaza as their true home and are always comparing those of their kin who came directly from the original village to Amman unfavourably with the Gaza branch of the family, saying that they are more conservative, do not care for education and treat their women badly. Muna often talks about her life in the refugee camp in Gaza with nostalgia. Life in the camp, she says, was more like village life, and relationships between men and women were simpler and freer. She used to spend the summer with other children at the beach. It often seems that Muna is really mourning her childhood rather than Gaza itself, for since the family came to Amman, Muna has had to take on increasing responsibility.

The family had a difficult time when they first came to Amman. They wanted to live close to their kin who had come in 1948, and stayed with their paternal second cousins, then living in one room and a kitchen in one of the large refugee camps. They lived in this house for two years until their maternal uncle bought them a shack where their present house stands for 9 JD and fenced the land around it. He arranged for his sister to live there so that she would not be beholden to anyone. Muna says that her maternal uncle was very fond of her mother and would often visit to make sure that she was well. She wonders if her own brothers will ever treat her in the same way.

When they came to Amman, Muna's father began working as a mechanic in a garage. He worked all day and came back very tired in the evenings, but still made time to supervise the children's studies. He used to sit with all of them around a table and coach them by the light of a kerosene lamp. Muna also improved her

English by reading to a blind relative who had studied at a British-run school for the blind on the West Bank. One day Muna's father met a friend of his from Gaza who was then working in Saudi Arabia and within a few weeks his friend had found him a job. He did not want to leave until Muna entered college and began teacher training. The whole family was looking forward to this, but Muna's paternal uncle was against her continuing her college education, and her father wanted to make sure that she was enrolled and had started the programme before he left the country. When Muna did not qualify for teacher training college, her father went with her to register her in the secretarial course instead. He left the next week for Saudi Arabia and they did not see him for two years, when he took his first leave to attend Muna's graduation.

The family continued to live in the shack. When her brother married, he and his wife lived close to them in another shack and they all had to struggle to make ends meet. There was no water or electricity. When the owner of the land offered to sell it, they bought the part they were living on for 2 JD per m². In order to do so, her mother sold her gold necklaces and bracelets and when her father came back from Saudi Arabia, they built the house. Muna helped with the expenses and gave her salary to the household. Within a few years both her mother and her father died.

At work, Muna is relaxed and confident. She has a desk in the typing pool room which she shares with three other typists, but often roams around the building and visits her friends in the other rooms. She is good at her job and sometimes takes on the work of the other typists because she is faster and more accurate. She boasts that the General Director asks for her personally when his secretary is on vacation. Muna is not very interested or involved in the work itself, but rather with the people and the relationships in the office. Recently, due to a fight between two other secretaries in which she was inadvertently involved, she received an administrative warning and her tenure was delayed. She was told that even if she had tenure, under certain circumstances she could still be fired. Muna feels bad about this and comments that it shows that hard work is not enough, that unfairness and discrimination exist about which she can do nothing. The threat of losing her job scared Muna badly and now she does not dare take vacations or days off until her relationship with her director becomes secure once again.

Muna supports her two younger brothers. One of them studied to become a pharmacist's assistant and recently began working in a pharmacy in the city of Salt. Muna went to make sure that he rented a suitable room there. When he settled, she visited him every week or so. Later he left this job and found another one in the Jordan Valley. Although he is making 150 JD per month, he is not contributing towards the household expenses, because he is a man and has to think of his future and to save up for it, especially for marriage. Her other brother is studying computer programming at a community college and is not doing very well. He failed several courses and has had to delay taking the general board exam by one year. In the meantime he helps out a friend of his as a shop assistant and occasionally gets paid. Muna is not pleased about her brother's college results but there is little she can do. As for her younger sister, Muna tried to convince her to finish school, but she refused. She then tried to convince her to learn sewing and registered her in a course, but her sister went a few times and then stopped going, preferring to stay at home and do housework. Soon after she got engaged and married.

Muna wears colourful dresses and puts bangles and ribbons in her hair. Her summer dresses are sleeveless and short, for which she sometimes is criticized by her sister-in-law. In reply, she says that God cares about people's hearts and not the way they dress, and that while it is true that she goes out a lot, at least she is not spending her time gossiping like her sister-in-law. Muna has many friends from the office, and also attends social functions sponsored by the company. She likes to have dinner in smart hotels when the company is hosting a conference, or to visit friends in the residential areas of Amman, where she is surprised by the lack of children in the streets. She wishes she could buy a car so that she could have more freedom of movement and not depend on her brothers accompanying her when she wants to go out at night. But she says that every time she saves up for a car, 'something happens', and she has to spend the money on something else. At the moment her savings amount to 500 JD.

In her free time, Muna sews and saves a lot of money in this way, since ready-made clothes are expensive. She wants to take a sewing course in order to learn how to improve making the more difficult parts, such as the collars. She also thought of taking a course in artificial flower-making but decided to take the sewing course instead because it is more useful.

Muna is often critical and caustic in her comments about the community in which she lives. 'They are living in the Middle Ages', she says. 'They want their sons to be mechanics and their daughters to get married at fifteen.' Muna considers herself a rebel, not only because she works outside the house. She herself lays more emphasis on the fact that she refused to marry her first cousin, explaining that it was impossible to marry someone she had known all her life as a brother and whose conservatism she dislikes. She points to the restrictions that he imposes on his present wife. She has also refused proposals from a couple of men who approached her through one of her cousins, a busy-body forty-year-old woman who has fifteen children. One of these men is already married and wanted her as a second wife, which Muna said was out of the question. The other was a widower with one daughter and Muna would not consider marrying him because she would not want to be unfair to the daughter – if she ever scolded or hit her, she would be criticized by others, and if the child did not deserve it, it would be a sin. Besides, she says, she wants to have two children herself, one son and one daughter. Her cousin the match-maker blames her employment for this attitude. 'Muna thinks she is something special because she works', she says. 'This talk about only two children! At her age all she can ever hope to have is two children.'

In spite of her untypical behaviour and ideas, Muna is also completely involved in the life and relationships of her immediate surroundings. She goes visiting, is visited in return, and exchanges sewing patterns, news and gossip with neighbours and relatives. In spite of her criticisms of the community's values, she says they are caring, good and simple people. When her young nephew had an accident all the neighbours helped take him to the hospital.

Muna is aware of her unusual position in the community. She says that, depending upon where she is, she changes her accent and manner of speaking: at work she speaks with a city accent and at home with a peasant accent, so that the family will not laugh at her. She says the community does not approve of her but still like her. It is difficult not to like Muna who has a pleasant personality and is always smiling. But Muna also has a local standing that goes beyond her personality. When a female relative is to be married, Muna is asked to inspect the flat the bridegroom will provide. She has the last word on this and other matters. She is seen as someone who knows and understands the world outside the community. When Muna's married younger sister quarrelled with her mother-in-law and came home 'in anger', she came to Muna and not her brothers, making it clear that Muna was the head of that household. In the negotiations to effect a reconciliation between mother and daughter-in-law, it was Muna who played the key role.

Muna says that the people of the community do not care about educating their daughters. If a daughter is not doing well in school and wants to leave, they do not try to dissuade her. Sometimes mothers force their daughters to leave school to help them with the housework and want their daughters to get married at fifteen so as not to become an old maid. She says:

> I am the oldest maid as far as they are concerned, but I don't care. I am convinced of the importance of education and work. If I were not working and earning a salary, I would have been taking orders fror. my sister-in-law. Education is important even if a woman is married, for she may be divorced or widowed and if she cannot work, then she will live a life of humiliation at the mercy of her sister-in-law.

IV. Conclusions

The two cases above present a picture of women's participation in the labour force which, admittedly, has many features specific to the particular environments studied, yet they clearly indicate a very low rate of participation in the formal wage-labour force within a population which has the highest need for women's contribution to the household economy. The attempt to define current trends in these communities also brings to light methodological problems in the study of this multifaceted issue.

There is a paucity of studies in Jordan, and the Middle East in general, that define the characteristics of the female labour force at national level and which relate these characteristics to the changing economy. Although some national surveys exist, these merely serve to determine the numbers of women in each sector of the economy. Over and above the fact that such surveys do not include the economic activities of women who are not engaged in the formal wage-labour force, this simple classification does not indicate patterns over time or permit the analysis of the changing features of women's work. The surveys do not give information on educational levels, marital status or class background of the women concerned. Nor do they give an indication of wage-level, the type of wages received by such women, or their job security. They are therefore of no use in predicting future trends or in understanding the impact of women's work upon their own and their family's lives.

However, even if surveys were to include this type of information, it would still not suffice to give a complete picture of the context of women's work or changes in status and roles in a particular community and in society as a whole. Problem-oriented, local-level and in-depth studies are also needed to delineate this context and to highlight its nuances. Research should concentrate on life-long and occupational-longitudinal studies in order to observe changes in occupational history. Surveys should include a new category for women who have 'ever worked', similar to the concept now used to collect data on 'ever married' women, to capture such shifts over time.

State policy towards women and development in Jordan has generated a substantial number of papers and reports (see Annotated Bibliography). The approach to the issue, however, is generally inadequate and women's work is discussed in general terms which do not take account of geographical or class differences. Generalizations are based on the limited data available in official statistics. The problems arising from the use of different definitions and concepts in the collection of such data, which usually aim at examining general issues rather than women's issues, are not recognized.

Furthermore, the approach adopted in these papers falls within the framework of modernization theory, where modernization is defined in terms of economic growth achieved through planning, knowledge and technology. Accordingly, the analysis of women's status is based on an assumption that their status improves with modernization. Therefore, education and participation in the labour force are the main variables measured as indicators of modernization and improvement in women's status. Judgments are often based on inaccurate premises: for example, in an article advocating increased educational and training opportunities for women, Masri and Abu Jaber criticize school books for tending to represent 'the traditional consumer role of women in society rather than the modern producer role' (1983: 12). This implies that they themselves accept the assumption that women's traditional role is not a productive one.

In addition to their simplistic modernization approach, most papers generally reflect the goal of the state, which is the integration of women in development without causing fundamental changes in the social structure on the level of the family or the legal system as a whole. As Hijab points out: 'There is most resistance in the Arab World to change anything to do with the family' (1988: 12). Most policy-oriented approaches therefore avoid examining social and family relations that may constrain women's participation in the labour force, and advocate the preservation of existing moral values and family relations.

Another trend, however, sees that the integration of women in development requires not only increasing the opportunities for female education and participation in the labour force, but also changing the laws pertaining to women. This 'legal-administrative perspective' (Kandiyoti, 1980: 121) argues that the existing laws, and especially personal status laws and labour laws, retard the process of integration and urges that they be changed to accommodate the changing role of women (Khadir, 1987). However, this approach is also restricted by its analysis of existing laws without acknowledging the socio-economic obstacles to the actual practice of the proposed new laws, nor the way in which these laws may influence women's status in the different classes or environments.

In the two cases presented above, we have tried to show the logic of the characteristics of women's work, given the particular context of the communities to which they belong. This also shows the participation of women in the wider economy both through their contribution to household economic activities and enterprises and to wage-earning employment outside the home. The changing patterns of women's work are different in the two contexts but both show the impact of developments in the regional economy. Finally, the perception of these communities, and of the women themselves, concerning their work was examined in order to assess the reciprocal relationship between social norm and economic need. The studies show that it is difficult to measure increases and decreases in women's labour-force participation due to its constant fluctuation. The rural case-study especially shows that a rate of participation that holds in a certain period or season may not do so in the next. Regional economic changes also cause shifts in particular directions.

In the urban case-study, the rapid rise of income levels during the oil boom resulted in the withdrawal of many women from the labour force, especially poorer unskilled and uneducated women whose employment potential could not promise an economic return that made their work outside the home a worthwhile endeavour. For skilled or educated women, however, the oil boom has led to increased opportunities due to the expansion of the local labour market through the growth of the state bureaucracy and the private sector. The distribution of employment in this cohort, therefore, reflects the top-heavy image of the national level. Women from the squatter areas also played a role in labour migration abroad. The trend in this setting is therefore towards decreasing participation in certain types of employment and also towards an emphasis on more secure, formal labour-force employment, moving away from insecure, part-time and intermittent work. The life-history of Muna illustrates the change of status of women holding regular employment, which increases their authority within the family and the community network. However, the obligations engendered by this status reaffirm and strengthen the subordination of women's labour to the needs of the family.

In the rural case, the irrigation development project and the transformation of the agricultural economy and its orientation towards export crops has led women to enter increasingly insecure spheres of agricultural labour. Even wage-labour in the setting examined was not a secure or stable form of employment. At the same time, work within the family, which at least provided the security of continuity, is made less viable by changes in the economy. Furthermore, educational services are not widely available and, more significantly, employment for women with a certain level of education is severely circumscribed. The life-history of Sa'diyah is one example of how social norms and the particular economic circumstance of the family determine the labour choices available to women at different periods of their life.

The future is, of course, tied to the economic situation of the region. Both studies were conducted at a time when the current recession had not yet manifested itself clearly. Although the situation had started worsening, the optimism of the oil-boom years generally prevailed. Women's education, especially in the urban areas, was often encouraged by parents for the purpose of ensuring their daughter's employment, and even for sending them to work in the oil-producing countries. The family income subsequently depended largely upon this daughter's contribution. Since then, opinions in policy-making centres have been voiced for the withdrawal of women from the formal labour force as a solution for the rapidly intensifying unemployment problem in the country. If this type of policy is pursued, then even the limited inroads that women have recently achieved in the formally acknowledged sectors of the economy will be threatened and they will be likely to disappear once again into the 'invisible' and unmeasured spheres of labour.

References

ANANI, J.A., 'The Labour Situation in Jordan', in API/ILO, *Population, Employment and Migration in the Arab Gulf States*, Kuwait: API/ILO, 1978

ANON, 'Jordan: Labour Migration Hampers Economic Development', *Arab Economist*, 10 (108), 1978: 19–20

BASSON, P., *Male Emigration and the Authority Structure of Families in North-West Jordan*, report submitted to IWSAW, Beirut University College, Lebanon, 1984

BIRKS, J.S. AND C.A. SINCLAIR, *International Migration and Development in the Arab Region*, Geneva: ILO, 1980

BISHARAT, L. AND M. TEWFIK, 'Housing the Urban Poor in Amman: Can Upgrading Improve Health?', *Third World Planning Review*, Vol. 7, No. 1, Feb., 1985

BISHARAT, L. AND H. ZAGHA, *Health and Population in Squatter Areas of Amman: A Reassessment After Four Years of Upgrading*, Amman: Urban Development Department, 1986

BISHARAT, L., 'Infant and Childhood Mortality In the Upgrading Areas of Amman' (Mss), n.d.

BURCKHARDT, J.L., *Travels in Syria and the Holy Land*, London: John Murray, 1822

CLARKE, J., 'Jordan: A Labor Supplier', paper prepared for the USAID Seminar on Labor Migration, Washington DC: US Agency for International Development, 1977

DEEB, M., *Household Structure as Related to Childhood Mortality and Morbidity Among Low Income Areas in Amman*, unpublished Ph.D Dissertation, Johns Hopkins University, 1987

DOAN, R., *Class and Family Structure: A Study of Child Nutritional Status in Four Urban Settlements in Amman, Jordan*, unpublished Ph.D Dissertation, Cornell University, 1988

FINDLAY, A. AND S. SAMHA, 'The Impact of International Migration on the Urban Structure of Amman', *Espace, Populations, Sociétés*, 1, 1985: 93–8

GULICK, J., 'Baghdad: Portrait of a City in Physical and Cultural Change', *Journal of the American Institute of Planners*, 33 (4), July 1967: 246–55

HALCROW FOX AND ASSOCIATES, *Jordan Urban Project: Final Report*, Jordan: National Planning Council and Municipality of Amman, 1979

HAMMOUDA, A.A., 'Jordanian Emigration: An Analysis of Migration Data', *International Migration Review*, Vol. 14, 1980: 357–82

——, 'Some Aspects of Emigration from Jordan: Use and Application of a Log-Linear Model in the Analysis of Migration Data', *Egyptian Population and Family Planning Review*, Vol. 15, No. 2, 1980a: 25–74

HARB, MOHAMMED, 'Goat Breeding by Rural Women in Soubehi and Um Al-Basateen Village', paper presented at the Regional Experts' Meeting on Women's Role in Food Production, organized by the Ministry of Social Development in co-operation with FAO; Amman, 22–6 October, 1983

HIJAB, NADIA, *Womenpower: the Arab Debate on Women at Work*, Cambridge: Cambridge University Press, 1988

HUTTEROTH, W-D. AND K. ABDULFATTAH, *Historical Geography of Pales-*

tine, Trans-Jordan and Southern Syria in the Late 16th Century, Erlangen: Erlangen Geographische Arbeiten, 5, 1977

THE JORDANIAN INSTITUTE FOR SOCIAL SERVICES, *The Conditions of Working Women in Factories in Amman City*, a report submitted to the Women's Department – Ministry of Labour, Amman, 1978

KANDIYOTI, D., 'Urban Change and Women's Roles: An Overview and Evaluation', in Helen Anne B. Rivlin and Katherine Helmer (eds), *The Changing Middle Eastern City*, New York: Center for Social Analysis Program in Southwest Asian and North African Studies, State University of New York at Binghamton, 1980

KARPAT, K., 'Ottoman Immigration Policies and Settlement in Palestine', in I. Abu-Lughod and B. Abu-Laban (eds), *Settler Regimes in Africa and the Arab World*, Illinois: The Medina University Press International, 1972

––––, *The Gecekondu*, Cambridge: Cambridge University Press, 1976

KEDDIE, N.R., 'Problems in the Study of Middle Eastern Women', *International Journal of Middle Eastern Studies*, 10, 1979: 225–40

KHADIR, ASMA, 'Women and Trade Union Laws and Regulations', paper presented at the Seminar on Women and the Proposed Jordanian Labour Law: Amman, 17–18 September 1983, Organized by the Association of Professional Women (published 1987)

KHASAWNEH, S., 'Status of the Labour market', paper presented to the Seminar on the Status of the Jordanian Labour Market, Amman, 20 October 1986, organized by the Association of Professional Women

KHOURI, R.G., *The Jordan Valley: Life and Society Below Sea Level*, London: Longman, 1981

KIRWAN, F., 'The Impact of Labour Migration on the Jordanian Economy', *International Migration Review*, Vol. 15, 1981: 671–95

––––, 'Labour Exporting in the Middle East: The Jordanian Experience', *Development and Change*, Vol. 13, No. 2, 1982: 63–89

LASLETT, P., *Household and Family in Past Time*, London: Cambridge University Press, 1978 (first published in 1972)

LEWIS, N., *Nomads and Settlers in Syria and Jordan 1800–1980*, NY: Cambridge University Press, 1987

LOBO, S., *A House of My Own: Social Organization in the Squatter Settlements of Lima, Peru*, Tucson: University of Arizona Press, 1982

LOMNITZ, L., *Networks and Marginality: Life in a Mexican Shantytown*, New York: Academic Press, 1977

LYNCH, W.F., *Narrative of the United States' Expedition to the River Jordan and the Dead Sea*, London: Richard Bentley, 1849

MADANAT, S., 'Housing Situation in Amman in the 1980's', in R. Keles and H. Kano, *Housing and the Urban Poor in the Middle East – Turkey, Egypt, Morocco and Jordan*, Tokyo: Institute of Developing Economies, 1987: 196–218

MANGIN, W., 'Latin American Squatter Settlements: A Problem and a Solution', *Latin American Research Review*, II (3), Summer, 1967: 65–98

MASRI, M. AND K. ABU JABER, 'Education and Training of Women', in K. Abu Jaber (ed.), *Major Issues in Jordanian Development*, Amman: The Queen Alia Jordan Social Welfare Fund, 1983: 9–45

MCCLELLAND, D.H., *Worker Migration and Worker Remittances – Jordan*, Amman: US Agency for International Development, 1979

MUJAHID, G.B.S., 'Female Labour Force Participation in Jordan', in J. Abu Nasr *et al.* (eds), *Women, Employment and Development in the Arab World*, Berlin: Mouton, 1985

OWEN, R., 'Government and Economy in Jordan: Progress, Problems and Prospects', in P. Seale (ed.), *The Shaping of an Arab Statesman: Sharif Abd al-Hamid Sharaf and the Modern Arab World*, London: Quartet Books, 1983: 85–104

PERLMAN, J., *The Myth of Marginality: Urban Poverty and Politics in Rio de Janeiro*, Berkeley: University of California Press, 1976

PRINCESS RAHMA DEVELOPMENT CENTRE – ALLAN, *The Comprehensive Pilot Study to Assess Community Basic Needs of Allan and Karaymeh Areas: Field Studies*, Amman: Ministry of Social Development, 1980

QUINN, N., 'Anthropological Studies on Women's Status', *Annual Review of Anthropology*, 6, 1977: 181–225

RASSAM, A., 'Introduction: Arab Women: The Status of Research in the Social Sciences and the Status of Women', in Unesco (ed.), *Social Science Research and Women in the Arab World*, London, Dover NH, and Paris: Unesco and Frances Pinter, 1984: 1–13

——, 'Towards a Theoretical Framework for the Study of Women in the Arab World', in Unesco, Ibid., 1984a: 122–38

ROYAL SCIENTIFIC SOCIETY (RSS), *Report on the Study Group on Worker Migration Abroad*, Amman: RSS/Population Council, 1978

SAKET, BASSAM, K., 'Promoting the Productive Use of Remittances', in ECWA, *International Migration in the Arab World*, Beirut: ECWA, 1982

——, *Economic Uses of Remittances: The Case of Jordan*, Amman: Royal Scientific Society, 1983

SAKET, BASSAM, K. (ed.), *Worker Migration Abroad: Socio-Economic Implications for Households in Jordan*, Amman: Royal Scientific Society, 1984

SECCOMBE, I.J., *Manpower and Migration: The Effects of International Labour Migration on Agricultural Development in the East Jordan Valley*, Durham: Durham University, Centre for Middle Eastern and Islamic Studies (Occasional Paper Series, II), 1981

——, 'Manpower and Migration: Key Issues in the Recent Demographic History of the Hashemite Kingdom of Jordan', in A.M. Findlay (ed.), *Recent National Population Change*, London: Institute of British Geographers, 1982

——, *International Migration for Employment and Domestic Labour Market Development: The Jordanian Experience*, unpublished PhD Thesis, Durham University, 1983

——, *International Labour Migration and Skill Scarcity in the Hashemite King-*

dom of Jordan, Geneva: ILO, International Migration for Employment Project (Working Paper 14), 1984

SHAMI, SETENEY, *Ethnicity and Leadership: The Circassians in Jordan*, unpublished PhD Dissertation, Department of Anthropology, University of California, Berkeley, 1982

——, 'Maternal Practices in Child Care in an Urban Area', a paper presented to the UNICEF Workshop on Girls in the Middle East and North Africa, Amman, 23–26 March 1985

SHAMI, SETENEY AND LUCINE TAMINIAN, *Reproductive Behaviour and Child Care in a Squatter Area of Amman*, Cairo: The Population Council Regional Papers, 1985

SHURAYDEH, KHALID AND AMAL SABBAGH, *Women's and Employer's Attitudes towards Female Vocational Training and Employment in Jordan*, Amman: Ministry of Labour and Social Development, 1985

TAMINIAN, L., *Rural Transformations and Their Impact Upon Women's Participation in Agricultural Labour: A Case-Study of Ghor al-Mazra'a/al-Haditha*, unpublished Master's Thesis, Department of Anthropology, Yarmouk University, 1988 (in Arabic)

URBAN DEVELOPMENT DEPARTMENT (UDD), *Summary Tables of Comprehensive Social-Physical Survey*, Amman: Urban Development Department, 1981

——, *A Baseline Health and Population Assessment for the Upgrading Areas of Amman*, Cairo: Population Council Regional Papers, 1982 (re-issued 1984)

——, *First Report, Amman Follow-Up Health Assessment*, Amman: Urban Development Department, 1985

VELEZ-IBANEZ, C., *Rituals of Marginality: Politics, Process and Culture Change in Urban Central Mexico 1969–1974*, Berkeley: University of California Press, 1983

ZAGHA, H., 'Housing Problems, Policies and Solutions in Jordan', in R. Keles, and H. Kano (eds), *Housing and the Urban Poor in the Middle East – Turkey, Egypt, Morocco and Jordan*, Tokyo: Institute of Developing Economies, 1987: 178–96

ZURAYK, H., 'Women's Economic Participation', in F. Shorter and H. Zurayk (eds), *Population Factors in Development Planning in the Middle East*, New York and Cairo: The Population Council, 1985: 3–58

ZURAYK, H. AND F. SHORTER, *The Social Composition of Households in Arab Cities and Settlements: Cairo, Beirut, Amman*, Cairo: The Population Council Regional Papers, 1988

Select bibliography of studies on women in Jordan

ABDEL JABER, TAYSEER. 'Female Labor Force and the Jordanian Labour Law', paper presented at the seminar on Women and the Proposed Jordanian Labour Law, 1983, organized by the Association of Professional Women, Amman, 17–18 October 1983.
An analysis of the female labour force, its distribution in the different sectors and the impact of the proposed law on women in the various sectors.

ABU GHAZALEH, HAIFA AND ABU TALIB TAGHREED. 'Jordanian Women in Leadership and Administration Spheres', paper presented at the Regional Seminar for the Assessment of Women's Needs in Leadership and Administration Spheres, organized by The Queen Alia Jordan Social Welfare Fund in co-operation with ICOMP, Amman, 11–13 June 1988.
A statistical study defining problems facing women in leadership positions in the public sector and voluntary organizations, and the characteristics of a female leader.

ABU GHAZALEH, HAIFA et al., 'Women's Education and Training in Jordan', paper presented at The National Conference of Jordanian Women: Current Status and Future Prospects, organized by The General Union of Jordanian Women, Amman, 14–16 May 1985.
A study of the educational system in Jordan and the status of female education in particular; based on statistics collected by the Ministry of Education in Jordan.

ABU JABER, KAMEL AND GHARAIBEH FAWZI. 'Conditions of some Working Women in Jordan', *Arab Journal of Public Administration*, Vol. 2, No. 2, July 1978.

ABU KHOURMA, KHALEEL. 'Women in Trade Unions', paper presented at the Women and Trade Unions Seminar, organized by The Association of Professional Unions, Amman, 12–14 December 1987.
Deals with the legal state of trade unions in Jordan and women's position within them and defines the constraints that hinder their participation in the trade unions.

ABU HILAL, AHMAD K., 'The Jordanian Working Woman and Family Affairs', paper presented at the seminar on The Role of the Working Woman in Society, organized by the Ministry of Labour – Department of Women in co-operation with UNFPA, 1980.
A descriptive study of female unpaid labour within the family enterprise and in the house, as well as their paid labour outside the family domain.

74

AL-AHMAD, AHMAD Q., 'The Role of Jordanian Women in Development', paper presented at the seminar on Population and Development, Amman, 7–9 August 1982.

AL-BASHEER, HAIFA. 'The Importance of Organization in the Enhancement of the Women's Movement in Jordan', paper presented at The National Conference of Jordanian Women: Current Status and Future Prospects, organized by the General Union of Jordanian Women, Amman, 14–16 May 1985.
A study of The General Union of Jordanian Women, its programmes, achievements and the difficulties it faces.

AL-BASHEER, HAIFA AND SHURAYDEH HIYAM. 'The Political Participation of Jordanian Women and Attitudes towards their Participation', paper presented at The National Conference of Jordanian Women: Current Status and Future Prospects, organized by the General Union of Jordanian Women, Amman, 14–16 May 1985.
A study based on interviews conducted with men in decision-making positions concerning their attitudes towards women's participation in public life.

AL-DAMEN, RIMA K., 'Women and Economic Development', paper presented at The National Conference of Jordanian Women: Current Status and Future Prospects, organized by the General Union of Jordanian Women, Amman, 14–16 May 1985.
A study of the constraints that hinder women's participation in economic development with suggestions for the enhancement of their participation in socio-economic development.

AL-KISWANI, SALIM. 'The Jordanian Woman Between the Achievement of Political Rights and the Practice of these Rights', paper presented at The National Conference of Jordanian Women: Current Status and Future Prospects, organized by the General Union of Jordanian Women, Amman, 14–16 May 1985.
A study of the legal status of women in the political system and public life and the difference between legal status and the practice of political rights.

AL-KURDI, MONAWWAR. *The Role of Jordanian Women in Development*, unpublished PhD Dissertation, The Institute of Economic and Social Studies, University of Tunis, Tunisia, 1983.

——, 'The Female Sector', study submitted to the Ministry of Planning, Amman, N.D.
An analysis of women's present status in education, health, the labour

force and public life. It suggests a plan for the integration of women into comprehensive national development plans.

AL-MASRI, MONTHER. 'The Opportunities for the Training and the Rehabilitation of Women', paper presented at the seminar on Community College and University Graduates: Future Professionals, Where To?, organized by The Ministry of Labour and Social Development in co-operation with The Association of Professional Women, Amman, 25–6 March 1985.
A study of the educational and vocational training opportunities available to women compared with those for men as well as the problems and difficulties encountered in planning vocational training programmes for women.

AL-MUTLAQ, AIDA. 'The Social and Psychological Factors that Constrain Women's Participation in the Labour Market', unpublished paper, N.D.
An analysis of the social factors, such as child socialization and traditions, that hinder the full participation of women in public life.

AL-RADAYDA, KHALID. 'Employment Opportunities, Female Graduates and their Job Performance', paper presented at the Seminar of Community College and University Graduates: The Future Professionals, Where To?, organized by The Ministry of Labour and Social Development in co-operation with The Association of Professional Women, Amman, 25–6 March 1985.
A statistical study of females employed by the state: their number, level of education and job performance as compared to men's.

AL-TEL, SOUHEIR. *Introduction to Women's Issues and Movement in Jordan*, Beirut: The Arab Foundation for Studies and Publications, 1985.
A study based on statistics collected by different state agencies in the fields of education, health and work; it also tells the history of the women's movement in Jordan.

——, 'Female Labour Force in Jordan', unpublished paper, N.D.
A descriptive study of the situation of the female labour force in Jordan and its development in the last twenty-five years.

AL-UTTUM, MANSOUR. 'Female Graduates and Employment Opportunities', paper presented at the seminar on Community College and University Graduates: Future Professionals, Where To?, organized by the Ministry of Labour and Social Development in co-operation with the Association of Professional Women, Amman, 25–6 March 1985.
A study of the labour market in the mid-1980s and job opportunities available to women, as well as the future status of the labour market. It

gives general suggestions for designing vocational training programmes for women.

ARAB WOMEN'S ASSOCIATION. 'Women and Development', unpublished Paper, 1975.
A descriptive study of the socio-economic conditions of Jordanian women, emphasizing the importance of their integration into national development plans.

——, 'The Status of the Family in Jordan', unpublished paper, N.D.
An impressionistic study of the socio-economic conditions of Jordanian bedouin, rural and urban families.

BADRAN, IBRAHIM. 'The Interrelation between Education and Industrial Development', paper presented at the seminar on Community College and University Graduates: Future Professionals, Where To? organized by the Ministry of Labour and Social Development in co-operation with the Association of Professional Women, Amman, 25–6 March 1985.

BARHOOM, MOHAMMAD. 'The Attitudes of University Students Toward Working Women in Jordan', Amman, 1980.

BASSON, PRISCILLA AND N. ABURUMEILEH. *Food Conservation in North-West Jordan*, report submitted to FAO, Rome, Italy, 1980.

BASSON, PRISCILLA. *Women and Traditional Food Technologies: Changes in Rural Jordan*, Irbid, Yarmouk University, Department of Humanities and Social Sciences, 1981.
The study investigates the impact of development (commercialized production of milk products and eggs) on the household resources and on rural, middle-aged women whose illiteracy and family ties make them ineligible for participation in the modern sector.

——, 'Women's Productivity in Rural Jordan: Methodology for Quantification of Work Roles', Irbid: unpublished Ms., 1985.
A study of male- and female-headed households in thirteen localities in the North-West plateau region, assessing women's domestic productivity and the factors that influence it. It argues that age, education and fertility, as well as cash-earning activities, have an impact on women's domestic productivity in the two types of households with the result that older, less educated and more fertile wives not involved in cash-earning activities are more productive.

BILBEISI, OSAMA. 'A Study of the Role of Women and Youth in Rural Development in Jordan Valley', unpublished paper, N.D.

77

DAHHAN, U., *Population and Labour Policies: Regional Program for the Middle East: An Examination of the Literature on Jordanian Women*, Geneva: ILO, 1981.

DEPARTMENT OF PUBLICATIONS. *The Jordanian Woman*, Amman: Department of Publications, 1979.
A brief account of the history of the women's movement in Jordan from the 1920s till late 1970s, and a description of women's status in education, the labour force, politics and voluntary social work at the end of the 1970s.

THE DEPARTMENT OF SOCIAL AFFAIRS – PLANNING AND STUDIES SECTION. *A Survey Study of the Conditions of Married Working Women in Balqa District*, Amman: unpublished report, 1979.
A survey of 250 working mothers with children below the age of six (pre-school age) in the area of Salt, specifying the mothers' needs for child care centres. It examines the characteristics of working mothers with regard to their age, educational level, number of working hours, number of pre-school age children and child care during the absence of mothers.

DEPARTMENT OF STATISTICS. *The Findings of the Labour Force Census*, Amman: Department of Statistics, 1975.

——, *The Multi Purpose Study of the Family*, Amman: Department of Statistics, 1975.

——, *Basic Demographic and Socio-Economic Characteristics of Women in Jordan*, Amman: Department of Statistics, 1981.

——, *Jordan Fertility and Family Health Survey*, Amman: Department of Statistics in collaboration with the Division of Reproductive Health Centers for Disease Control, Atlanta, 1983.

EL-ASSAD, SHUJA' AND ATEF KHALIFA. *Family Structure in Relation to Fertility in Jordan*. Amman: Department of Statistics, 1977.

——, 'Fertility Estimates and Differentials in Jordan 1972–1976', *Population Bulletin of the United Nations Economic Commission for Western Asia*, 12, 1977.

FAKHOURI, HAIFA. *Position and Role of Working Women in Amman, Jordan: A Sociological Study*, unpublished Master's Thesis, Wayne State University, USA, 1974.

——, *Women, Change and Development in Jordan*, UNFPA-Ministry of Social Development and Labour: Amman, 1985.

GHAZWI, FAHMI S., *Modernization and Social Change in Family Life in Jordan*, unpublished PhD Thesis, University of Virginia, USA, 1985.

HAMMOUDA, AHMAD, A., 'The Jordanian Woman: An Evaluation of Woman's Status and Role during the Last Decade. A Strategy for the Enhancement of her Role till the End of this Century', unpublished report prepared for the Ministry of Labour and Social Development, 1985.
A descriptive study of women's position from 1975–1984 in the fields of education and the labour force, and of social constraints on women's participation in the labour force.

HARB, MOHAMMED. 'Goat Breeding by Rural Women in Soubehi and Um Al-Basateen Village', paper presented at the Regional Experts' Meeting on Women's Role in Food Production, organized by the Ministry of Social Development in co-operation with FAO, Amman, 22–6 October, 1983.
An evaluative study of an income generating project and its socio-economic impact on the ten families who benefited from it.

HIJAB, NADIA. *Womenpower: the Arab Debate on Women at Work*, Cambridge: Cambridge University Press, 1988.
An informative study on the experience of the Arab World in integrating women into the labour force illustrated by case-studies of Jordan and the Gulf States. It argues that the women's issue should be analysed within a framework that draws on the sociology of religion as well as the Arab quest for national and economic independence and development. It examines the existing personal status laws in different Arab countries and development policies that influence women's integration into development. In the case-study on Jordan, the emphasis is on state policy and its response to the economic need for increasing the participation of women in the labour force.

IBRAHIM, OTHMAN. 'Changes of the Urban Family in Jordan', *The Journal of Social Sciences*, Vol. 14, No. 3, 1986: 153–77

ISTEITIYEH, D.M., 'The Social and Economic Status of the Inhabitants of Ghor Dhra' and its Impact on the Growth and Development of the Local Community: A Field Study', unpublished paper, N.D.
A field study based on interviews and questionnaires, which examines the socio-economic conditions in a given village, and suggests measures to be taken to improve the living conditions of villagers.

JALAL AL DEEN, M.N., 'Sexual Discrimination and its Impact on Women's Status and Role: A Case of Jordan and Sudan', *The Journal of Social Sciences*, Vol. 12, No. 3, 1984: 7–35

JARDANEH, B., 'Jordanian Women in the Labour Force', paper presented to the National Conference of Jordanian Women: Current Status and Future Prospects, organized by the General Union of Jordanian women, Amman, 14–16 May, 1985.
A statistical study of working women in Jordan: their education and distribution in different sectors.

——, 'Female Labour in Jordan and the Arab and International Labour Agreements', paper presented to the National Conference of Jordanian Women: Current Status and Future Prospects, organized by the General Union of Jordanian women, Amman, 14–16 May 1985.
A brief account of all the Arab and International Labour Agreements that have been approved by Jordan and the impact of these agreements on female labour in Jordan.

——, 'Women's Status in Development', paper presented at the Seminar on Mass Media and Their Role in the Support of Women's Role in Development, organized by the Ministry of Social Development and Princess Rahma Centre for Development, Amman, 21–2 January 1984.
A brief account of the socio-economic changes in Jordan through the last twenty years and their impact on the labour market and on women's participation in the labour force.

——, 'The Jordanian Female Labourer and her Role in Agriculture, Industry and Trade', paper presented at the 11th session of the Arab Women's Committee, Amman, 24–28 April 1984.
An account of the characteristics of the female labour force with some emphasis on female agricultural labour.

——, 'The Achievements of Jordanian Women and Future Ambitions', paper presented to the seminar on Working Women and Population Issues, organized by the Ministry of Labour in co-operation with ILO and UNFPA, Amman, 1984.
A study of the demographic changes in Jordan in the last twenty years and their impact on the status of female labour. It also describes the social constraints on female labour.

JARDANEH, INTISAR. 'Voluntary Societies and Working Woman', paper presented at the Workshop on The Role of Working Woman in the Jordanian Society, organized by the Ministry of Labour – Department of Women in co-operation with ILO and UNPAF, Amman, 26–9 April, 1980.
A brief account of the development of voluntary societies in Jordan and of women's participation therein. It describes the role of voluntary societies in the enhancement of women's participation in the labour force.

JARDANEH. B. AND SALWA AL-MASRI. 'The Association of Professional Women and its Role in the Preparation of Women for Development', paper presented at the National Seminar on Population and Development, organized by The Ministry of Labour and the Association of Professional Women in co-operation with ILO and UNFPA, Amman, 26–7 May 1984.
A description of all the activities carried out by the Association of Professional Women with a view to enhancing women's participation in the labour force.

THE JORDANIAN INSTITUTE FOR SOCIAL SERVICES – RESEARCH AND STUDIES UNIT. *The Conditions of Working Women in Factories in Amman City*, report submitted to the Ministry of Labour – Department of Women, Amman, 1978.
A survey study of 293 female labourers working in twenty factories in Amman specifying their characteristics with regard to family structure, types of job, vocational training and attitudes towards labour.

THE JORDAN VALLEY AUTHORITY. *A Preliminary Study on Women and Labour in The Jordan Valley*, unpublished report, Amman: The Jordan Valley Authority, N.D.
A feasibility study to assess the availability of a female labour for the 'Arda marketing project. It covers 185 women living within the area, 95 of whom do not work. It investigates the reasons for this and the type of work the others do: paid/unpaid, seasonal/permanent.

JWEIHAN, MAJIDA. *The Investigation of the Impediments for the Qualified Jordanian Woman's Work Outside the House*, unpublished MA Thesis, University of Jordan, Jordan, 1985.

KELDANY, V., 'Problems Facing Working Women in the Field of Education in Amman', Amman: Social Work Department, 1972.

KHADIR, ASMA. 'Women and Trade Unions Laws and Regulations', paper presented at the seminar on Women and Trade Unions, organized by the Association of Professional Unions, Amman, 12–14 December 1987.
A study of the legal status of professional unions in Jordan, the position of women within them and the discriminatory laws which constrain women's roles.

——, 'Working Women in Jordan: Reality and Legislations', paper presented at the seminar on Women and the Proposed Jordanian Labour Law, organized by the Association of Professional Women, Amman, 17–18 September 1983.

A brief account of the proposed labour law and its impact on working women in the different sectors.

KHALAF, REEMA. 'Developmental Planning and Women in Jordan', unpublished paper, 1987.
A brief account of the different approaches adopted in the national plans towards the female labour force and the socio-economic reasons behind them.

KHAYRI, MAJDUDDIN O., *Attitudes Towards the Changing Role of Women in Jordan*, unpublished Master's Thesis, American University of Beirut, Lebanon, 1975.

——, *Social Relations in Some Jordanian Nuclear Families*, Amman: Jamiyyat Al-Matabi Al-Taawiniyyeh, 1985.

——, 'Modernization and Emancipation of Women in Jordan', unpublished paper, N.D.

——, et al. 'A Socio-economic Study of Self-Supporting Activities Conducted by Jordanian Women in Low Income Areas in Amman', study prepared for ECWA, 1982.
A survey of self-supporting activities of 99 households from two low-income areas in Amman, which investigates the contribution of these activities to the family's basic needs and specifies the networks that are formed as a result of them.

LAYNE, LINDA L., 'Women Wage-Earners: The Case of Factory Workers', Monograph, Amman, 1980.

——, 'Women in Jordan's Work Force', *MERIP Reports*, March–April 1981.

MALALLAH, M. (ed.), *Proceedings of the Second Symposium on Manpower Development: The Role of Jordanian Women*, Amman: Ministry of Labour, April 1978.

MALHAS, HIND. 'The Jordanian Woman in Rural Areas', paper presented at the National Conference of Jordanian Women: Current Status and Future Prospects, organized by the General Union of Women in Jordan, Amman, 14–16 May 1985.
A brief account of income-generating projects designed and implemented by the Ministry of Social Development in rural areas in Jordan.

MINISTRY OF LABOUR AND SOCIAL DEVELOPMENT. *National Document Submitted by the Hashemite Kingdom of Jordan to the World Conference to*

Review and Appraise the Achievements of the U.N. Decade for Women, Amman: Ministry of Labour and Social Development, 1985.

MINISTRY OF LABOUR AND VOCATIONAL TRAINING CORPORATION. 'Survey Study on Employment Opportunities and Training of Women in Jordan', Amman: Ministry of Labour, 1981.

MUJAHID, G.B.S., 'Female Labour Force Participation in Jordan', in J. Abu Nasir, *et al.* (eds), *Women, Employment and Development in the Arab World*, Berlin: Mouton, 1985.
A comprehensive evaluation of the statistical information available from different censuses and surveys on the female labour force and its characteristics. It also explores the main cultural, religious, demographic and economic factors that constrain women's economic activities and prescribes possible measures to facilitate and promote their participation in the labour force.

NASIR, RABIHA D., 'Women in Leadership Positions and Decision Making', paper presented at the National Conference of Jordanian Women: Current Status and Future Prospects, organized by the General Union of Jordanian Women, Amman, 14–16 May 1985.
A survey study of 102 women in leadership positions aiming at specifying female perceptions of leadership characteristics.

NASIR, SARI. 'Working Women in the Jordanian Society', *Faculty of Arts Journal*, University of Jordan, 1969.

NASRAWI, FATIN E., *Factors Influencing the Female Leadership Role in Jordan: Male and Female Perspectives*, unpublished Master's Thesis, Yarmouk University, Department of Education, Jordan, 1986.
A study based on interviews of 240 male and female Jordanians in leadership positions in private and public sectors, to delimit the socio-economic factors that constrain women from achieving leadership positions.

NEVIES, ISABELLE. *Income Generating Projects for Rural Women in Jordan: An Evaluation*, Amman: Unpublished report, 1985.
An evaluation of a dress-making workshop project which employs twenty-four women of low income. It specifies the characteristics of these labourers, and the social problems and difficulties facing female wage labourers in general.

PRINCESS RAHMA DEVELOPMENT CENTRE – ALLAN. *The Comprehensive Pilot Study to Assess Community Basic Needs of Allan and Kraymeh Areas: Field Studies*, Amman: Ministry of Social Development, 1980.
The study defines the basic needs of the local community and the natural

and human resources available in order to draw up development projects and design and implement training programmes for the participants in these projects. It studies family structure, socio-economic situation, education, health, attitudes towards, and participation in, development.

——, *A Study of Employment Opportunities of Rural Women in the Jarash Area*, Amman: Ministry of Social Development, 1982.
A study of job and employment opportunities available to women to accordingly design and implement vocational training programmes.

——, *A Study of Women and Childhood Status in Allan and Al-Deereh Towns*, Amman: Ministry of Labour and Social Development, 1988.
A feasibility study of income generating projects for women. It specifies women's attitudes towards work, their skills and the social constraints on their participation in development.

QUEEN ALIA JORDAN SOCIAL WELFARE FUND. *A Study of the Socio-economic Conditions of Rural Women in the Kerak Area*, Amman: Queen Alia Jordan Social Welfare Fund, 1981.
A survey study of 308 rural women from six villages in Karak areas. It is based on interviews and collects data needed for designing and implementing income-generating projects.

QUMEI', RULA. *A Feasibility Study of Income Generating Projects in Jordan*, Amman: Catholic Relief Services, 1984.

QUTIFAN, WAFA. *Family, Kinship and Economy in a Village in Northern Jordan Valley: (Qada Bani Kanana)*, unpublished Master's Thesis, Yarmouk University, Institute of Archaeology and Anthropology, Jordan, 1988.
An anthropological study examining the structure of the household economy in a rural area and the role of women in the domestic economy.

RASHDAN, NA'ILA. 'Women and Legislations', paper presented at the National Conference of Jordanian Women: Current Status and Future Prospects, organized by the General Union of Jordanian Women, Amman, 14–16 May 1985.
A descriptive study of women's status in Jordanian legislation in general and in labour law; election law as well as civil service regulations.

SABBAGH, AMAL A., 'The Role of Working Woman in Development', paper presented at the seminar on Working Woman and Population Affairs, organized by The Ministry of Labour in co-operation with UNFPA and ILO, Amman, 9–13 August 1981.
The paper focuses on the importance of the integration of economic and

social development, the implications of this for women and the importance of female vocational training and participation in decision taking.

SAE'D, NIMRA. 'The Changing Role of Women in Jordan', paper presented to the Research Committee on Sociology, Toronto, 1974.

SAE'D, NIMRA *et al.*, 'Women's Extra Work Outside the House', paper presented at the second seminar on The Development of Manpower: the Role of Jordanian Women, Amman, 4–7 April 1976.
A survey study specifying the characteristics of part-time female labourers in regard to their age, educational level, marital status, and skills, as well as the nature of the establishments that employ such labourers. The data covers 150 female labourers and thirty-nine establishments.

SAE'D, NIMRA. 'Education and Sex Roles in Jordan', paper presented at the 9th World Congress of Sociology, Uppsala, Sweden, 14–19 August, 1978.

SAKET, BASSAM K. (ed.) *Worker Migration Abroad: Socio-Economic Implications for Households in Jordan*, Amman: Royal Scientific Society, 1984.

SHAMI, SETENEY. 'Maternal Practices in Child Care in an Urban Area', paper presented at the Workshop on Girls in the Middle East and North Africa, organized by UNICEF, Amman, 23–6 March 1985.
Examines child bearing and child rearing in squatter areas of Amman with special emphasis on the role of young girls in child rearing and other household activities.

SHAMI, SETENEY AND LUCINE TAMINIAN. *Reproductive Behavior and Child Care in a Squatter Area of Amman*, Cairo: The Population Council Regional Papers, 1985.
An anthropological study of a squatter area in Amman. It focuses upon aspects of the social environment including household structure, kinship group and community which determine reproductive behaviour and child care in a squatter area of Amman.

SHURAYDEH, HIYAM, AND ADEL LUTFI. 'Working Woman in Jordan: A Study and Analysis of Her Characteristics', paper presented at the National Conference of Jordanian Women: Current Status and Future Prospects, organized by the General Union of Jordanian Women, Amman, 14–16 May 1985.
A study of the characteristics of working women and their participation in the labour force in accordance with their age. It specifies the social factors influencing women's work as well as its social and economic impact on family income, child care and age at marriage.

SHURAYDEH, KHALID, AND AMAL SABBAGH. *Women's and Employer's Attitudes towards Female Vocational Training and Employment in Jordan,* Amman: Ministry of Labour and Social Development, 1985.
A survey study that investigates the socio-economic factors affecting female attitudes towards education and certain careers, as well as employer's attitudes towards female employment.

THE SOLDIERS' FAMILIES' WELFARE SOCIETY. *A Survey Study of Women in Gwerieh Area,* Amman: unpublished report, 1982.
A survey study of 153 households specifying the major demographic socio-economic characteristics of women aged 20–39 who can participate in income-generating projects.

TAMINIAN, LUCINE D., *Rural Transformations and Their Impact on Women's Participation in Agricultural Labour: A Case Study of Ghor Al-Mazra'a/Al-Haditha,* unpublished Master's Thesis, Department of Anthropology, Yarmouk University (in Arabic).
An anthropological study examining the impact of the integration into the world market and of development projects on agricultural production in the Jordan Valley with special emphasis on the role of females in different forms of agricultural production.

TUTUNJI, RIMA. 'The Status of Women in Jordan', Amman: USAID, 1978.

VOCATIONAL TRAINING CORPORATION. *Survey of the Labour Force in Jordan,* Amman: Vocational Training Corporation, 1986.
The data collected by the Vocational Training Corporation covers 1,092 female students in the 3rd preparatory class from Amman and Zarqa areas and 149 employers from industrial and service establishments operating in the same areas.

YAHYA, KHAWLA. 'Women's Participation in Public Life', paper presented at the National Conference of Jordanian Women: Current Status and Future Prospects, organized by the General Union of Jordanian Women, Amman, 14–16 May 1985.

2

Rural women, work and gender ideology: A study in Egyptian political economic transformation

Soheir A. Morsy

I. Introductory remarks

This comparative study of rural women in two Egyptian villages of the Nile Delta focuses on work, social position, and gender ideology in relation to transformations in the Egyptian national and regional political economy. Informed by a holistic conception of work which transcends remunerative wage labour, it examines women's roles in production and social reproduction (cf. Tucker, 1976; Harris and Young, 1984; Beneria and Sen, 1981; Croll, 1986). Fieldwork conducted in the villages of Fatiha and Bahiya[1] during the mid-1970s and early 1980s respectively, provided some of the data on which this study is based. Attention is focused on the social conditions, material and ideological, which produce and reproduce the gender division of labour among local social collectivities as well as on male–female power relations in the communities under study.

1. Thanks are given to Hanan Sabea and Petra Kuppinger for their assistance in library research and to Unesco's Division of Human Rights and Peace for commissioning this comparative study as a follow-up to the Unesco Regional Working Group on Women's Participation in Public Life in the Arab States region (Irbid, Jordan, 13–16 December 1986). The study draws *inter alia* on some of the data collected during previous fieldwork by the author. The support of the Wenner-Gren Foundation for Anthropological Research and the American Research Center in Egypt for fieldwork conducted in Fatiha is acknowledged, as well as the grants from the National Endowment for the Humanities and the American Research Center in Egypt for fieldwork in Bahiya.

It should be noted that Fatiha and Bahiya are pseudonyms given by the author. The ethnographic present will be used in the case-studies of these two villages.

The study draws upon political economy as a methodological complement to an empirically based analysis of socio-culturally embedded gender differentiation. This illuminates national and regional influences which originate far beyond the boundaries of local communities, yet affect rural women's lives profoundly. By linking micro-sociological ethnographic analysis to the macro-analytical level of political economy, the study presents an alternative to the idealist socio-culturalism which has long characterized much of the literature on Arab women (e.g. Flory, 1940; Patai, 1969; Antoun, 1970; Ginat, 1981; cf. Tomiche, 1968; Hammam, 1980; Tucker, 1986).

Furthermore, epistemologically this study derives from a feminist orientation and from related efforts to rectify an androcentric bias in social studies (Reiter, 1975). Calling for historical specificity in the study of Arab women's work and social position, it also adopts the anti-orientalist stance which rejects classification in terms of *the* 'Islamic culture' (Abdel Malek, 1963; Abou-Zahra, 1970; Naim, 1978; Patai, 1969; Said, 1978).

In the decade after the completion of the anthropological research on which the account of women's social position in Fatiha is based, many changes have occurred in the Egyptian economy. Populist development has given way to 'open door' state policies and associated more complete reintegration of Egypt into the global political economy (Abdel Khalek, 1977; Morsy, 1980; Cooper, 1982; Abdel Khalek and Tignor, 1982; Waterbury, 1983). Concomitant changes have been noted for rural Egypt (Richards, 1980; Morsy, 1981; Korayem, 1982; Richards and Martin, 1983; Hopkins, 1987), and in relation to certain dimensions of the gender system (Khattab and El Daeif, 1982; Hatem, 1983; Khafagy, 1984; Awni, 1984; Morsy, 1985). Such changes, notably those related to labour migration and the regional petro-economy, are detailed in the examination of women's social position in the village of Bahiya.

Within the comparative framework of the study, the earlier account of Fatiha provides a background for judging the relatively more recent illustration of Egyptian rural women's work and social position derived from Bahiya. More generally, the comparative orientation adopted here tests the validity of the assertion that 'rural women's roles underwent *considerable* change' during the last decade, particularly with regard to alleged empowerment and new found 'emancipation' (Khafagy, 1984, as quoted in Abdel Khader, 1987: 131, emphasis added).

This study now continues with an examination of theoretical

issues related to women's work in the Third World and in the Egyptian context (Part II), followed by Part III which situates the analysis within the framework of changes in Egyptian state policies towards rural areas and the gender implications resulting therefrom. Results of fieldwork in the two Nile Delta villages, Fatiha and Bahiya, are presented in Parts IV and V. Part VI provides concluding remarks comparing the experiences of rural women in these two communities.

II. Women, work and gender ideology: Theoretical considerations

A. Beyond eurocentric conceptions of work

Over the course of the United Nations Decade for Women (1975–85), researchers and policy makers extended considerable attention to ways of 'integrating' women into the development process (Beneria and Sen, 1981). Within the framework of developmentalist strategies, women were targeted as potential sources of increased productivity with a consequent raising of the gross national product, an outstandingly economistic index of development. Increasing women's participation in the salaried labour force formed an important component of women in development programmes designed to enhance women's social position.

As the United Nations Decade for Women drew to a close, the assertion of empowering women through 'development' no longer enjoyed its once privileged tone. With the abandonment of the modernist assumption that the development process in the Third World is inherently beneficial and 'progressive', strategies for the empowerment of women, including salaried employment, no longer struck the same earlier notes of optimism. The critical analytical orientation, adopted by researchers to document the adverse impact of colonial surplus appropriation on Third World women, now extends to studies of women in independent, post-colonial nation states integrated in the international economy (e.g. Boserup, 1970; Remy, 1975; Smarakkody, 1979; cf. Bossen, 1975; Nash and Fernández-Kelly, 1983).

Critical appraisal of conceptions of women's work in the Third World has prompted researchers to note the failure of development policies to recognize the value of women's contribution to production and reproduction in both rural and urban societies. It is argued that:

the apparent invisibility of women's worth, as well as their work, is widespread and persistent. Women's work has, on the whole, been severely devalued by a universal ideological framework that regards them as inferior bearers of labour. . . . This perception appears to be at its strongest in many rural areas in underdeveloped countries, where a coincidence of interests between capital and male policy-makers has resulted in the creation of a female domain in subsistence agriculture responsible for reproducing and nurturing a large reserve army of cheap labour (Afshar, 1985: ix).

A number of recent studies of women's work reveal how euro-centric interpretations of women's economic activities in the Third World derive from a reductionist definition which equates work with wage labour. In documenting the variety of conceptions of work cross-culturally, anthropologists have shown that the definition of work extends even to the ritual arena. As Diane Bell has noted in her study of central Australian Aboriginal women: 'Rituals are indeed work for aborigines for it is here that they locate the responsibility of maintaining their families and their land' (1986: 78).

By relegating women's non-remunerated labour to the domain of the unseen and theoretically irrelevant, the modernist orientation conceals the relation between women's non-wage labour and the more 'public' domain of 'formal' economies. Ideological implications aside, such an economistic focus on wage labour hides not only women's domestic labour, but also their more 'public' contribution to the so-called informal sector (Tiano, 1981; Jules-Rosette, 1982; Bujra, 1984; Martella, 1985); as well as their double burden of domestic and non-domestic work (Eisenstein, 1979; Hammam, 1979; Gallin, 1986; Wallerstein *et al.*, 1982: 438).

With the failure of development programmes to empower women or to develop their societies, attention turned to the under-lying processes of development into which women were to be 'integrated'. Informed by a conception of development which recognizes the power asymmetries associated with global political economy (S. Amin, 1973), researchers have begun to analyse the effects of the internationally dominant mode of production on Third World women. While some recent studies of women's work have concentrated on the techniques of resistance to capitalist values and institutions (Long, 1984), others emphasize the transformation prompted by capitalist development (Afshar, 1985). Overall, accounts show that capitalism does not everywhere have the same effects on women (Bujra, 1984: 17).

Contrary to developmentalist jargon, scholarly accounts reveal that women are *already* integrated in the development process, albeit not exclusively in a manner consistent with the ideological definition of work as remunerated labour. Beyond the limitations of deceptive labour statistics, historical as well as contemporary studies document women's direct contributions to the economies of their local societies, and indirect subsidization of national and international economies (Arizpe and Aranda, 1981). Indeed, women, in addition to their roles in production, bear the brunt of reproduction. They are responsible for the provision of 'basic needs', ranging from contributing to food production and processing, to responsibility for fuel, water, health care, child rearing and sanitation (DAWN, 1985: 16–17). Even within the restrictions of gender-based subordination, women have managed to participate in various forms of associations and establish co-operative networks with clear economic functions. It is only in light of a certain restrictive conception of work that such activities are relegated to the 'informal' sector of 'developing' economies (March and Taqqu, 1986).

B. Arab women and work: Between idealist assertions and political economic analysis

Compared to the proliferation and theoretical sophistication of women's studies in other parts of the world, 'data on Arab women . . . is extremely limited and fragmentary, much of it based on second- and third-hand impressions rather than on direct field contact with Arab women' (Shilling, 1980: 117). However, since the 1970s an increasing number of empirically grounded studies of the Arab world have focused on women's once 'muted structures' (e.g. Dwyer, 1978; Davis, 1982; Eickelman, 1984; Abou Lughod, 1986; Al-Torki, 1986; cf. Nelson, 1986). While the consideration of economic activities in such studies has been limited, they nevertheless reveal the variety of women's economic contributions. It is noted that: 'The economic aspects covered in studies are manifold, ranging from migration and its effects on women . . . to traditional work organization in villages, including recent changes. . . . There are articles on women workers . . . and urban petty traders . . . and also . . . studies of upper class professionals.' (Kuppinger, 1988: 1)

Empirical research on Arab women's economic contributions, including that which documents women's productive and reproductive activities, although limited, nevertheless represents a welcome corrective to the mystification of statistically based studies of women's 'labour force participation' (Youssef, 1974; Sullivan,

1981; Lesch and Sullivan, 1986). Data presented in empirical studies stand in contrast to the restrictive definition of work as remunerated labour. Women have been shown to engage in a variety of income-generating activities apart from wage labour, participate in inter-household co-operation, and manage craft production (Rugh, 1979; Balfet, 1982; Glavanis, 1984; Lynch and Fahmy, 1984; Koptiuch, 1985; Abaza, 1987a, 1987b; Nelson and Saunders, 1986). Documentation of women's work patterns associated with male migration has likewise formed a major focus in recent studies (Khafagy, 1984; Myntti, 1984; El-Solh, 1985; Morsy, 1985).

Recent historical and micro-sociological accounts of women's position in the Arab world pose a challenge to universalistic models of male–female power relations, notably those derived from the modernist paradigm (Baer, 1964: 43; cf. Tucker, 1983; Koptiuch, 1985), and the allegedly universal opposition of the public and private domains (Rosaldo and Lamphere, 1974; cf. Nelson, 1973; Joseph, 1975; Sutton *et al.*, 1975; Sukkary-Stolba, 1985). The bifurcation of spheres, which is nothing less than a eurocentric construct traceable to the Aristotelian state power-politics paradigm (Elshtain, 1974), has been demonstrated as problematic in the study of women in the Arab world. Hammond and Jablow's claim that women's work is always private, while roles within the public sphere are the province of men (quoted in Leacock, 1975: 606) illustrates this position. In addition to undermining the relation between the two 'spheres', such an approach obscures the fact that in this part of the world, 'the domestic sphere is a lively area of economic action' (Joseph, 1986: 4).

In spite of the recent increase in women's studies in the Arab world (Mernissi, 1975; Wikan, 1982; El-Atteyah, 1983; Fernea, 1985; Gadant, 1986; Sullivan, 1986), research on the gender division of labour remains 'embryonic' (Keddie, 1979: 240; cf. Abdel Fatah, 1984; Rassam, 1984). Not unlike the case of women in other parts of the so-called developing world, Arab women's work generally remains hidden from view until it enters the market, where its exchange value is established. Only then is the work of 'economically active' women honoured with statistical notation. Based on such documentation, and the related restricted conception of work, it is alleged that women's participation in the labour force is 'limited' (Youssef, 1976, 1978).

In contrast to universalistic paradigms, it has been suggested that 'instead of making generalizations about women in any cultural area such as the [Arab world], it is profitable to analyse comparatively the types of networks and political-economic systems in which women are found' (Aswad, 1978: 476). When such political economic studies have been undertaken in the Arab world, they have revealed the variability of historically specific female productive and reproductive activities. Thus, modernist interpretations and ahistorical idealist approaches to the study of homogenized 'Muslim' women have been effectively challenged (J. Gran, 1977; Hammam, 1977; Hale, 1981).

Some recent studies have adopted a political-economic analytical framework which places Arab women's experiences in a historical context and differentiates them in the light of their class position (e.g. Hammam, 1980; Tucker, 1986; cf. Al Qazzaz, 1978: 377; Keddie, 1979: 240; Hatem, 1987). Commenting on Egyptian female workers during Egypt's early phase of industrialization in the nineteenth century, Mona Hammam indicates that the political-economic transformation of the time undermined cultural prescriptions:

> The fact that women faced the same responsibilities as men points to the correctness of the view that economic need (on the part of women) and the need to exploit cheap labour (on the part of the employer) is a much stronger force in determining women's roles than are the cultural biases dictating female confinement and seclusion. Not only did women fulfil their responsibilities to the employer as men did, but they also . . . engaged in defending their rights *vis-à-vis* their employer, confirming once again that cultural biases constitute only a contributing factor in defining women's roles and not a determining one. (Hammam, 1977: 34)

When historically specific political-economic conditions are considered, Arab women's allegedly 'unhealthy' and 'negative' attitude towards work, as impediments to their labour force participation (Korayem, 1981a), also appears in a different light. Nineteenth-century accounts of peasant women indicate that under Mohamed Ali's system of statist industrialization:

> When draft animals were forced to be given up by the peasants as payment towards government levies, women were substituted for traction. . . . Not only did women do the work of draft animals but the scarcity of labour at the national level drew women into public works construction: irrigation networks, canals, dams, etc., through corvée drafts. They were assigned, alongside men, to clear the earth, carrying and transporting the heavy loads of mud and sand on their heads (St John, 1841, and Hamont, 1843 as quoted in Hammam, 1980: 16).

While historical studies have been significant in shedding light on

how women have already been 'integrated' into capitalist development in Arab social formations, many questions related to women's
social position in contemporary Arab society remain unanswered, and
many more remain to be raised in the light of new data. For Egypt, a
survey of published accounts of rural areas indicates that: 'research
that highlights the role and contribution of women and children has
not yet been done. Survey research is unlikely to produce this kind of
information, for practical reasons, and a fairly high degree of famil-
iarity with one or another village seems necessary' (Hopkins and
Mehanna, 1981: 65).

The present study aims to contribute towards 'highlighting' the
role of Egyptian rural women.

III. Egyptian state policies, agrarian transformation and rural women (1952–1981): An historical note

In contrast to the dominant idealist orientation which has guided
much of the study of Arab women, historical studies have revealed
the significance of state interventions (Hammam, 1977; J. Gran,
1977; Morsy, 1978a: 146–58; Abdel Khader, 1987; cf. Bybee, 1978).
Given the present study's theoretical orientation, it partakes of this
line of analysis. Thus the focus of this chapter on agrarian
transformation in relation to state capitalism and Open Door
Economic Policies (ODEP) contextualizes the micro-sociological
accounts of the two Nile Delta villages (Fatiha and Bahiya) in
macro-level political-economic transformation. This consideration
of the impact of state policies is analytically indispensable, given the
central function of the state in the process of capital accumulation,
and its role as direct agent in the production process in the
post-1952 era.

A. Populist state policies and rural transformation

At the time of the July 1952 Free Officers' Coup, Egypt had been
integrated into the global capitalist system for several decades (S.
Amin, 1976, 1978; Clawson, 1978; Davis, 1975; Gran, 1979; M.
Hussein, 1973; Radwan, 1975). Contrary to modernist assertions,
colonial domination led to the country's underdevelopment, and
the interruption of the process of proletarianization of Egyptian
women in its incipient stage (Abdel Malek, 1968; Hammam, 1977;
Radwan, 1977). Upon coming to power, Gamel Abdel Nasser set
Egypt on the road of state capitalist development. The conse-

quences for rural Egypt and peasant household production were most significant. In an attempt to break up the power of the ruling oligarchy in the countryside, the new leaders undertook to win the support of the rural masses through a programme of land redistribution. Beneficiaries of this programme included peasants from Fatiha and Bahiya. The allocation of land reflected the state's androcentric bias. Priority was thus given to male heads of household with large families. Unlike collectivist agrarian programmes in other parts of the world, the Egyptian reforms were designed to expand small family holdings (Abdel Fadil, 1975: 8).

While improvements in income and legal status for the majority of agricultural producers stand out as the most valuable achievements of the Nasserist agrarian reforms (Warriner, 1962; cf. Radwan, 1977: 28), peasant families, including women, continued to bear the burden of the state's programme of economic development. As the state regulated access to productive resources through the distribution of expropriated land, it proceeded to appropriate its surplus products to finance the development of other sectors of the Egyptian economy. Agricultural surplus was extracted through a 'double squeeze' of taxation and claim to part of the crop yield (or all of it in the case of cotton). Agricultural co-operatives functioned primarily to execute government policies in the management of agricultural cycles, appropriation of surplus, and taxation of the peasants to ensure a steady flow of revenues to finance state capitalist development.

According to the statistics of the Central Bank of Egypt, the state paid the peasant 18 Egyptian pounds (£E) per *qantar*[2] of cotton and sold it raw on the world market for £E 33.4. For broad beans the peasant received £E 8.7 per *ardáb*[2] when the world market price was 51.3. Thus peasant production was further integrated into the national, and in turn, the international economy.

Contrary to unilineal modernist or marxist models of societal development, the continued integration of Egypt as part of a dependent region in the global capitalist economy did not produce the predicted, uniform outcome:

> [Although] such an integration challenged the survival capabilities of former subsistence-oriented peasant communities, [it] did not result in homogeneous forms of peasant production and social organization. Instead earlier structures mediated and enhanced the integration of former peasants into the world-economy and national societies, so that

2. One *qantar* is equivalent to 157.5 kilograms, one *ardáb* to 19.1 kilograms.

paths of integration exhibited a variety of outcomes ranging from full proletarianization to partial proletarianization and to independent commodity production. (Glavanis and Glavanis, 1983: 15; cf. Abdel Fadil, 1975, Byres, 1977, Richards, 1982)

Cognizant of alternative 'paths of rural transformation' (Keyder, 1983), anthropological studies of historically specific peasant responses to capitalism have undermined the assertion that the 'agrarian transition' (to capitalism), allegedly associated with the Nasser regime, has occurred in Egypt (Glavanis, 1984; Hopkins, 1987; cf. Abdel-Fadil, 1975). Such studies have demonstrated that the capitalist path is but one of a number of major alternatives including familial petty commodity production, as well as agrarian transformation associated with state programmes and exemplified by the case of the reclaimed New Lands (Sabea, 1987). While individual villages may be *dominated* by one or another of these paths of agrarian transformation, this does not exclude other forms (Hopkins, 1987: 5).

In this regard it is worth remembering that agrarian reforms were designed to create a regime of small peasant properties and provide beneficiaries and their families with bare subsistence expenses (Abdel Fadil, 1975: 8). Owners of small plots and members of their families, including females, were often forced to supplement their income through wage labour. Long after the implementation of the state programme of land distribution, landholdings under five *feddans*[3] continued to predominate numerically as individual peasant households consolidated themselves over the years. State policies thus reinforced the small peasantry, and household production, as the *backbone* of Egyptian agriculture. Aside from assertions regarding agrarian transition to capitalism, empirically based studies suggest that: 'the salient feature of agrarian social structure and economy [continued to be] the small peasant producer oriented towards the production of basic subsistence crops within a household where labour remains *unremunerated* . . . [Moreover], . . . informal co-operation is a vital aspect of village reality' (Glavanis and Glavanis, 1983: 69, emphasis added).

Within the framework of populist state policies the rural poor, women included, came to enjoy a form of security previously unknown to them. In addition to access to means of production (including private property and state-regulated tenancy) and related

3. One *feddan* equals 1.038 acres or 0.42 hectares.

culturally valued secure subsistence (Saad, 1987), peasants benefited from state services, notably public education and health care
(Harik, 1974; Mayfield, 1974; Baker, 1979), as well as urban
industrial and bureaucratic employment. However, small peasant
households, reinforced by state policies, continued to bear the
brunt of national development. Within the framework of state
capitalist development, the state's control over the productive
process did *not* mean undifferentiated allocation of surplus. In fact the
state imposed on small producers of traditional crops a disproportionate burden of taxation to finance state capitalist development.

During the 1950s and 1960s women's work remained a vital part
of small peasant household *unremunerated* labour. It continued to be
inseparable from non-capitalist forms and relations of production
articulated with dominant capitalism in the agrarian economy
(Glavanis, 1984). Given the predominance of small peasant household production based on family unremunerated labour, women's
productive and reproductive activities, within the framework of
internationally articulated state capitalist development, remained
far from 'limited'.

Contrary to statistically based assertions, women's work, as part
of small peasant household production, integrated into the national
and international economy, continued to help subsidize wage
labourers and rich peasants in rural areas as well as workers and
capitalists in urban areas, while also contributing to capital accumulation on a world scale.

Within the framework of this integration, the continued significance of women's contributions renders unilinear predictions and
universalistic models of women's roles doubtful.

B. Egypt's 'economic opening': capitalist reorientation and state agrarian policies

From the mid-1970s, Egypt witnessed a re-orientation in capitalist
development, popularly designated 'the economic opening', which
would bring about its more complete reintegration into the global
market economy (Mursi, 1976; Hussein, 1981; Abdel Khalek,
1982). Signalled by the paper of October 1974, the state's Open
Door Economic Policies (ODEP) introduced a series of measures
aimed at attracting foreign capital, encouraging Western and Arab
private investment in previously nationalized sectors of the economy, and providing new employment opportunities for Egyptian
labour.

Within the framework of economic liberalization rooted in earlier state capitalist development, the state's role in rural Egypt
remained considerable. Its subsidization of agricultural inputs,
system of forced deliveries, and regulation of access to means of
production through control of the land tenure system remained
firmly established. In addition legislation was introduced legalizing
advantages enjoyed by the upper strata of rural society (Abdel
Fatah, 1981), which was followed by the dramatic 1974 ruling by
the Highest Court of Appeal decreeing that the sequestration of
land from large landlords by the Nasser government was illegal
(Saad, 1987). These various measures, as well as subsidies, credit
and tax exemptions, have clearly favoured the upper strata of the
peasantry and capitalist farmers. While Egypt continued to be
plagued with shortages of essential food items and became a net
importer of agricultural commodities for the first time in its history
(Richards, 1980), the state supported the expansion of fruit orchards, meat and milk production for urban consumption as well as
aromatic plants (Al-Ahram al-Iqtisadi, 1981; Federation of Egyptian Industries, 1981).

During the latter part of the 1970s, state interventions were
correlated with certain outstanding trends in Egyptian agricultural
production. While the area planted with traditional field crops
amounted to 9,753,000 *feddans* in 1960 and 9,794,000 *feddans* in
1978, these represented 94.0 per cent and 87.8 per cent of total
cultivated areas, respectively, indicating a net decline in the proportion of traditional field crops (Abdel Fatah, 1981). Statistical
data from the Ministry of Agriculture also indicate that for the
period from 1960 to 1978, while the area planted with field crops
showed a net increase of 0.4 per cent, vegetables increased by 91.5
per cent, fruits by 158 per cent and medicinal and aromatic plants
(such as jasmine grown in the village of Bahiya) by 2,133.3 per cent
(ibid.).

Notwithstanding the obvious increase in areas planted with
aromatic plants, this form of cultivation constituted a minor proportion of Egyptian agricultural production, amounting to no
more than 0.44 per cent of the total field crop area for the period
between 1974 and 1976 (Mohamed, 1980). Of the combined area of
medicinal and aromatic plants cultivated in Egypt during this period,
only 27 per cent or 13,000 *feddans* were devoted to the cultivation of
aromatic plants. But although cultivation of the latter is limited, their
economic value is considerable, particularly after the raw vegetation is
processed and exported to Europe and the United States in the form
of aromatic concentrates and oil (Abdel Fatah, 1981). It is this relative

profitability of aromatic plants, associated with world market prices, which renders their cultivation attractive to local producers, including the peasants of Bahiya.

In general the increase in the area of non-traditional crops has been associated with rich peasants who have channelled their investments into non-traditional agricultural production. Since the late 1950s the cultivation of profitable, capital intensive orchard crops and flowers had been exempted from taxation. Although in 1978 parliament legislated the taxing of profits from orchards, poultry and livestock on holdings of three or more *feddans*, this ruling was put aside by a 1981 revision of the law. Moreover, owners of five or more head of cattle continued to be entitled to insurance for their animals, as well as fodder amounting to 150 kg. per month at subsidized prices. Large landowners also continued to partake of the state's subsidized credit for the purchase of livestock, which increased from £E 440,000 in 1970 to £E 21.5 million in 1978. Furthermore, state policies maintained support for wealthy agrarian elements by encouraging large-scale poultry and egg production, and providing customs exemptions on imported chicks and equipment (Waterbury, 1983: 296).

While the upper strata of agrarian producers has benefited from the state's programme of economic liberalization, landlessness and rural poverty increased during the decade following the state's 1974 policy declarations (Radwan, 1977; Harik, 1979; Korayem, 1987). The tremendous increase in agricultural wages during this period did not alleviate the deprivation of the rural poor; labour demand remained highly seasonal. With the exceptions of the early summer and autumn months, labour supply has still been in excess of demand. Under these circumstances migration to the petroleum producing countries (PPC) of the Arab World has come to represent a primary, relatively viable option (Waterbury, 1983: 296). State policies have in turn contributed to encouraging this form of individual solution to the societal problems of rural Egypt, thereby permitting the extended reproduction of family-based peasant forms of production which had characterized rural Egypt during the course of its state capitalist development.

C. ODEP, regional petro-economy, and the internationalization of Egyptian labour

In the post-1973 period, the regional petro-economy had a profound impact on Egyptian society. Of the many changes which have accompanied the oil boom, the out/inflow of skilled and unskilled labour from the poor countries of the region into the rich oil-producing states stands out as a significant development affecting Egyptian society. Egypt has traditionally supplied labour to the Arab world and Africa (Birks and Sinclair, 1979: 291), and has predominated numerically in the international labour movement within the Arab region (Choucri, 1977, 1983; Imam and Zayda, 1983; Suleiman, 1983). Although the estimates of those involved in international labour migration vary greatly, ranging between 1.4 million persons, according to the 1982 census of the Central Agency for Mobilization and Statistics, and 2.658 million according to the National Councils (El-Gabry 1983: 87–8), there is no doubt about the significant increase in the number of migrants as a correlate of the state's ODEP.

Within the framework of the 'economic opening', the labour exodus to the oil producing states increased dramatically. New state policies facilitating labour migration have been propagated by the mass media which describes migration as a 'constitutional right of every Egyptian' (*Mayo*, 11 May 1981). Although Egypt has not had an official migration policy in recent years (United Nations, 1982), the Government has definitely encouraged the exodus of both skilled and unskilled Egyptians. Laments about the 'brain drain' are contradicted by state support of the migration of professionals and technicians, an appropriate policy within the framework of ODEP and associated development strategies (Morsy and El-Bayoumi, 1980).

During the period of Egypt's state capitalist development, based on public sector industrialization, migration to neighbouring Arab countries was restricted. It was argued that anyone who could find work abroad would be greatly needed at home (Waterbury, 1983: 204). This should not suggest that Egyptian migration to the Arab states was non-existent prior to the 'economic opening'. Current migration patterns involve changes primarily in the rate of increase and in the technical profile of migrant labour (Choucri, 1977, 1983; El-Bakry, 1981; Suleiman, 1983). During the 1950s and 1960s, Egyptians working in the PPC were primarily professionals recruited to contribute to a 'unitarian national construction' (S. Amin, 1988: 21) through education and technical assistance. Relatively unskilled workers represented a small proportion of migrants.

Unlike earlier inter-Arab long-term or permanent migration, that during the 1970s and early 1980s consisted largely of temporary flows (United Nations, 1982: 40). Moreover, labour movement to the oil-exporting countries has been male-dominated. Several factors have contributed to this general pattern, including the restrictions of the labour-importing countries on permanent migration and citizenship, as well as prospective employers' unwillingness to provide housing and transportation indemnities for their Egyptian workers (Khattab and El Daeif, 1982). Since Egyptian labour migration has been, by and large, of the 'foraging' type (people migrating in order to establish specific goals within a specific time period and then returning home), lone male migrant workers, unhampered by economically dependent family members, have the opportunity to maximize their savings and expedite their return home. Leaving women and children behind has additional perceived benefits, including the management of production and family property (where applicable) at home. Women left behind likewise ensure the supervision of children's education and, more generally, the reproduction of Egypt's labour.

In cases where single female professionals seek employment in the PPC, their departure from Egypt has often been restricted by the host government's stipulation that they be accompanied by a *mahram* (a male blood relative), thereby reinforcing male control over women (Hatem, 1983: 11; cf. Ibrahim, 1982).

Whether they migrate as companions of husbands or as employees themselves, Egyptian women, in adjusting to the social environments of the labour-importing states, find themselves compromising certain rights related to personal emancipation which they had taken for granted at home (Hatem, 1983: 11). Such restrictions and related ideological support are also imported into Egypt by migrants returning from the Gulf. Contrary to modernist predictions (Sedghi, 1976; Youssef, 1976; cf. Ebeid, 1985), veiling and the call for Egyptian women's 'return to the home' stand out as expressions of 'petro Islamism' (Zakariya, 1986, as quoted in Abaza, 1987b: 3; cf. El Baz, 1988; Shafiq, 1988).

Within the framework of on-going debates surrounding the overall impact of labour migration on Egypt's development, it is often argued that migrants' remittances are an important contribution to the country's balance of payments. Indeed, remittances exceed other sources of foreign exchange and cover a large part of the country's import charges. But as has been frequently pointed out,

individuals enjoy considerable flexibility with their foreign currency. It is by no means certain that all foreign exchange saved by migrant workers is remitted to Egypt. . . . Apart from noting that remittances to Egypt enjoy an uncertain future, it should be noted that remittances are not a source of foreign exchange comparable with say Suez Canal dues, . . . workers' remittances are at the disposition of individual migrant workers, who may choose to invest them or spend them as they please. Thus it is only in an accounting framework that remittances are comparable with other sources of foreign exchange. . . . In an economic sense they can more usefully be seen as an enhancement to personal income and as an increase to the money supply. (Birks and Sinclair, 1982: 41; cf. Abdel Fadil, 1980)

Migrants' remittances (and other sources of income such as tourism and the Suez Canal), which have been critical for a surge of growth in the Egyptian economy since 1975 and which have undoubtedly had an effect on the increasing inequality of income distribution (Waterbury, 1983), are themselves symptomatic of constrained development. Reliance on these sources of income indicate that Egypt is 'turning once more into a dependent economy, relying on the export of raw materials (and now also on services) rather than on the growth of the domestic market, and on foreign capital rather than domestic savings' (G. Amin, 1981: 434).

The Egyptian case approximates the general international patterns of failure of migrant remittances to catalyse development. While migrant labourers send portions of their earnings home, thereby increasing local family consumption, there is no evidence of investment in industrial infrastructure (Swanson, 1979; Wojno, 1982; United Nations, 1982). Personal savings by no means ensure national economic development (United Nations, 1982: 42).

In Egypt, a 'consumer craze' rather than productive investment predominates. A low level of domestic capital formation is maintained despite increased individual savings. These have contributed to a housing boom in both urban and rural areas, including the village of Bahiya, a related rise in land values, encroachment on agricultural land for non-agricultural exploitation, increased mechanized agriculture and transportation in the rural areas, as well as increases in small-scale commercial enterprises, the province of 'informal' sector family labour.

In sum, the European experience of primitive accumulation through migration during the mercantile phase of capitalist development has not been replicated for Egypt. Accumulated savings have not been transformed into capital for industrial development and the agrarian transition remains blocked. The persistence of peasant household production based on family labour remains a vivid manifestation of this blockage.

D. Labour migration and agrarian transformation

Beyond the suggestion that migration has resulted in a local shortage of skilled labour in the modern industrial sector (Birks and Sinclair, 1982: 47), this shortage likewise has repercussions on agricultural labour. As rural workers replace urban skilled labour (thereby contributing to reduced industrial productivity), or take the migrant route across Egypt's borders, at least seasonal labour shortages occur in certain rural areas. Rural labour shortages and attendant surges in agricultural wages have contributed to a decline in agricultural production. Labour shortages during the cotton-harvesting season reach such proportions that the Ministry of Education has postponed the opening of schools for two weeks so that schoolchildren can help harvest the cotton. In one of Egypt's governorates, it was estimated that 8,000 *feddans* were left fallow because of labour shortage (El-Gabry, 1983: 88).

While the specific impact of labour export may be expected to vary from one community to another as a function of peasants' class positions and related family labour patterns, the consequences for national agricultural production and food security have been catastrophic (Chaney, 1983). As food production per capita has been falling (Birks and Sinclair, 1980: 221), Egypt's imports have increased at an alarming rate (Goueli, 1978). The reduction of agricultural labour, artificially low government-imposed prices, low levels of investment in land reclamation, and loss of land to urban growth and rural housing construction have all contributed to lowered agricultural productivity. Moreover, the increasing reliance on food imports undermines migrants' foreign exchange remittances through its contribution to balance of payment deficits. As rural households' self-sufficiency declines, an increasing proportion of remitted income is allocated to the purchase of market goods (Hammam, 1981: 10).

Supported, indeed encouraged by state policies, a widespread response to the rural labour shortage has been the resort to capital-intensive production techniques involving the use of machinery, the cultivation of citrus fruits, and dairy farming. While this form of adaptation remains an option for relatively wealthy producers, including the rich peasants of Bahiya, it does not represent a viable alternative for the majority of rural Egyptians. Among small peasants, the massive flow of labour to the oil-based sectors of the region and derivative income have permitted the extended reproduction of 'traditional' forms of production based on family labour (Glavanis and Glavanis, 1983; Abaza, 1987a).

While adult rural male exodus has led to an increase in the agriculture workload of women, official statistics suggest a decline in women's overall labour force participation from 5.5 per cent in 1976 to 4.4 per cent in 1986 (Abdel Wahab, 1988). But besides the reliability of such statistical estimates, micro-sociological studies indicate that a large portion of female (and child) sustained economic activity remains oriented towards subsistence production. Women are being only partially absorbed into the monetized sector of the economy as a result of male labour shortage, while continuing to reproduce labour power at below its exchange value, thereby continuing to subsidize capital accumulation. For example, in the Upper Nile Egyptian villages of Beit Alam and Hagara, where male out-migration ranges between 50 and 75 per cent of the economically active men, labour shortages and dramatic increases in wages have accentuated dependence on the unpaid family labour of women and children (Hammam, 1981: 10).

While there is general agreement that male out-migration increases women's workload and prompts them to assume certain responsibilities considered the province of males (Abou Mandour *et al.*, 1988), the consequences of increased dependence on women's work for family welfare and authority patterns have been controversial. Contrary to the assertion that increased workload and responsibilities result in 'greater sexual power and self assertion' (Ibrahim, 1982: 40; cf. Khattab and El-Daeif, 1982; Khafagy, 1984), it has been argued that the prevalence of female-headed households is not necessarily conducive to female empowerment, and may be a sign of the feminization of poverty (Myntti, 1978; Taylor, 1984; Morsy, 1985; cf. Hatem, 1983: 15).

The material rewards for women's involvement in agricultural production have not simply 'continued to be weak', but have been further weakened by out-migration of able-bodied men. Mona Abaza's anthropological study of the village of al-Warda points out that 'the process of migration *itself* devalues the spheres now left to women, namely agriculture and local dealings' (Abaza, 1987a: 5; emphasis added).

IV. Fatiha in 1974/5: Smallholder familial production

A. *Overview of the community*

Fatiha, with a population of 3,200 inhabitants, is located in the province of Kafr el-Sheikh in the north-western corner of the

Egyptian Nile Delta, nearly midway between Alexandria and Cairo. Administratively, the village is part of the district (*markaz*) of Kallin. Villagers frequent this administrative centre for various official business purposes and to obtain goods and services which are not available in the village. A variety of mechanisms integrate the village into the encompassing society. Networks of transportation and communication, public education, and government operated medical care facilities shatter the image of the isolated rural community. Migration to the urban centres and the maintenance of kinship ties also link the village to the major cities.

In addition to their Egyptian identity, the villagers of Fatiha identify themselves as being 'of the religion of Muhammad'. They define the practice of Islam as a series of rituals which include fasting, prayer, and the payment of *zakat* (alms). Pilgrimage to Mecca is a highly desired goal which is fulfilled only by a few older male and female villagers who hoard their life savings for this long awaited journey. While most adult males and females fast during the month of Ramadan, the majority of villagers do not pray. Those who do are mostly men. Collective religious practices, including the weekly Friday noon prayer, are confined to males. Popular religion remains associated with women in particular (Morsy, 1988).

Occupational specialization in Fatiha is minimal. With the exception of the village barber and the carpenter, all the inhabitants of the village engage in some form of crop production, such as cotton, corn, wheat and rice. This includes the 13 per cent of landless peasants who attempt to rent some land or share-crop for family subsistence purposes whenever possible. They, however, remain heavily dependent on the wage-labour of all family members. Even the few government employees, army draftees, grocers and students with resident families are to varying degrees involved in agricultural production. Families cultivate privately owned or rented land ranging in size from between 0.125 and 8 *feddans*. Of the total number of cultivators, 43.4 per cent have access to less than 2 *feddans* of arable land, 42.2 per cent to between 2 and 5 *feddans*. Less than 1 per cent of village households control between 6 and 8 *feddans*.

In agricultural production the peasants of Fatiha rely on family labour and inter-household co-operation. A minority of resident peasant families hire labourers, and then do so only occasionally. The household labour process consists of family-centred subsistence activities and petty commodity production, providing for daily consumption as well as the reproduction of human labour and means of production. Since the household, indeed the entire community, is integrated into a larger system governed by capitalist relations of production, the family-centred labour process is conditioned by the demands of dominant political economic structures (Friedman, 1980; Bernstein, 1981; Redclift, 1985; Newcomer, 1977: 18; Hopkins, 1987; Sabea, 1987). Thus, beyond family needs, the village household labour process yields a surplus which is appropriated by the state, or paid in the form of cash or agricultural product in return for access to land. The combination of differential access to land, household composition, as well as degree of reliance on exchange and wage labour accounts for different labour processes. Given the limited differentiation of the peasantry in Fatiha, such variation is largely a function of the developmental cycle of the family.

In Fatiha social differentiation is minimal, pertaining primarily to distinctions between the resident descendants of the village's original Turkish rulers and former *kibar a'yan* (rural upper stratum), from among whom *umdas* (headmen) are drawn to this day (Ansari, 1986), on the one hand, and the remaining majority of villagers on the other. Nearly 90 *feddans* of village agricultural land are owned by descendants of the former Turkish rulers. While most reside mainly in the major urban centres of Cairo and Alexandria, some live on the outskirts of the village. Most of their land is rented out to peasants but some areas are left under the guardianship of a *nazir* (overseer). He supervises the total process of cultivation, harvesting, turning in the required government surplus, and selling the agricultural products, in return for a stipulated portion of the harvest.

The life-style of the descendants of the Turkish élite differs drastically from the majority population of land-tilling peasants in Fatiha. Those residing in the village work in the government bureaucracy in the nearby town. Their children, both male and female, attend school in the nearby towns or leave the area for extended periods to acquire a university education in the major centres of Egypt. Some professionals from these families work in neighbouring Arab countries. One of them is known to have taken a young peasant woman from the village to work as a domestic helper for his family. The contrast between the life-style of women of this élite group and the majority of women in the village emphasizes the significance of economic status in defining the position of women in 'Islamic' Egyptian society (Smock and Youssef, 1977). At the opposite end of the social ladder, men and women of households using less than 2 *feddans*, including 'landless' peasants who try to lease tiny plots or share-crop, are generally unable to raise enough crops to maintain their families and find it necessary to resort to seasonal wage-labour to supplement their incomes.

B. *State institutions in Fatiha*

The village of Fatiha is integrated into a wider economic, social and political structure with which it engages in relationships marked by power asymmetry. While the household economy is characterized by relative self-sufficiency, the provision of surplus to the state represents a major burden on peasant producers (Rosenbury, 1976).

The role of the state is clearly visible in village social life. As a result of the national programme of land reform developed in the post-1952 period, a large portion of families in Fatiha were given access to productive resources. Land from the holdings of the royal family in the vicinity of the village was expropriated and allocated to some families in the village. Moreover, the government imposed tenancy regulations providing villagers with legal protection which they had not previously enjoyed.

In addition to regulating access to productive resources, the state appropriates surplus products from Fatiha to finance the development of other sectors of the economy. Through the local agricultural co-operative, agricultural surplus is controlled by the state. Thus, while the villagers of Fatiha are held responsible for the cultivation of their plots, the local co-operative (*gam'iya*) implements government regulations regarding crop consolidation and rotation, and co-ordinates activities for fumigation of crops and pest control. As in the case of other Egyptian peasant communities, the village agricultural co-operative is the only source of credit, seeds, fertilizers and pesticides, where men, and to a lesser extent, women, spend hours 'looking after [their] interests'.

At the end of each harvest the peasants of Fatiha, men and women, turn in the required amount of crops to the agricultural co-operative. They receive payment for their produce, from which deductions are made for loans used to obtain the necessary inputs for cultivation, and the servicing of the land. While peasants are paid for the yields of crops which they turn over to the agricultural co-operative, the stipulated requirement for rice and wheat prevents them from providing for the needs of their families. They are forced to buy some of these very products of their labour on the open market at considerably higher prices.

In short, the agricultural co-operative functions primarily to execute government policies regarding management of the agricultural cycle, appropriation of surplus, and taxation of the peasants to ensure a steady flow of revenues to finance other sectors of Egyptian society. They leave the villagers of Fatiha, male and female, isolated from formulating and executing policies which influence their own lives. For although the agricultural co-operative is managed by an elected council of villagers, members are subject to the directives of the government-appointed technicians and bureaucrats who staff the co-operative in the village. One educated female villager is employed as a clerk.

The people of Fatiha are well aware of their role in subsidizing the national economy. Villagers state that their work is basically for the benefit of people in urban areas. They feel that these people despise them and exploit them. As one woman noted:

> We only like city people because we are from the same shore, but we hate them because they take all [the products of] our efforts and our struggle. The agricultural co-operative charges tax for rice, even though we work very hard and we do not have enough rice for our home and children. The government takes our rice and we end up having to buy rice from the market. But buying from the market is very expensive.

The surplus product produced by the peasants of Fatiha, and appropriated by the state in the form of agricultural commodities (rice, wheat, cotton) is distributed to the local urban population or exchanged on the world market. Thus peasant household non-capitalist production is integrated into the national and global capitalist economy in ways which affect both modes (Rosenbury, 1976: 47). This underlines the significance of the contention that any explanation of the status of rural women cannot be divorced from an understanding of the structural principles which regulate the development of the rural sector of Egyptian society in general (Arizpe and Batey, 1987).

The state regulates the election of the *umda* and two *sheikh-el-balad* (village elders). These government officials settle most disputes within the village, including those related to land utilization and conflicts between women and their husbands.

In Fatiha, political participation is limited and kinship affiliation is the primary basis for political support. Only relatively wealthy men become involved in political contests. Of the ten representatives elected to the committee of the local chapter of the Arab Socialist Union (ASU), all own land, none controlling less than 2 *feddans*. Among the entire local membership of the ASU there is only one woman, the one who works for the agricultural co-operative as mentioned earlier.

Those who are elected to the ASU are expected to have urban connections and be capable of dealing with the bureaucracy at higher levels of government. Villagers are well aware of their relative powerlessness vis-à-vis the external government bureaucracy and constantly seek mediators. In expressing her perceived powerlessness an older woman remarked: 'Inside my home and in the village I have a long tongue but outside [in town] I cannot do anything.' Indeed political control rests with urban élites whose patronage is actively sought by local men and women in their pursuit of personal goals. Women in particular turn to descendants of the former Turkish rulers when seeking a position for their kinsmen in the local government bureaucracy, urban employment for their male relatives, medical care, financial assistance and a variety of other favours.

The state provides local residents with a variety of services. With the exception of about six households which have running water, relatively clean water is provided by two large taps installed by the government. When available, water from these public taps is used extensively by the women for cooking and drinking, but clothes are usually washed in the canals.

Local state representatives regulate the collective responsibility of villagers for the annual cleaning of village ponds. Families are expected to contribute one person per *feddan* according to the number of *feddans* they cultivate. Men and young women join the work parties. Those who fail to do so are charged according to the amount of land they cultivate, £E 0.25 a day per person. Cleaning of the *masarif* (major drainage channels) is the responsibility of the government which employs migratory male wage-labourers for this purpose.

Villagers appreciate the services of the government-established and supervised elementary school. For while land is considered a valued source of security, education is recognized as a significant means of social mobility. But despite the eagerness of village parents to enrol their children in school, the economic constraints of the family interfere with the fulfilment of such a desire. Many children who do attend school are absent from classes during periods of heavy agricultural work. Only a minority of school-age children ever complete even the elementary level of school education, fewer still ever complete secondary school. Only one male has completed university and enrolled in a programme of graduate study.

Although the enrolment of girls in the local primary school has increased tremendously, their number remains about one-third of male pupils. Education of girls is a mark of their families' relative wealth. In 1975 a female villager entered university for the first time. Like her younger cohorts, this educated woman belongs to a relatively wealthy family. She enjoys freedom of movement and respect within the household not ordinarily extended to females of her age. Like other female students from the village her dress is urban in style and she does not wear the traditional head cover of peasant women.

The equal opportunity in education provided to males and females by the state does not extend to other dimensions of village economic and social life. Male peasants have had privileged access to land redistributed under the agrarian reform plan (Deere and Leon de Leal, 1982; Tadesse, 1982; Croll, 1986). Furthermore one notes the priority given to village men for employment on government projects outside the village, and wage differentials between male and female workers. The average daily wage of women is about two-thirds of that paid to men. The favoured position of males in Egyptian society is likewise reflected in the Code of Personal Status which is imposed on all sectors of the Egyptian population, including the village of Fatiha. This code, which regulates marriage, divorce and child custody, favours men in all these areas of matrimonial relations. Local women, like their urban counterparts, suffer the consequences.

The government requirement that those standing for elections to the agricultural co-operative board and to the local chapter of ASU in the village must be literate discriminates against the majority of peasants and even more so against women, who are most likely to be illiterate. And yet when government efforts are undertaken to 'obliterate illiteracy' in the village, females are excluded. During our research in the village, a directive from the Ministry of Education instructed the *umda* to compile a list of illiterate *males* for whom a tutor from the village would be provided.

C. Access to land

Land tenure may be freehold (*khalas*), or utilisation obtained through cash rent (*naqd*), *shirka* and *zara'a wahda*. In the *naqd* or cash form of rent, the amount is fixed by the government at seven times the tax per *feddan* (amounting to between approximately 23 and 26 £E *feddan* per year). In the *shirka* (partnership) type of tenancy (also known as *muzar'a* or planting together), the share-cropper provides the labour, the owner provides the land and each provides half of the seeds and chemicals. The products are likewise shared. In the

case of *zar'a wahda* ('one planting only'), the owner has greater
control over his land, although in some cases the tenant may go
ahead with a second planting and the consequent sharing of the
harvest products. But no matter what form access to land takes,
family exploitation is the norm. Although males 'seal the deal' for
such access, women play an important role in the informal negotiations leading up to the agreement and contribute to cultivating
the land.

Ideally, land and other forms of accumulated wealth are passed
on from one generation to the other according to the Islamic *sunna*
(teachings). The female is supposed to receive a *kum* (pile) and the
males *kumin* (two piles). In actual fact, however, the terms of the
sunna are ignored. Disputes over inheritance are common in the
village and a lot of the time of the *sheikh-el-balad* (village elder) is
known to be spent settling such disputes. He recounted his role in
such a settlement as follows:

> I have a case of a man who is threatening his wife that he would divorce
> her if her brothers do not give her her father's inheritance. Some people
> do not follow the *shari'a* [Islamic law] and will write for the boys only
> and exclude the girls. In this particular case, before the father died, he
> sold over the land to his sons and kept the registration with a friend to
> ensure that his sons would not abuse him during his lifetime. When his
> daughter's husband found out about it after his father-in-law's death, he
> came to me. There is not much that I can do except try to tell the
> woman's brothers to fear God and give her her rightful share. I have
> only one girl and I even gave her *kumin*.

Evidently, Islamic prescriptions regulating women's access to
property are not always upheld in the village of Fatiha.

Religious directives aside, control over valued instruments of
production, notably land, and over the products of agricultural
labour is vested in males. Although women contribute heavily to
agricultural activities, one notes a marked asymmetry in the distribution of productive resources, which are controlled by men and
only sporadically available to women. In the commoditized economic system of the village, control over goods and services which
have exchange value constitutes a significant power-base for men.

Since control of land and other means of production and agricultural products is skewed in favour of males, women only have
access to such resources through their kinsmen whose own power
is primarily based on material wealth, measured by land holdings.
Women who do inherit may either retain formal ownership of the

entire plot inherited, or turn over legal control of part or all of it to their husbands. In some cases women may choose to turn over their share of inheritance to their male kinsmen who in return cultivate the land. Aside from the different options exercised by women who inherit land, those who do gain access to this valuable resource enjoy a relatively powerful position in their husbands' households, compared to their less materially endowed cohorts. In the few village households where women, rather than their husbands, control productive resources, it is the female who is the authority figure. A husband in this situation is clearly in a position of dependence and may suffer deep emotional distress (Morsy, 1978a, 1987b).

D. Gender relations and the developmental cycle of the family

In Fatiha, individual males and females derive the primary dimension of their identity from family affiliation. As a villager noted:

> If a man does not have relatives, he picks a wife who will give him good connections. . . . A man stays close to relatives and picks connections to make an *'izwa* [support group] for himself; as the saying goes, 'one hand does not clap alone'; . . . the woman who has *'izwa* is supported by her relatives. She is courageous in her relations with women and men, including her husband and his family.

The importance of derivative power for women who can rely on the support of their families was underlined by a female participant in the research project who noted:

> My father was poor, so I cannot rely on him [i.e. for support], thus I am good with my husband. I control my tongue and I never go to them [her family] when I am in trouble with him. A woman who has *wid* [support] from her family complains to them and they talk to her husband; they may even hit him.

In Fatiha, phases of the family developmental cycle produce three major types, the predominant nuclear family, the extended family, and the fraternal joint family. These kinship units form the primary framework of village-centred production relations only if their members occupy the same household. In a few cases, however, members of extended and fraternal families may continue to occupy a room in the family household while having their separate *ma'isha* (livelihood). More generally, kinship is a significant basis of inter-household co-operation.

In Fatiha, the selection of a marriage partner is a family undertaking, with the man's mother playing a major role. Villagers generally agree that a good bride must be polite, a *good worker*, healthy and beautiful. In defining the quality of beauty, a female participant in the research project remarked: 'a woman's beauty is in her cleverness. She should be able to withstand hard work in the sun. All our women look alike, they are all related, they only differ in their capacity for hard work.'

The payment of bridewealth to a woman's kinsmen symbolizes, as is the case in their role as guardians of her 'honour', men's control over women and the transfer of their productive and reproductive capacities to their husband's kin group. However, marriage does not terminate a woman's ties with her relatives. In fact, these ties are maintained throughout her life and she may utilize the support of her male and female kin in production, and to bring pressure against her husband and his family. However, the support of kinsmen is subject to variation. A woman may count on the aid of her brother; in fact, she is in a position to demand it with 'an open eye' (that is, without shame) if he is 'indebted to her generosity'. But a woman may be beaten by her brother or father and sent back to her husband's household when she turns to kinsmen of limited resources with complaints of illness or maltreatment. In fact, the woman's own relatives may condone the husband's action and blame his fury on her repulsive attitude and her 'long tongue'.

As a married adult, a man is expected to provide his wife and children with shelter, food and clothing. This is, in fact, the most significant role of an adult male. The birth of children is generally believed to cement matrimonial ties. Barrenness in women and sterility in men are generally regarded as legitimate grounds for divorce.

The early years of marriage are usually stressful for young brides. They are subjected to orders from older sisters-in-law and are clearly subservient to the authority of their husband's mother. In this extended family setting, the products of their domestic and agricultural labour, like those of other members of the household, are under the control of the senior male and senior female (mother and father-in-law in extended family households, and older brother and his wife in fraternal joint family households). Senior males and females are the centre of authority.

As long as the father is alive, his married sons and their wives are at the mercy of the mother who is the primary locus of authority. At this stage of the family developmental cycle, as a married woman's male children reach adulthood and take on responsibility for agricultural labour from their father, her own labour efforts gradually become confined to the home. She begins to feel that she can rely for material and moral support on her grown children, especially her male offspring.

Freed from the burden of agricultural labour and of most of the domestic work, the mother-in-law manages the household. She organizes the division of labour and the distribution of resources and may even direct her sons' agricultural activities. This is clearly a case where authority rests on performance and evidence of power rather than on legitimacy as such. Having taken over nearly all agricultural functions from their father, a woman's adult male offspring carry out these functions in consultation with their mother and her kinsmen. Evidently, when the senior male member of the family, who is vested with authority, fails to perform accordingly, his authority is challenged by the senior female who is usually younger and in better health than her husband.

A senior woman maintains control over extended family labour and its products until the death of her husband. At this time, with the help and support of her kinsmen, she may maintain her husband's property intact and continue to be the principal locus of authority in the extended family. If she owns property of her own, this may encourage her sons to remain as part of an extended productive unit. Alternatively, her sons may demand their share of their father's property, which brings about fragmentation of the family property and, with it, the power base of the mother-in-law.

The break-up of the extended family unit is often blamed on women in pursuit of personal gain, but it is incorrect to characterize domestic quarrels by reference to women's manipulative actions. Quarrels between women in domestic groups reflect the conflicts and tensions between the men upon whom they are dependent. The men experience the stress of subordination to the authority of dominant older brothers, mothers or fathers, but under threat of certain cultural sanctions, they are curtailed from engaging in open conflict and therefore voice their dissent through the women. Thus, it is through his wife that a subservient male expresses his dissatisfaction with a reward which he considers disproportionate to his nuclear family's input into the labour pool of the extended kinship unit. The relatively powerless husband cannot voice his dissatisfaction' with those who control the family's economic resources. In this case, then, the woman and her dependent husband strive for the same goal but the eventual breakup of the extended family household is blamed on women.

Soheir A. Morsy

E. Gender differences in early age socialization

In Fatiha, preparation for adult sexual division of labour is manifested at a very early age. Child-play is clearly a preparation for adult gender roles. Little girls are seen playing with pieces of dough given to them by their mothers while they are baking; little boys play with a whiplike toy and imitate men in leading oxen for ploughing. Mothers, in justifying the preferential treatment and feeding of their male children, say 'we want our son to grow up quickly so that he will help his father in the field'.

Boys between four and six years of age load donkeys and feed the animals, which they also accompany back and forth from the fields. A child of this age may help his father sow crops during the planting season. When a boy does not have any older sisters, he may take care of younger siblings. If his mother sends him on an errand related to domestic affairs he may refuse, but if his father orders him to perform any task related to agriculture he will promptly comply. At a comparable age a girl sweeps, cleans the cooking utensils, fetches water for household needs, accompanies animals and their loads to the fields, and helps her mother in baking and child care.

In their mid-teens, young people take on a larger share of adult responsibilities. At this stage, a girl is ready for at least preliminary considerations of marriage. It is said that at this age she shows herself off to people by walking forcefully and by doing all sorts of tasks with effort. This is the time when young men start to notice girls and begin to choose their prospective brides. A good part of a young woman's day is given up to domestic work. In addition, she is involved in agricultural labour, either on her father's land, or as a day labourer. At this age, she learns to perfect the tasks which she learned as a child, with the important thought in the back of her mind that it is such skills which please a potential mother-in-law.

At a similar age, the boy takes over the major part of his father's field tasks. He likewise thinks of marriage, confiding in his mother and asking for her opinion of the girl whom he has picked out. Mothers usually prefer their sons to marry a relative over whom they may exercise control. But if a son refuses his mother's advice or marriage to a relative, she cannot force him to comply.

F. Division of labour in agricultural production within the family

During fieldwork it was observed that men and women work in agriculture together and with other family members, there being a

115

variation in the division of labour according to the crops and agricultural operation involved. Only ploughing is viewed as a male activity. When necessary, as in the case of women whose husbands are sick for an extended period of time, those who are widowed, or have no adult sons, women will even plough their land and irrigate it.

Cultivation is a year-round undertaking involving continuous work centred around the preparation of the soil, planting, irrigation, harvesting and processing of agricultural products. Cotton is considered the most important crop and one which needs 'lots of servicing'. The land is ploughed three times. Eight days afterwards the soil is watered, the seeds are planted by male and female children. Following heroic efforts by the peasants to keep the plants free of parasitic organisms, harvesting starts in September. Men, women and children join the harvesting parties. During this period wage labourers may be paid as much as £E 0.40 per day as opposed to the usual daily wage of £E 0.25.

Cotton harvesting is followed by the planting of wheat. Men usually plant the wheat seeds, while the harvest in May involves all members of the family. Villagers rent machines either from private owners or from the agricultural co-operative to separate the grain from the straw. Generally, village households' involvement in mechanized structures of production is minimal (Hopkins, 1987).

Rice is planted after the wheat harvest. *Shitla* (sprouts) of rice are prepared on a small portion of the field and then transferred and spread throughout the entire field by men, women and children, who stand almost knee deep in muddy water for hours. Weeding keeps all the family busy until the harvest around October when all members of the household, except the elderly (and the few relatively well-to-do) participate. The rice crop is in turn replaced by clover which is harvested four times. Cattle are fattened at this time and they produce lots of milk which is either sold, consumed or made into cheese by the women. A corn crop then completes the agricultural cycle.

In addition to their contribution to these major agricultural crops, women cultivate vegetables between other crops for household consumption. While women have primary responsibility for processing subsistence crops, other household members generally contribute to this task. For example, it is not unusual to find older males helping women to remove corn from the husk and pull the kernels off the cob. Agricultural processing in fact takes up hours of women's time. They wash, dry and store grain, and are responsible for having the wheat and corn ground at the public mill.

Thus in Fatiha, the image of secluded Arab women is shattered. Ideally, women's labour should be confined to the domestic sphere and men are expected to engage in agricultural work. With the exception of very old women or those who are heads of extended families, the economic realities of the peasants' situation prevent them from upholding this ideal. The degree of female participation in agricultural activities is furthermore directly related to the age of women, their marital status, and the socio-economic status of their kinship group. Apart from the few unmarried young adult females who attend school, all single women work in the fields with their brothers in one capacity or another. With the exception of the few 'big families' of the village who control land in excess of 5 *feddans*, married females in households which own or rent agricultural land contribute to its cultivation in various degrees, ranging from daily labour in the fields to supplementary help during the harvest.

Perhaps the only status which normally exempts a woman from agricultural work outside the household is advancing age. But the lowly economic existence of peasants in Fatiha makes many exceptions to this rule. Evidently, cultural prescriptions are subordinated to pragmatic considerations of daily consumption and the reproduction of the peasant household, including the working capacity of its members. Given the limited differentiation of the peasantry in Fatiha, this applies to the great majority of villagers. Women whose labour is confined to domestic activities are indeed exceptional.

G. *Household income pooling in Fatiha*

In addition to the limited number of villagers who are employed in urban industrial state-operated enterprises, wage income likewise constitutes an important source of livelihood for many residents of Fatiha. Locally, the labour market draws household members to varying degrees. Child and female wage-labour constitutes a particularly important source of income among the 'landless'. More generally, contributions to household income from this source are inversely proportional to the size of landholdings. Both females and males work as wage labourers in the village or are part of migratory labour forces working away from the village for as long as one or two months.

According to the migratory labour system, *tarhila*, a contractor rounds up nearly a hundred villagers, including females. Some couples and their children also join such expeditions, as well as poor unmarried women. Recognizing the economic hardship suffered by such women who have no alternative means of support, villagers say 'she is such a good daughter, she runs on her parents and her siblings' (i.e. supports them). Married women do not usually join such groups unless accompanied by kinsmen. However, a woman who is separated from her husband or divorced may leave her children with her mother and go on a *tarhila*, although this seldom happens.

In 1974 and 1975 opportunity for income generation outside Egypt was just starting to be the focus of considerations and deliberations among villagers. Some village men were examining the possibility of migrating to Iraq within the Egypt–Iraqi agreement for permanent settlement of Egyptian peasant families there (El-Solh, 1985). Although the idea of leaving Egypt permanently was not accepted, some villagers did start to consider temporary migration. The case of the young woman who had migrated to Kuwait with the family of a professional from the village élite provided an example of the *kheir* (prosperity) that could be derived from such ventures.

Whether male or female, from inside or outside the village, wage-labour has become an economic necessity. Female wage-labour in particular is indicative of household poverty. The ideal of restricting women's work to domestic activities is highly cherished, but the less than favourable economic conditions of the peasants may force some men to abandon their culturally stipulated responsibilities as sole breadwinners. Women with chronically ill husbands, for example, may find themselves the sole providers for their families as is the case of widows with no adult male offspring.

In using their hard-earned income, the peasants of Fatiha value thrift and constantly strive to save money, with the ultimate goal of gaining access to expanded areas of land. Women accumulate cash by raising chicks or growing chickens and selling their products for a profit. When enough money is saved from this undertaking, a woman may invest in a goat whose kids are eventually sold for what is generally considered a large sum of approximately £E 10. Goat's milk may be used by the woman's family or she may make cheese which is either used by members of her household or sold for profit.

Cattle raising is particularly profitable. Women who can afford to raise water buffaloes and cows are those who have a little money of their own. They are able to invest in the feeding and upkeep of animals, sometimes through partnership (*shirka*). Others who do not have access to private cash cannot maintain such a chain of savings. Their husbands and older connections expect them either to yield the products of purchased animals for direct consumption by household members, or sell them and buy other household necessities.

Accumulated cash may be wrapped inside a rag, then buried in a wall in the house and covered over with mud. As soon as a woman accumulates enough cash, she may supplement it by the sale of jewellery received from her family when she married; she then invests her savings in land. Even those who buy jewellery use it only as an intermediate form. They buy gold when it is cheap and sell it when it is expensive.

While nearly all household members contribute to income generation in one capacity or another, ranging from the sale of vegetables for profit, and dressmaking by women, to a few adult males reciting the Koran at funerals, control over household revenues is culturally vested in males, although this may vary with the developmental cycle of the family. In the case of 'landless' peasants, among whom male–female power relations are relatively egalitarian, a woman is less restricted by her husband in disposing of income generated for household use.

Among families with unmarried male and female wage labourers, the former turn over their earnings to parents after keeping part for themselves, usually for the purchase of cigarettes. Young women, on the other hand, generally turn over their entire wages to their parents. While young men in particular are expected to support their parents through 'whatever means possible', young unmarried women who have no male siblings likewise take on this responsibility. In some cases a daughter is judged an important source of material and emotional support. For example, Fatma, who was the oldest of five children, including two males, and who considers herself as strong and clever as any male, described her role in the support of her parents as follows:

> There was not a job I did not do to get money to make my parents comfortable. I would work in construction, in the fields; I used to buy *hatab* [dried branches] and strip off the leftover cotton and sell it. I raised chickens, I cleaned our house, I did everything. My father used to say, 'you are better than any man Fatma . . . may God bless you with two daughters who would take care of you as you have taken care of me'.

Aside from limited accumulation of wealth, the fragmentation of property through its division upon inheritance is notable. The limited opportunities available to villagers for accumulating wealth make them reluctant to invest their savings in any venture not considered foolproof. Purchase of land and cultivation of the standard crops of cotton, wheat and corn is the general rule. Innovation entailing the cultivation of aromatic plants for the international market has been undertaken by relatively richer cultivators from the nearby village. The family which introduced this new form of cultivation also introduced the cultivation of potatoes as a cash crop in the area. Villagers recognize that it is only the well-to-do who can take such risks and experiment with new crops.

H. Forms of inter-Household co-operation

In addition to the various forms of income generation which contribute to the reproduction of peasant household production units, a variety of forms of inter-household co-operation involving women serve this end. Labour exchange, as well as borrowing farm equipment, household utensils and food, enable small-holders to be less dependent on wage income. Through such co-operation, those with larger areas of land are able to spend less on hired labourers, particularly at harvest time and other periods of heavy agricultural work.

Co-operation among peasants in Fatiha is particularly evident in the collective ownership of the *sagya* (waterwheel). The *sagya*, which may cost up to £E 350, a sum beyond the means of the majority of the villagers, is owned and maintained by a group of five or six families. People who cultivate adjacent fields and who collectively own and operate a *sagya* take turns watering their land by opening up the appropriate channels. Men are generally responsible for this task, but women may co-operate in watering each other's fields when necessary.

Beyond the formalized sharing associated with *shirka* tenancy, in Fatiha there is a form of exchange labour and co-operation known as *zamala* (partnership). According to this mutual, non-contractual form of co-operation, people help their friends, neighbours, and relatives in a variety of agricultural work including planting cotton, harvesting wheat and corn, or lending draft animals for ploughing. It is evident that this form of co-operation is undertaken by those who cannot afford to hire wage labourers. Villagers say that 'the person whose arms are wide does not become a partner, he hires labourers'. Women engage in *zamala* for baking, and to a certain extent for child care.

Younger unmarried women also co-operate with girl friends during planting and harvesting. Some of the older village women who take care of children receive small gifts of bread, some rice or sugar from parents.

Neighbours and relatives borrow food items such as corn, rice or wheat. After harvesting their own crops, they return the loans, thereby avoiding market purchases. Women and men develop reputations for their generosity (or otherwise) in lending to others in time of need. On an almost daily basis several other food items such as sugar, onions, or tea are borrowed and equivalent amounts are returned at a later date. Women sometimes use each other's ovens. If a woman has no time to bake, she asks her neighbour to lend her a specific number of loaves which she returns when she bakes. The person who borrows animals is responsible for supplying their feed.

Services may be paid for in kind rather than in cash. Women who help others bake take home with them some of the baked bread as payment when there is no intention of reciprocating such services. During the harvest season, agricultural products are exchanged for a variety of goods and services ranging from children's sweets to the payment of field labourers, help in baking, the circumcision of a child, or reciting the Koran at funeral services.

I. Reproduction of labour: procreation and use-value production

The peasants of Fatiha define adult females in terms of domestic functions, which includes their principal culturally defined function of bearing and raising children.

In the relatively simple technological system of peasant agriculture, human labour is by far the most significant form. Children's labour is exploited almost as soon as they are able to run about and communicate with their elders. Thus, the birth of children ushers in the rise of women's power in the family. For although the ultimate control over their reproductive function and its product (human labour) rests with men, the actualization of this culturally valued function and the loyalty which a mother builds in her children is a woman's most significant and relatively durable power-base. Mothers of female children express their yearning for a male child who, unlike daughters who marry out, is expected to attend to his parents' needs in their old age.

Compared to women's contribution to the generation of nationally and internationally appropriated surplus, their role in petty commodity production is easily recognized. In addition, while the local sale of their labour-power is obvious, use-value is less evident. Nevertheless, this form of contribution is at least equally important, given its significance for household *reproduction* and surplus accumulation. In some village households such accumulation allows access to larger areas of land, and even the purchase of the labour-power of members of other households. The potential for accumulation of surplus is thus further enhanced.

The married woman is responsible for all domestic labour and all aspects of child care. The neglect of any of her children's many needs is viewed as laxity on her part and will incur the wrath of husband or mother-in-law.

Single and unmarried women undertake a variety of unremunerated tasks in the course of daily maintenance of the household. Women's responsibilities include preparing meals and taking lunch to the males of the household in the field. During harvest time, and on occasions of labour exchange, meal preparation and the repeated offering of rounds of tea to helpers takes up a good part of a woman's day. Women are also responsible for fetching water, washing and baking, nursing and feeding children, cleaning stables and making dung-cakes for fuel, as well as occasionally repairing household structures and undertaking family-centred healing.

The time allocated by women to use-value production differs from one household to another, depending on such factors as household composition, ratio of male to female residents, distance of residence from public water tap or canal, and the willingness of males to help out, particularly in purchasing commodities from nearby provincial towns, or accompanying family members to biomedical specialists.

Beyond noting that women spend hours in use-value production, it is worth considering women's culturally mediated orientation towards different types of work. Although the 'task' of going to the weekly market in the nearby town or further away is doubtless a time-consuming activity which keeps women away from domestic chores or work in the fields, it is nevertheless a welcome opportunity for 'recreation'. Women in extended households make sure that they do not miss their 'turn' to go to market. The same holds true for washing clothes by the canal, which often provides women with their only opportunity for socializing outside the household or the field.

J. Power relations and gender ideology

In spite of women's great contribution to agricultural and domestic work, their help is considered only complementary. Female domestic labour is not considered vital; it is male field labour which is deemed prestigious. In contrast to the few older participants in the research project who refer to the complementarity of male and female work in the 'old days' (Abaza, 1987a, 1987b), most village men do not appreciate the efforts made by women in the running and maintenance of the household.

The differential valuation of male and female labour, and the exchange values of the two forms, extends to personal autonomy and decision-making powers. From 'childhood, a female perceives males as her guardians and protectors. Indeed, some of the most crucial decisions relating to women are delegated to their male kinsmen. She may even have to marry against her own will. Moreover, women are often under the threat of divorce, especially during the early years of marriage. When faced with the possibility of repudiation, a woman may mobilize the support of her kinsmen and seek the help of intermediaries. The husband, however, has the final word over the termination of the matrimonial relationship and is supported by the legal codes of Egyptian justice (Mohsen, 1974: 38–42).

Further evidence of differential autonomy is detected in relation to freedom of movement within and outside the village. Men socialize with friends on the village streets in the evening. Women on the other hand are not supposed to leave their homes after nightfall, unless on an urgent errand. Permission must be sought from husband or mother-in-law to pay a visit to relatives or neighbours. Women are obliged to travel to market in groups or be escorted by their children. Only some older women dare transgress this cultural restriction on female movement outside the home.

The pattern of power asymmetry related to gender identity which the foregoing account has brought into focus is clearly reflected in the villagers' ideology. Differential valuation of males and females extends to physical and moral status. Women are said to be incapable of rational decision-making. It is argued that 'a woman's opinion, if it is correct, causes a year's worth of destruction'. As noted in other studies on Egypt, women are supposedly 'lacking in mind and religion' (Maher, 1974: 91).

In Fatiha, where Islam is composed of an infusion of Koranic directives and a variety of popular values and customs traceable to pre-Islamic ancient Egypt (Blackman, 1927), male dominance is often justified by reference to the *sunna*. However, the villagers' aforementioned belief that 'women are lacking in mind and religion' actually contradicts the Koranic stipulation of equal potential piety of men and women (Sura IX, 71) and the common nature of all believers (Sura IV). Moreover, the Islamic prohibition of female infanticide is contradicted by benign neglect of female infants, reflected in their mortality rate for Egypt as a whole (Valaoras, 1972).

Women themselves verbalize belief in their own physical and mental inferiority. However, such beliefs do not necessarily guide their daily activities. In fact, some women reject such characterization outright and note that such ideas are made up by men who use them to control women.

Beyond ideological declarations of male dominance or rejections thereof, women's and men's power is based on control over power-bases which are accorded cultural recognition. Thus the few male villagers who are involved in public political contests have a power-base in land and kinship relations. In the case of the female member of the Arab Socialist Union (ASU), her education is the significant resource on which her power in the community resides. Finally, in the case of the descendants of the former Turkish élite, their power derives from their descent (*asl*) which, translated into concrete power indices, means access to communication channels through kinship ties and incurred obligations.

The developmental cycle of the family which mediates power asymmetry illuminates the dynamics of male–female relations. In this regard, the limitation of equating authority with legitimacy is brought to light. It is evident that the patterned, generalized authority of mothers-in-law in extended family households rests on performance, or the actual exercise of power, rather than on legitimacy of cultural prescriptions. This is also manifest when the extended family breaks up upon the death of the senior male. While, according to custom, married sons are obliged to honour their mother, and while a mother may legitimately demand that her adult sons attend to her needs and comfort until her death, a woman succeeds in keeping the extended family intact after her husband's death and continues to enjoy the prestigious status of senior female if she owns property of her own. Similarly, although cultural ideals emphasize brothers' support of their sisters and the latter's right to depend on their male kinsmen, economically and otherwise, a woman is more likely to partake of such familial obligations if she turns over her inheritance to her brothers. In short, cultural prescriptions are not a substitute for a durable power-base.

K. *Some concluding remarks on women in Fatiha*

This analysis of Fatiha throws light on some theoretical issues raised in Part II of this study. Contrary to universalistic explanatory schemes of male dominance, political concerns in Fatiha are anything but extra-familial. Furthermore it is not women's association with the private sphere (in the few cases of those who can afford it), or childbearing, which limits their public political participation (Rosaldo and Lamphere, 1974). In general, political participation in this peasant community is limited for *both* men and women. Males of limited means do not participate in public political contests. Political control rests with urban élites whose patronage is actively sought by the local inhabitants, male and female, in their pursuit of personal goals.

As for the assertion that gender asymmetry is rooted in the procreative functions of women, this is equally invalid for Fatiha where motherhood is a culturally venerated status which constitutes one of women's most durable power-bases (Dwyer, 1978: 170). Neither can the confinement of women to the domestic sphere be realistically defined as the basis for their relative powerlessness. In fact, the rise of women's power in the family occurs at a stage of its developmental cycle when a woman becomes the mother of married sons, a stage which corresponds to an increased confinement of her activities to the domestic sphere.

Contrary to orientalist reification of Islam as a unitary social force, it is evident that in Fatiha Islam is marshalled to support variable ideological positions. Thus, while one father opposes his daughter's education and forces her into marriage by stating that religion directs her to obey her parents, another justifies his daughter's university education away from the village by reference to Islamic directives regarding literacy and knowledge.

Beyond individual cases, gender ideology is made more or less probable by structural constraints. For Fatiha, and other parts of rural Egypt, an outstanding structural element is the control exercised by the state. The structure of the Egyptian social formation, dominated by capitalism, is supportive of ideologies which reproduce the devaluation of women's use-value production and render invisible their contribution to production and reproduction locally, and capital accumulation nationally and internationally.

V. Bahiya in 1980/1: Regional labour migration and familial production

A. Overview of the community

The village of Bahiya is located in the Nile Delta, approximately 30 kms north of Tanta and nearly 30 km. west of the industrial centre of Mihala. With a population of about 8,000, the village is under the administrative jurisdiction of the district (*markaz*) of Qutur, famous as a major centre for the cultivation and partial processing of aromatic plants.

Bahiya is connected to major Egyptian urban centres through a transportation network which is crucial for the marketing of a variety of commercial crops. Public education, health clinics and hospitals, as well as state employment of local residents also integrate the village into the encompassing society.

Like Fatiha, Bahiya is known as a community of ancient origin. Up to 1952 most of the village land was administered by the Ministry of Awqaf (religious endowments). Older villagers still remember the days of the Awqaf when *zir'a 'ala il zima* was practised, whereby peasants were given access to a *feddan* of land which was cultivated by family labour, including women's work, in return for work on the Awqaf land. Following the army coup in 1952 and the dissolution of Awqaf land, nearly two-thirds was sold to the villagers.

Bahiya is also a Muslim peasant community. As many as six mosques are to be found in the village. The oldest was built by the Ministry of Awqaf as early as 1901, while donations from migrants returning to the village from neighbouring oil-rich Arab countries have been used to build the others. Prior to 1952, particularly up to the mid-1940s, the village was an important centre of popular religion with as many as fifty Sufi *tariqas* (religious orders) represented. Since the latter part of the 1970s, the popular religious ceremony of *zar* (spirit possession) has returned to the village. In addition to the local residents, the weekly ceremony draws those afflicted with spirit possession from surrounding areas. While many women attend the *zar*, they do not participate in the collective weekly Friday noon prayers held in the mosques of the village. Compared to Fatiha, however, many women do pray regularly at home. Many of the village's young female students have taken up Islamic dress, and, unlike the women in Fatiha, most of them cover their heads in public.

Occupational specialization in Bahiya is more diverse than in Fatiha. Many of the children of the relatively wealthy landowners hold intermediate or university degrees and work as teachers. Some villagers work in the industrial centre of Mihala, and others, including young women, are employed in the local bureaucracy or in the nearby provincial towns. However, all these are members of households involved in agricultural production in one capacity or another.

As in Fatiha, access to land is highly desirable. Given the peasant 'subsistence ethic', the approximately 10 per cent of landless peasants constantly strive to control a piece of land, however small and however brief the duration of the contract. Officially, approximately 93 per cent of peasants in Bahiya cultivate under 3 *feddans* of land; 5.5 per cent of landholdings are between 3 and 5 *feddans*; 1 per cent between 5 and 10 *feddans*; 0.5 per cent between 15 and 25 *feddans*; and one tenant operates over 25 *feddans*. Such official statistics underestimate the percentage of landholdings over 3 *feddans*. In order to avoid taxes, household heads register part of their land in the names of their wives. In addition, approximately 30 per cent of landholders registered with the agricultural co-operative are female. This practice is designed to facilitate the task of women who must procure agricultural inputs from the village co-operative while male members of their households are away from the village as migrant labourers.

Migration from the village in pursuit of non-agricultural employment is no longer restricted to urban Egypt. Within the framework of the state's 'economic opening', many villagers have left Bahiya to seek their fortune in the petroleum-producing countries of the Arab world. In addition to teachers and other professionals, including a few females, the *sheikh el-balad* (village elder) estimates that between forty and a hundred peasants leave the village annually as part of the generalized trend of seeking individual resolutions to Egypt's economic problems. With the exception of the few female teachers who have been accompanied by male relatives, men leave the village without their wives and children. This male migration causes seasonal labour shortages, aggravated by mass government employment of army draftees following their discharge.

B. State institutions

In Bahiya, as in other Egyptian villages, the role of the state is evident in various forms including the provision of educational and health services. Beyond the introduction of electricity of Bahiya in 1966, and four public water taps in 1967, this is particularly pronounced, as in Fatiha, with regard to the regulation of the agricultural cycle, extraction of surplus, and extension of credit.

While the state, through the local agricultural co-operative, appropriates the surplus of traditional fieldcrops, its control does not extend to vegetables and aromatic plants. Of the village's total cultivated area, 19.2 per cent is devoted to these commercial crops. In addition to being free to dispose of their products as they wish, and enjoying the full profitability of production, cultivators of such agricultural products are taxed only nominally. Since it is the upper stratum of the peasantry which is capable of enjoying this type of cultivation, and by extension such tax exemption, it is evident that the state has contributed to the differentiation of the peasantry and consolidation of rich peasant production. This is not to suggest that the agrarian transition to capitalism has occured in Bahiya. Far from leading to proletarianization, state policies related to tenancy and surplus appropriation, and more recently migration, have consolidated the small peasant household in Bahiya, as elsewhere in Egypt.

Closely associated with the agricultural co-operatives is the system of village banks established by the state within the framework of the ODEP. The *Bank al-Karya* (village bank), located in a nearby community, serves Bahiya and four other villages. In addition to authorizing the allocation of cultivation inputs and cash advances, the bank gives out loans to those farming no less than 3 *feddans*. These are used for the purchase of a variety of agricultural machinery and consumer durables ranging from water pumps to sewing-machines and pick-up trucks. The village bank, through the provision of loans, contributes to the implementation of the state's policies favouring the mechanization of agriculture. Local elders opposed to such policies, and the more general trend of economic liberalization, consider village banks to be nothing less than conduits for surplus production in the West, which is 'dumped on Egypt'.

The state's representatives for maintenance of public order in Bahiya include two *sheikh el-balad*. Compared to their counterparts in Fatiha, these men play a more limited role in settling family disputes in this relatively large village. A newly acquired role of these local state representatives is the issuing of official documents for men wishing to work outside Egypt. The two *sheikh el-balad* assist the *umda* (headman) and his deputy and are all held accountable to the Ministry of the Interior.

As in the case of Fatiha, involvement in public political contests is limited to males who are associated with the ruling National Democratic Party and opposition political parties. None of the village women are politically active. Neither are the less well-endowed male peasants who consider such involvement more suitable for those 'who can afford it'. Like their counterparts in other rural communities they recognize the urban élites and their local representatives, the rich peasants, to be the locus of political control.

C. *Migration and the social organization of agricultural production*

Anthropological studies of the impact of labour migration on agricultural production and the role of women in the household labour process indicate different outcomes (Abaza, 1987a). For Bahiya the impact varies as a function of the differentiation of the peasantry. More precisely, labour migration bears a reciprocal relation to variable access to means of production, household composition and family structure, and forms of income generation. For some women, migration has led to restriction of their labour to use-value production, and the reproduction of family labour power. Others have become increasingly involved in commodity production to various degrees; in some cases their own labour power becomes commoditized as they enter the wage labour arena.

1. Access to land and differentiation of the peasantry   In Bahiya, official records of the agricultural co-operative suggest that the range of land distribution varies between under 1 *feddan* and 25 *feddans* per single owner or operator. But an extended family household may in fact collectively own up to 75 *feddans* of land. Such large areas of land owned by extended family households are not, however, exploited on the basis of capitalist principles involving wage-labour and mechanical power.

During the 1960s cultivation of aromatic plants by more well-to-do peasants proceeded according to capitalist relations of production based on wage-labour. More recently, labour migration to the petrol-producing countries of the Arab world, and changes in international market demands for local aromatic plants, have affected the pattern of land utilization. As a result of seasonal labour shortages associated with migration, rich peasants have increasingly resorted to exploiting their large landholdings through share-cropping arrangements. Moreover, in some cases, the dissolution of capitalist landholdings-in-formation can be foreseen. As educated descendants of rich peasants migrate from Bahiya, land fragmented through inheritance may be either sold or parcelled out for share-cropping or cash rent.

Share-cropping is more profitable for landowners than cash rent, as rent is subject to state regulation while share-cropping is negotiated informally. Cash rent per year for 1 *feddan* ranges from £E 45 to £E 60. On the other hand the 'landless peasant', anxious to provide subsistence for his family, may be obliged to pay up to £E 160 every six months to obtain the right to share-crop. In some cases such families are willing to pay equally exaggerated prices for access to land for the short duration of *zar'a wahda* (one planting season) to grow corn, wheat or clover.

Share-cropping is used particularly in the cultivation of rice. The relatively wealthy peasant finds it troublesome to grow rice because of labour shortages. In some cases, he may have to pay up to £E 3 per day for a wage-labourer. The poor peasant/share-cropper does not face the same labour shortage problem. In addition to the labour power of his entire family, he relies on exchange labour (*muzamla*), which the young men and women of the household are particularly active in arranging with friends and relatives.

Under share-cropping arrangements, the labour power of the whole family is exploited by the landlord. Although contractual relations and the specification of conditions of surplus appropriation are arranged by men, or by male relatives in the case of migrants, the poor tenant in fact commits the labour of his entire family to cultivation.

Given the 'subsistence ethic' of peasants, 'landless' families whose members derive income as wage-labourers constantly strive to gain access to land. The pattern of wage-labour in Bahiya belies the assumption of a land consolidation–proletarianization dichotomy and by extension the allegation of a completed transition to capitalism in Egyptian agriculture as discussed earlier. The designation 'landless' peasant is seasonally highly variable for any given peasant. Access to land may be realized in the form of short-term share-cropping arrangements or through informal (and illegal) short-term land leases at exorbitant prices.

In Bahiya there is a greater variation in the relative wealth of village households than in Fatiha. But beside differences in standards of consumption (as indicated by the various degrees of comfort found in village dwellings, food consumption, dressing habits, education of children and cash remittances from village migrants), there is a noticeable contrast at the more fundamental level of production. In other words, there is greater differentiation of the peasantry. This is evident in the variation of access to productive resources (and related differential control of surplus products and accumulation of resources, i.e. differential investment capacity), the extent of employment of wage-labourers, differences in crop mixes, and agricultural mechanization. Migrants' remittances represent a significant input in this regard.

2. The sexual division of labour In Bahiya the impact of male migration on women's contributions to social production is correlated to the social differentiation of the peasant household (De Los

Angeles Crummett, 1985). Among 'landless' peasants, the pre-
dominantly male labour exodus increased dependence on women's
work as part of the more general intensification of self-exploitation
of family labour.

For women who replace men as wage-earners, integration into
capitalist production has meant that the virtually unlimited labour
service offered to landlords' households has declined. While some
female wage-labourers continue to be exploited by families of rich
peasants (e.g. helping out with baking, cleaning and shopping),
this occurs to a much more limited extent than was the case
formerly or is even so currently for share-croppers' kinswomen.

The redivision of labour resulting from seasonal adult male
labour-shortage has also meant an increased work burden for
children at low pay. This is particularly evident with regard to the
cultivation of jasmine. Children, and to a lesser extent women,
predominate in the harvesting of this aromatic plant for a fraction
of the pay received for picking cotton. It is indeed a wonder that
child labour power is committed by parents to the harvesting of
jasmine at lower wages. Children and women engage in the
harvesting of jasmine on the land of rich peasants so that the latter
will guarantee regular employment for family members during the
slack agricultural season in the winter months. Additionally, the
harvesting of jasmine by children and women is often a form of
repayment of loans (and other favours) extended by rich peasants to
these workers' kinsmen or to female heads of household during the
absence of migrant male relatives. Evidently the 'comparative
advantage' of jasmine cultivation and international marketing of
the partially processed aromatic plant are closely associated with
the 'comparative disadvantage' of peasant women and children
(Arizpe and Aranda, 1981).

Some of the malnourished and overworked female and male
children who harvest jasmine in Bahiya succumb to what local
inhabitants describe as 'jasmine illness', a form of anclystomiasis or
hookworm disease, which has been on the decline over the past few
years as decreasing international market demands for jasmine and
aggravated labour shortages have forced many cultivators to up-
root their jasmine shrubs.

While 'landless' peasants, during certain periods, earn their income as wage-labourers, the poor peasants' household labour force
(those with less than 1 *feddan*) is also semi-proletarianized, supplementing income with wage-labour. They are not proletarian in the
full sense of the word since they have certain control over the
means of production and the production process. Among these

poor peasants, family labour, including women's non-capitalist production, subsidizes the wages of the semi-proletarian villagers. In fact, the involvement of these peasants in subsistence production is a means of reproducing their labour-power. The women of wage-labourers and poor peasant families, in addition to contributing to the cultivation of subsistence crops, often sell their labour-power as wage-earners, depending on the size of landholding accessible to their families from one agricultural cycle to another.

For proletarianized and semi-proletarianized families, remittances from migrants may allow women to forego wage-labour employment and confine their efforts to family agricultural production. On the other hand, in the early days of a male's migration, when remittances are irregular, or non-existent, a woman whose labour was once confined to family production may be forced to become a wage-earner for varying periods of time, depending on the consequent pattern and amount of remittances.

Among poor peasants, in contrast to their less poor and rich counterparts, women take on major responsibility for agricultural production. These poor peasant-women are now burdened with obligations that were previously shouldered by males, including the time-consuming and unpleasant charge of dealing with the state bureaucracy. In some cases, as mentioned earlier, semi-proletarianized men who are heavily involved in wage-labour, or who migrate temporarily, register land in the names of their wives to facilitate their interaction with the staff of the agricultural co-operative.

Aromatic plant cultivation, once a lucrative source of income, has seldom been a realistic option for poor peasants. Although poor peasants, under seasonal labour-shortage conditions and through increased exploitation of family labour, are well-suited to maintain the daily harvest of jasmine, they cannot devote the whole of their small area of land to aromatic plants or any other commercial crop cultivation. Aromatic plants require more than one season to mature, and poor peasants cannot ordinarily survive on income from their land for this period. More important still, they cannot give up subsistence crops such as wheat, rice and corn, nor can they abandon cultivation of fodder for their animals.

Migrants' remittances may in some cases allow poor peasant households to forego subsistence production in favour of commercial crop agriculture. The family may use remitted cash for food purchases and devote land to commercial exploitation. In such cases, women's contributions are likely to be confined to domestic work. Their contribution to commercial crop cultivation is only supplementary and is evaluated as such. Family production thus evolves in a different way, depending on the amounts of savings accumulated and possible investment options and decisions.

Among less poor peasant households, characterized by the relative self-sufficiency of labour requirements, the women's contribution is usually confined to family labour. Their only work on land controlled by other households is within the framework of exchange labour at times of heavy agricultural work. Commoditization of women's labour is not characteristic of less poor peasant households. In fact, only on rare occasions do they resort to engaging others as day-labourers for supplementary help.

Migrant savings may alter the less poor peasant family's pattern of sexual division of labour if this permits expansion of landholdings. In such cases, depending on the size of newly acquired holdings and available remittances for their management, women's work may actually increase as their activities as family producers intensify. Or, on the other hand, they may retreat to prestigious domestic production as their efforts in agricultural production are replaced by hired non-family labour.

When landholdings expand beyond the capability of family labour, as is the case among rich peasants, the landowner's role in production gradually becomes a supervisory one with wage-labourers (male and female) hired to do the work. The women of rich peasant households are secluded and confined to use-value production. Large-scale aromatic plant cultivation and citrus fruit production is an option for rich peasants as well as for the agrarian bourgeoisie in the outlying regions of Bahiya. Their access to productive resources beyond their subsistence requirements and their access to cash for market purchases permit them to forego the product of their land for extended periods of time.

During their husband's migration, women peasants replace them in carrying out manual operations, including ploughing. Migrants' remittances have, however, contributed to increased mechanization of agriculture in Bahiya. The use of these new agricultural instruments (tractors, reaping and threshing machines, water pumps) remains the prerogative of the male peasant. Women nevertheless do appreciate the labour- and time-saving machinery which replaces the back-breaking work of manual threshing and driving the animals that turn the water wheels.

In Bahiya reliance on mechanical devices is, however, far from universal. Men and women have not abandoned traditional cultivation methods, such as the traditional plough pulled by animals which still serves a very important function and is considered essential when ploughing wet land. While this task continues to be the responsibility of men, the planting of rice, once a family affair, as in Fatiha, has now become the responsibility of female members of the household.

3. Household income pooling and the reproduction of household labour
Compared to Fatiha, relations of commodity production and exchange are much more pronounced in Bahiya. Here cash crops which are marketed locally, nationally and internationally provide a significant direct or indirect source of income for village households. Out of the 340 *feddans* used for cash-crop production, 108 are devoted to aromatic plant cultivation, 52 to fruit, including oranges, apples and mangoes, and 180 are used to grow potatoes.

As mentioned previously, commercial crop production is an option for those who have investable capital and who can forego the product of their land for at least two harvest seasons. Oranges, apples and mangoes require relatively large areas of land and continuous access to it, thus eliminating small peasant households and 'landless' share-croppers. As for jasmine, the young plants are planted in May and it is not until two summers later that they are ready for harvesting.

In describing the comparative profitability of different commercial crops, poor peasant women lament: 'money begets money'. It is estimated that while the average profit from a *feddan* of cotton is approximately £E 100, that derived from potatoes is about £E 250. A *feddan* of jasmine used to generate a net profit of approximately £E 2,000. In 1981, due to labour shortage and decreasing demands for this aromatic plant on the international market, it still provided at least £E 800 in profit. As for violets, the profit derived from 1 *feddan* in one year is estimated to be £E 1,500.

Given the profitability of cash crops, small peasant households do their best to allocate at least a tiny area of their land for their production. Such economic diversification constitutes an important adaptive strategy which helps foster the reproduction of the peasant household. While men are responsible for the planting of jasmine shrubs, it is the responsibility of women and children to harvest the flowers daily before sunrise and to turn over the yield to middlemen who take it to the processing plant near the village.

In addition to deriving income from aromatic plants either as wage-labourers or by cultivating tiny plots, women generate income from cultivating and marketing vegetables locally and in the surrounding areas. Although this draws upon the labour of all members of the household, marketing is often the responsibility of women. Pick-up trucks, purchased with migrants' savings, facilitate transportation, and village women take other household products, including dairy products, eggs and poultry to the weekly market near the village. A few of the village women who trade in cattle may not own these animals but have a 'partnership' with wealthier villagers in return for responsibility in raising them.

Income from agricultural wage-labour is not readily available to household members all the year round. From November to March agricultural work is relatively limited. In April the demand for wage-labourers increases and continues until October. It is during this period of relative labour shortage that wages increase substantially, ranging from between £E 1.5 to £E 3 per work session of about three to four hours for men, and between £E 1.5 to £E 2 for women. At times of extreme labour shortage, for example during the planting of rice, the harvesting of cotton, wheat and rice, men and women may receive equal pay. In fact, during the cotton picking season, even a child gets the same pay as an adult.

Savings from migrant labour are considerable by peasant standards and have contributed to the development of a pattern of consumption hitherto unknown among the majority of peasants. Income generated in the PPC is invested in real estate, agricultural machinery, and transport vehicles ranging from carts to cars, all of which have facilitated both the production and the marketing of non-traditional crops.

While some of the men returning from work abroad may invest in land, this option is rather restricted in view of high prices, a *feddan* costing as much as £E 7,000. More realistic investments include crop diversification, cattle raising and the purchase of sewing-machines, all of which provide women with still more work, but also the opportunity for generation of additional income.

Women's use-value production and contribution to the reproduction of household labour is a year-round exercise. Along with wage-labour and share-cropping, it is essential for the reproduction of 'landless' and small-peasant households, including the consolidation of land ownership (Keydar, 1983). As a result of migration, and within the framework of the articulation of capitalist and non-capitalist production, women, in addition to being drawn into the wage-labour arena as substitutes for absent males, remain oriented towards subsistence production. It is indeed this and their role in maintaining their families that permits the release of men into migrant salaried labour.

As in Fatiha, adult women, in spite of their agricultural and seasonal wage-labour earning activities, are primarily defined and judged in terms of their maternal and domestic work functions. In addition to feeding, cleaning and attending to the numerous needs of children, women are expected to 'discipline' their children in the absence of the head of household, and to draw upon support from male kinsmen when necessary. For women with children in school, the failure of any of them to perform satisfactorily in the father's absence is blamed on the mother.

Peasant women, in addition to their involvement in agricultural exchange-value production in the absence of their menfolk, continue to perform a variety of domestic functions ranging from cleaning stables, to healing, repairing the walls of the house, washing and fetching water. Among 'landless' as well as small and less small peasant households, females, particularly young women, actively arrange labour during the peak agricultural season. Through this *zamala* women avoid the payment of wages, and in the long term contribute to the consolidation of household production.

Among rich peasants, the contribution of women to use-value production is by no means insignificant. Although they are often assisted by women of 'landless' and poor peasant households, rich peasant women are nevertheless burdened with a variety of domestic responsibilities. It is only the female students in such households who are spared the drudgery of housework, and then only during the school year. Otherwise rich peasant women are expected to manage their relatively large homes and extended families in a manner befitting their men's prestigious position in the village. Their workload, like other women in Bahiya, has also been affected by migration. Given the associated seasonal labour shortage, the households of rich peasants, in competing for wage-labourers, attract them by providing plenty of good food, numerous rounds of tea, tobacco, and gifts on festive occasions. During the harvest, wives of rich peasants, in addition to gifts of food, distribute lengths of cloth to their regular labourers.

D. *Power relations and gender ideology*

In spite of the obvious contribution of women to the generation of household income, shouldering the burden of intensified use-value production and preservation of the household as a production unit, it is the migrant men who are considered 'breadwinners', even if the man's savings have been accumulated through the performance of what is ordinarily considered women's work, such as baking.

When both man and woman are wage-labourers *within* Bahiya, or its rural vicinity, the woman's contribution to family income is more readily recognized, given its obvious and comparable remuneration. In terms of the community at large, 'landless' male and female wage-labourers are the least prestigious but, among themselves, more equal.

With increased labour migration, the very definition of the 'breadwinner' has changed from agricultural producers, provider of familial subsistence, to migrant labourer, generator of cash savings, giver of gifts, particularly consumer durables such as fans, tape-recorders and washing-machines.

While recognized, the extra responsibilities assumed by women in the household of migrant workers in the absence of their husbands do not constitute a durable, culturally significant power-base, except in a derivative sense. Women themselves do not consider the extra work a means of 'self-fulfilment', but a burden which they attribute to the misfortune of being peasants. But, for them, as for others, 'filling in' for a male migrant is considered much less strenuous and taxing than the life men are believed to live away from home.

Beyond improved standards of family consumption and status within the village, women of migrant households look forward to being spared from work in the fields. But they do not necessarily look on their work as a means of achieving more egalitarian relations with their husbands. In fact, women may joke with one another and say 'you work for his relatives, and you raise his kids, who knows who is with him now!' They may also remark jokingly, 'he will come back and kiss your hand when he brings you a *dura* [co-wife]'. While less than a handful of the twenty polygamous marriages in the village were contracted by migrants, this is nevertheless a precedent which women recognize and fear.

As in Fatiha, the differential valuation of male and female work in Bahiya, which now includes local agricultural production versus migrant non-agricultural labour, extends to personal autonomy. When a man departs from the village, he leaves a woman under the protection of his kinsmen and guardianship of her kinsmen whose duty it is to protect the family honour, as well as under the watchful eye of the village as a whole. Whereas women of 'landless' and poor peasant households are likely to live in the predominant nuclear family, independent of the direct control of mothers-in-law or older sisters-in-law, this opportunity for relative autonomy may be curtailed by property considerations, kinship obligations or the inaccessability of housing. In some cases migrants' remittances or savings may accelerate the dissolution of the extended family, thereby undermining the power of the mother-in-law (Morsy, 1988).

Gender ideology in Bahiya bears great resemblance to that in Fatiha. Here too women are said to be 'lacking in mind and religion' and male authority over women is justified by reference to the *sunna* while the devaluation of women's piety contradicts Koranic prescriptions, as does the barring of women from inheriting their fathers' property. But different from Fatiha is the returning migrants' idealized image of the veiled Muslim sister associated with women of the Gulf where they worked (Abaza, 1987b). Veiling has spread since the mid-1970s, and become an urban Egyptian practice in association with the ODEP and integration into the regional petro-economy. Young female students in Bahiya and surrounding rural areas are seen wearing head-veils and long dresses over trousers which cover their legs. Female clerks in the state bureaucracy around the village are similarly attired. This type of dress is no more modest than the traditional peasant style, but it does stand out as a status-marker, symbolizing not simply its wearer's piety but her 'de-peasantization'.

E. Some concluding remarks on rural women in Bahiya

In Bahiya, the departure of men to the PPC has left women with new responsibilities, ranging from sowing seeds in family plots to dealing with the agricultural co-operative, ultimately contributing to the reproduction of peasant household-production among the 'landless' and small peasant households which constitute the majority in the village.

In Bahiya there are no signs of women's alleged 'empowerment' as a result of increased workload. Women's (and children's) work continues to be devalued in comparison to that of the men. Since some of the work that women engage in is traditionally men's work, this suggests that devaluation is not simply a matter of the sexual division of labour. Agricultural production in its entirety, whether male or female, has become devalued in comparison to non-agricultural employment in which migrant males engage while they are abroad (Abaza, 1987a). Thus it is not only women's work which is relatively devalued, but also the work of male villagers whose productive activities do not approximate the new definition of 'breadwinner'.

The idealization of work in the PPC extends to the image of the 'respectable' veiled women in these countries. Income generated by migrant labourers allows their kinswomen to approximate this image. As a pre-existing sign of wealth and prestige, the restriction of women's labour to domestic production is welcomed by the women themselves.

The devaluation of women's productive work, and migrants' coveted culture of consumption are indicative of the general national and regional trends discussed in Part III of this study. Just as the women of Fatiha in 1974 were the product of state populist development, those of Bahiya in 1981 were the offspring of the ODEP and regional petro-economy.

VI. Conclusions

Beyond statistical estimates of 'economically active' rural women, the foregoing accounts of the Egyptian villages of Fatiha and Bahiya reveal women's often underestimated contributions to production (Balfet, 1982; F. Hussein, 1984; Mernissi, 1984; Abou Nasr, 1985; Ferchiou, 1985). Moreover, these anthropological accounts link women's work to primary and secondary reproduction, associated with household and social formation, respectively (Evers *et al.*, 1984). For while labour migration has brought into focus women's role in production, their role in *reproducing* the peasant household as a subsistence and surplus-producing structure still remains relatively neglected in studies on rural Arab women. It is therefore important to stress that whether men's remunerated labour is confined to rural Egypt, transferred to its urban centres, or exported to the PPC, within the framework of the articulation of capitalist and non-capitalist forms of production, it continues to be subsidized by various forms of women's (and children's) use-value production and their income-generating activities in the 'informal' sector. Given the appropriation of peasant surplus by the state, and Egypt's integration into the regional and global economies, women's household labour and locally generated income likewise contribute to capital accumulation nationally, regionally and internationally (cf. Cho and Koo, 1983).

Besides specific adaptive strategies of women in Fatiha and Bahiya, and associated differences in migration patterns, commercial crop production, differentiation of the peasantry and marketing of commercial products (all more developed and pronounced in Bahiya), it is evident that women in both villages are actively engaged in multiple tasks of production and reproduction. The work patterns of women in Bahiya are not qualitatively different from those of their counterparts in Fatiha. More generally, flexibility in the division of labour between women and men characterizes small-holder agricultural production in rural Egypt (Glavanis, 1984: 49). This is recognized by elders in Fatiha who take pride in the complementarity of men and women's work 'in the old days' reciting the proverb: '*il ragil bahr wil mara gisr*' (man is a river and woman a dam).

In fact the contribution of women to productive activity and public transactions are by no means new to the Egyptian rural scene, and certainly pre-date the regional petro-economic boom. The nineteenth-century Egyptian feminist Qasim Amin described a rural woman's 'wealth of knowledge through her work and business dealings' (Q. Amin, 1970, quoted in Abdel Khader, 1987). Women's involvement in the 'rural venture' (Marsot, 1978) has furthermore included responsibility for reproducing the family as a productive unit in the absence of male members, temporarily isolated from household production by the increasing demands of the larger society. These have ranged from Mohamed Ali's conscription programme to the current drafting of young able-bodied peasant men to serve in the national Central Security forces. As men pursue non-agricultural employment, women continue to forestall the gradual disappearance of the peasantry.

With male migration to the PPC, women in rural Egypt carry out traditional roles of both sexes. Evidently, a redefinition of the value of different forms of labour has been emerging and cultural valuation, now measured by cash remuneration, has been transferred to so-called 'modern' work, primarily the province of men.

The consequences of increased dependence on women's work for family welfare and authority patterns has stimulated much debate in the literature on women in development (Youssef *et al.*, 1979). For rural Egypt, Khattab and El Daeif, on the basis of an anthropological study, hypothesize that: 'wives of labour migrants who are forced to make independent decisions during husbands' absences concerning management of property and remittances will gain high status relative to husband and in-laws, whereas women who are deprived of managing husbands' remittances and property will experience little or no change in their roles and status' (1982: 68; cf. Khafagy, 1984; Mohieddin, 1987). They also assert that: 'Egyptian labour migrant wives are experiencing definite changes in their traditional array of roles which in turn is affecting their status within their families and the community at large' (Khattab and El Daeif, 1982: 52). Khattab and El Daeif conclude their study questioning: 'Will the wife of the migrant retain this egalitarian relationship in terms of decision-making . . . and authority after the return of her husband? Will she retreat to familial roles and abandon involvement in the public domain?' (ibid.: 71).

In contrast, Mervat Hatem offers a more definitive evaluation. She states that:

> Increased dependence on women's work in the labour exporting economies . . . [has] . . . not significantly changed women's position in the family and vis-à-vis men, in general . . . while changes in women's work roles could be observed . . ., they did not constitute a sufficient basis for challenging the character of the existing patriarchies. Social/ sexual relations maintained their autonomy and succeeded in adapting the new roles to the existing partriarchal value system (Hatem, 1983: 1).

In the same vein, Cynthia Myntti has observed that: '[in Yemen] . . . male relatives remaining behind make the decisions as surrogates for the absent emigrant' (1978: 30).

Moreover, it has been argued that the prevalence of female-headed households is not necessarily indicative of improved conditions for women. According to Hatem:

> Even though women had taken over new agricultural tasks, the tendency had been for them to work under the auspices of younger or older men. In other words, the adoption of new work roles did not necessarily lead to greater independence, but substituted the missing head of the household with the next male in line whether a son, a father, or a brother-in-law. More importantly, the decision on how to spend this money from the remittances was often a male decision either by the migrant himself or his family. In other words, women might not necessarily gain any new decision-making power within the family as a result of the absence of the male head of the household and/or the availability of new sources of income . . . the general promotion and acceptance of work as a societal response to change had not materialized. . . . The social and material rewards for women's involvement continued to be weak (Hatem, 1983: 15–16).

In the light of observations concerning Bahiya, one aspect of Hatem's assumption requires clarification. While it is true, as suggested by Khattab and El Daeif, that not all migrant wives will gain new decision-making powers, it is nevertheless important to recognize that some of them do acquire at least temporary decision-making powers.

Hatem's expectation of the substitution of the missing head of the household with the next male in line is not uniformly borne out by observations in Bahiya. While women usually function with some degree of male support during the absence of heads of household (or other significant male relatives), such support, even when readily accessible, does not necessarily curtail women's temporarily delegated decision-making powers. Female household heads often seek and secure the support (material and moral) of males (and females), particularly cognates, during the absence of their husband, but it is the wife herself who acts as surrogate. While the legitimacy of her decision-making powers may be accepted by some and rejected by others in certain cases, she is nevertheless the source of the decision.

In some cases, power delegated to women by men takes on a legal character and thereby becomes more lasting. In Bahiya this occurs when husbands register land that they own, or control on a contractual basis, in the names of their wives.

This clarification aside, observations in Bahiya support Hatem's contention that 'while changes in women's work roles could be observed . . . *they did not constitute sufficient basis for challenging the character of the existing patriarchies*' (emphasis added). Stated differently, the case of Bahiya indicates that male out-migration has not produced a fundamental change in the social relations of production and attendant male–female power relations. *Control* over the valued instruments of production remains vested in males; productive resources are only sporadically available to women. Variation between strata of the peasantry aside, control over goods and services that have exchange value rests with men. Women's increased workload, usually involving increased use-value production, has not altered male–female authority patterns in a meaningful way.

Although, as Khattab and El Daeif conclude, 'migrants' wives are experiencing *definite* changes' (emphasis added), these are by no means *fundamental* (Awni, 1984). Legal codes regulating access to productive resources through inheritance are still male biased, and the ideology that legitimizes female subordination still thrives in both rural and urban Egypt. In rural areas, legalized polygamy remains a weapon with which presumably independent migrants' wives are threatened (ibid.). It is not unheard of for a returning migrant to 'invest' his savings in a new marriage, thereby withdrawing authority delegated to his wife at his convenience.

Some evaluations of the consequences of male migration on women's power imply certain assumptions about the definition of power, but these are seldom made explicit (Nelson, 1975; Morsy, 1978a, 1978b). The absence of a clear definition of power in much of the literature on Arab family relations has often contributed to the creation of a mirage of power even when women's access to culturally meaningful power-bases is blocked by structural barriers. Temporary assumption of delegated responsibility is certainly not equivalent to acquiring (or seizing) control over culturally significant, durable power-bases that involve permanent modification of social status.

The important determinant of women's power is not their involvement in work *per se*, or their assumption of new economic roles; it is the framework of social relations of production into which their contributions are channelled and the related cultural evaluation of such contributions.

As for the assumption that 'male labour migration has presented the wives left behind with opportunities to play alternative roles to their familial ones' (Khattab and El Daeif, 1982: 54), it is useful to look at variations in the different strata of the peasantry. In contrast to Khattab and El Daeif's observation that '[only] in very few cases were rural women relieved of the necessity to work' (ibid.), observations in Bahiya as well as the village of Suad (a pseudonym) in the governorate of Gharbiya indicate that among the upper strata of the peasantry, wealth accumulated through migrant remittances prompts families to confine the labour of their women to the household. Women's isolation in the sphere of reproduction remains a mark of status in rural Egypt (Tucker, 1983: 330).

In evaluating the impact of migration-related changes on women's roles and on power relations in the family, it is not sufficient to consider women's participation in new economic activities and decision-making powers when appropriate family structures, residence and remittance patterns permit. Neither is it adequate to note 'the manner in which the husbands and relatives acknowledge their efforts and accomplishments' (Khattab and El Daeif, 1982: 64). To assess the significance of certain of women's newly acquired roles properly, one must move, conceptually, outside the analytical boundaries of roles themselves and evaluations thereof to consider the structural elements that maintain or constrain their evolution. This takes us beyond individual familial adaptations, social mobility, and family structure and residence patterns to consider the framework of production relations and related class structure. Migration studies, by focusing on social and status mobility and consumerism, have characteristically ignored class structure (Wojno, 1982). While there is no doubt that social mobility, newly acquired roles, and patterns of consumption constitute important migration-related changes, they do not contribute sufficiently to an understanding of the linkages between local social structure and the broader class relations in which they are subsumed (ibid.: 16).

In Bahiya variation in the contribution of women to social production is correlated with the social differentiation of the peasant household, which did not commence with migration. Within the existing framework of agrarian transformation, labour migration only perpetuates existing patterns, which is not to say that agrarian transformation has followed a unilinear path. On the contrary, in the early days of the recent wave of migration to the PPC, migrants' remittances and income derived from cultivating jasmine allowed some villagers to engage in capitalist production. Labour shortages in recent years have reinforced certain precapitalist relations of production. In short, migration has not transformed the class structure of Bahiya; only shifts over class segments have occurred. To the extent that migration-related social mobility among men and women has involved nothing more than 'horizontal social mobility', migration has not produced fundamental structural change. The structural boundaries of the social relations of production and the related sexual division of labour and family power relations have been maintained. Men's culturally prescribed authority continues to be upheld by their control over culturally valued power-bases ranging from privileged access to property, control over the products of women's labour, including that generated in their absence, to their association with nonagricultural migrant labour in the PPC, and bureaucratic employment or the operation of 'modern machinery' locally.

Beyond assertions of women's 'empowerment' and 'emancipation', and suggestions that 'rural women's role has undergone considerable change' during the last decade, it is evident that women's lives are affected by forces which transcend the boundaries of their peasant communities and which have varied historically.

Family household labour is by no means the only factor contributing to the reproduction of the peasant household as a subsistence and surplus-producing structure. State policies constitute significant influences through price regulation and surplus appropriation which often force peasant families to intensify self-exploitation of household labour (Korayem, 1981b; Larson, 1984; Khafagy, 1986:19). Women's inclusion in or exclusion from social production are the outcome of structural mechanisms involving state policy and the location of national and regional economies in the world system (Rubbo, 1975; Smith *et al.*, 1984; Sell, 1987: 70–75). The cases of Fatiha and Bahiya are illustrative of the operation of such historically specific structural mechanisms.

Contrary to the shifts in cultural orientations predicted by the proponents of a traditional–modern analytical dichotomy (Smelser, 1970: 37, and Goode, 1970: 242–3, quoted in Tiano, 1981: 2; Patai, 1969: 1; cf. Bossen, 1975), older people in Fatiha take pride in the complementarity of women's work 'in the old days' while in Bahiya women whose labour is confined to the household are envied as *mitsateteen* (lady-like) (Abaza, 1987b; Hoffman-Ladd, 1987). This idealization of the 'householding activities' (Friedman, 1984) is a cultural mechanism which contributes to the reproduction of the subsistence sector, and is thus compatible with the consolidation of peasant household-production under conditions of increasing 'formal' sector unemployment, as is the case in Egypt today. This household-production, although mystified and devalued, nevertheless reduces the social cost of maintenance and reproduction of the agrarian labour force and indirectly subsidizes national and international development. Indeed, as Beneria observes, 'a local economy survives thanks to women's involvement in subsistence production' (1982: 140). So much for rural women's 'limited' economic activity, anticipated integration in development, and the allegedly universal opposition between the public and private domains.

References

ABAZA, MONA, 'The Changing Image of Women in Rural Egypt', *Cairo Papers in School Science*, 10, 1987a: 3

——, 'Feminist Debates and "Traditional Feminism" of the Fellaha in Rural Egypt', Working Paper 93, Sociology of Development Research Centre, University of Bielefeld, 1987b

ABDALLAH, ISMAIL-SABRI, 'The Reverse Oil Shocks: Harsh Effects and Mild Responses', Dossier 61, 1987: 15–26

ABDEL-FADIL, MAHMOUD, *Development, Income Distribution and Social Change in Rural Egypt, 1952–1970*, Cambridge: Cambridge University Press, 1975

——, 'The Impact of Labour Migration to Oil Rich Countries on the Disparities in Income and Expenditure Patterns in Arab Labour Exporting Countries', *Oil and Arab Co-operation*, 6 (1), 1980: 87–111 (in Arabic)

——, 'Islamic Dress "Imported from London"', *Sout al-Arab*, 26 April

1987a (in Arabic)

ABDEL FATAH, CAMILIA. *Psychology of the Working Woman*, Beirut: Dar al-Nahda a-Arabiya, 1984 (in Arabic)

ABDEL FATAH, MAHMOUD MANSOUR, 'The Future of Egyptian Agriculture: A Study of the Contribution of the Egyptian Agrarian Sector in Realizing Self-Sufficiency'. Study presented to the 6th Annual Conference of Egyptian Economists, Cairo, Arab Republic of Egypt (ARE), 26–8 March 1981

ABDEL KHADER, SOHA, *Egyptian Women in a Changing Society: 1899–1985*, Boulder: Lynne Rienner, 1987

ABDEL KHALEK, GOUDA, 'Development Patterns and Increasing Dependency on the Outside World: A Study of the Egyptian Experience 1969–1974', in *Development and International Economic Relations, Proceedings of the First Conference of Egyptian Economists*, Cairo, ARE, 1977 (in Arabic)

——, 'The Open Door Policy: The Roots, the Harvest, and the Future', Cairo: Arab Centre for Research and Publication, 1982a (in Arabic)

——, 'The Open Door Economic Policy in Egypt: Its Contribution to Investment and Its Equity Implications', in M.H. Kerr and S. Yassin, (eds), *Rich and Poor States in the Middle East*, Boulder, Colorado: Westview Press, 1982b: 259–83

ABDEL KHALEK, G. AND R. TIGNOR (eds), *The Political Economy of Income Distribution in Egypt*, New York: Holms and Meier, 1982

ABDEL MALEK, ANWAR, 'Orientalism in Crisis', *Diogenes*, 44, 1963: 107–8

——, *Egypt: Military Society*, New York: Random House, 1968

ABDEL WAHAB, LAILA, 'Social Participation of Egyptian Women', paper presented at the Conference on the Impact of Petro-Economy on the Conditions of Arab Women, Cairo, ARE: Egyptian Committee for Afro-Asian Peoples Solidarity, March 1988 (in Arabic)

ABOU LUGHOD, LAILA, *Veiled Sentiments: Honor, Modesty and Poetry in Bedouin Society*, Berkeley: University of California Press, 1986

ABOU MANDOUR, M., M. HELMI NAWAR AND EZZAT AL-BENDARY, 'Socio-Economic Effects of Labour Migration on the Family and Roles of Peasant Wives', paper presented at the Conference on the Impact of Petro-Economy on the Conditions of Arab Women, Cairo, ARE: Egyptian Committee for Afro-Asian Peoples Solidarity, March 1988 (in Arabic)

ABOU NASR; N.J. KHOURY AND H. AZZAM (eds). *Women, Employment and Development in the Arab World*, The Hague: Mouton, 1985

ABOU-ZAHRA, N., 'On the Modesty of Women in Arab Muslim Villages: A Reply', *American Anthropologist*, 72, 1970: 1079–88

AFSHAR, HALEH. *Women, Work and Ideology in the Third World*, London: Tavistock, 1985

AL-QAZZAZ, AYAD. 'Current Status of Research on Women in the Arab World', *Middle Eastern Studies*, 14 (3), 1978: 372–6

AL-TORKI, SORAYA. *Women in Saudi Arabia: Ideology and Behavior among the Elite*, New York: Columbia University Press, 1986

AMIN, GALAL, 'Some Economic and Cultural Aspects of Economic Liberalization in Egypt', *Social Problems*, 28 (4), 1981: 430–41

——, 'External Factors in the Reorientation of Egypt's Economic Policy', in M.H. Kerr and S. Yassin (eds) *Rich and Poor States in the Middle East*, Boulder, Colorado: Westview Press, 1982: 285–315.

AMIN, QASIM, *The Emancipation of Women*, Cairo: Dar al-Ma'arif, 1970 (in Arabic)

AMIN, SAMIR, *Unequal Development: An Essay on the Social Formation of Peripheral Capitalism*, New York: Monthly Review Press, 1973

——, *Unequal Development*, New York: Monthly Review Press, 1976

——, *The Arab Nation*, London: Zed Press, 1978

——, 'The Conditions of Autonomy in the Mediterranean Area', paper presented at the Xth International Colloquium on the Impact of World Economy on the Arab, the Middle East, and World System, Cairo, ARE, 11–13 February 1988

ANON., 'Thorns in the Path of Egyptian Flowers', *Al-Ahram al-Iqtisadi*, 637, 1981: 26–9 (in Arabic)

ANSARI, HAMIED, *Egypt: The Stalled Society*, Albany, New York: State University of New York Press, 1986

ANTOUN, R., 'On the Modesty of Women in Arab Muslim Villages: A Study in the Accommodation of Tradition', *American Anthropologist*, 70, 1970: 671–97

ARIZPE, L. AND J. ARANDA, 'The Comparative Advantages of Women's Disadvantages: Women Workers in the Strawberry Export Agri-Business in Mexico', *Signs*, 7, 1981: 2

ARIZPE, L. AND CARLOTA BATEY, 'Mexican Agricultural Development Policy and its Impact on Rural Women', in Carmen Diana Deere and Magdalena Leon (eds), *Rural Women and State Policy: Feminist Perspectives on Latin American Agricultural Development*, Boulder, Colorado: Westview Press, 1987, 67–83

ASWAD, BARBARA, 'Women, Class, and Power: Examples from the Hatay, Turkey', in L. Beck and N. Keddie (eds), *Women in the Muslim World*, Cambridge, Massachusetts: Harvard University Press, 1978: 473–81

AWNI, ELISABETH TAYLOR, 'Egyptian Migration and Peasant Wives', *MERIP Reports*, 124, 1984: 3–10

BAER, G., *Population and Society in the Arab East*, New York: Praeger, 1964

BAKER, RAYMOND, *Egypt's Uncertain Revolution Under Nasser and Sadat*, Cambridge, Massachusetts: Harvard University Press, 1979

BALFET, H., 'Travail feminin et communauté villageoise au Maghreb', *Peuples Mediterranéens*, 18, 1982: 109–17

BELL, DIANE, 'Central Australian Aboriginal Women's Love Rituals', in E. Leacock and H. Safa (eds), *Women's Work: Development and the*

Division of Labour by Gender, South Hadley, Massachusetts: Bergin and Garvey, 1986: 75–95

BENERIA, L., 'Accounting for Women's Work', in Lourdes Beneria (ed.), *Women and Development: The Sexual Division of Labour in Rural Societies*, New York: Praeger, 1982: 119–48

BENERIA L. AND G. SEN., 'Accumulation, Reproduction and Women's Role in Economic Development: Boserup Revisited', *Signs*, 7(2), 1981: 279–98

BERNSTEIN, HENRY, 'Concepts for the Analysis of Contemporary Peasantries', in Rosemary Galli (ed.), *The Political Economy of Rural Development: Peasants, International Capital and the State*, Albany, New York: State University of New York Press, 1981: 3–24

BIRKS, J.S. AND C.A. SINCLAIR, 'Egypt: A Frustrated Labour Exporter?', *Middle East Journal*, 33, 1979: 288–303

——, *Arab Manpower: The Crisis of Development*, London: Croom Helm, 1980

——, 'Employment and Development in Six Poor Arab States: Syria, Jordan, Sudan, South Yemen, Egypt, and North Yemen', *International Journal of Middle Eastern Studies*, 14, 1982: 35–51

BLACKMAN, WINIFRED S., *The Fellahin of Upper Egypt*, London: George C. Harrap, 1927

BOSERUP, ESTHER, *Women's Role in Economic Development*, London: Allen and Unwin, 1970

BOSSEN, LAUREL, 'Women in Modernizing Societies', *American Ethnologist*, 2 (4), 1975: 587–601

BUJRA, JANET. 'Class, Gender and Capitalist Transformation in Africa', *Africa Development*, 1984

BYBEE, DOROTHY ANN, 'Muslim Peasant Women of the Middle East: Their Sources and Uses of Power', PhD. Dissertation, Department of Anthropology, Indiana University, 1978

BYRES, T.J., 'Agrarian Transition and the Agrarian Question', *Journal of Peasant Studies*, 4 (3), 1977: 258–74

CAULFIELD, MINA, 'Universal Sex Oppression? A Critique from Marxist Anthropology', *Catalyst*, 10/11, 1977: 60–77

——, 'Equality, Sex, and Mode of Production', in J.D. Berreman (ed.), *Social Inequality: Comparative and Development Approaches*, New York: New York Academic Press, 1982: 201–219

CHANEY, ELSA. 'Scenarios of Hunger in the Caribbean: Migration, Decline of Smallholder Agriculture and the Feminization of Farming', Women in International Development, Working Paper No. 18, Michigan State University, East Lansing, Mich., 1983

CHO, UNN AND H. KOO, 'Capital Accumulation, Women's Work, and Informal Economies in Korea', Women in International Development, Working Paper No. 21, Michigan State University, East Lansing, Mich., 1983

CHOUCRI, NAZLI, 'The New Migration in the Middle East: A Problem for Whom?', *International Migration Review*, 11(4), 1977: 421–43

——, 'The Dynamics of Contemporary Migration in the Middle East', *Al-Siyasa al-Dawliya*, 73, 1983: 52–68 (in Arabic)

CLAWSON, PATRICK, 'Egypt's Industrialization: A Critique of Dependency Theory', *MERIP Reports*, 72, 1978: 17–23

COOPER, MARK, *The Transformation of Egypt*, Baltimore: Johns Hopkins University Press, 1982

CROLL, ELIZABETH, 'rural Production and Reproduction: Socialist Development Experiences', in E. Leacock and H. Safa (eds), *Women's Work: Development and the Division of Labor by Gender*, South Hadley, Massachusetts: Bergin and Garvey, 1986: 224–52

DAVIS, E., 'Political Development or Political Economy?: Political Theory and the Study of Social Change in Egypt and the Third World', *Review of Middle East Studies*, I, 1975: 41–62

——, 'State and Class Formation in Modern Egypt', paper presented at the Annual Meeting of the Middle Eastern Studies Association, New York, NY, 9–12 Nov. 1977

DAVIS, S., *Patience and Power: Women's Lives in a Moroccan Village*, New York: Schenkman, 1982

DAWN, *Development Crises and Alternative Versions: Third World Women's Perspectives*, New Delhi, India, 1985

DEERE, CARMEN DIANA AND M. LEON DE LEAL, 'Peasant Production, Proletarianization, and the Sexual Division of Labour in the Andes', in Lourdes Beneria (ed.), *Women and Development: The Sexual Division of Labour in Rural Societies*, New York: Praeger, 1982: 65–94

DEERE, CARMEN DIANA, 'Rural Women and the State Policy: The Latin American Reform Experience', Women in International Development, Working Paper No. 81, Michigan State University, East Lansing, Mich., 1985

DE LOS ANGELES CRUMMETT, MARIA, 'Class, Household Structure and Migration: A Case Study from Rural Mexico', Women in International Development, Working Paper No. 92, Michigan State University, East Lansing, Mich., 1985

DORSKY, S., *Women of Amran – A Middle Eastern Ethnographic Study*, Salt Lake City: University of Utah Press, 1986

DWEYDAR, MOHAMED, 'The Agrarian Question and the Development of Capitalism in Egypt', *Qadaya Fiqriya*, 3/4, 1986: 78–123 (in Arabic)

DWYER, D., *Images and Self Images: Male and Female in Morocco*, New York: Columbia University Press, 1978

EBEID, JOAN, 'Women at the Centre of Social Change: An Egyptian Case', *British Society for Middle East Studies*, 12 (1), 1985: 42–4

EICKELMAN, C., *Women and Community in Oman*, New York: New York University Press, 1984

EISENSTEIN, Z., *Capitalist Patriarchy and the Case for Socialist Feminism*,

New York: Monthly Review Press, 1979

EL-ATTEYAH, FAWZIYA, *Women and Social Change in the Arab World*, Baghdad: Institute for Arab Studies, 1983 (in Arabic)

EL-BAKRY, KHAMIS, 'The Egyptian Employee as Migrant', *Al-Ahram*, 7 July 1981 (in Arabic)

EL-BAZ, SHAHIDA, 'Arab Women and the Value System of the Oil Era', paper presented at the Conference on the Impact of the Petro-Economy on the Conditions of Arab Women, Cairo, ARE: Egyptian Committee for Afro-Asian Peoples Solidarity, March 1988 (in Arabic)

EL-GABRY, ABDEL FATTAH, 'The Economic Consequences of Egyptian Labour Migration', *Al-Siyasa al-Dawliya*, 73, July 1983: 67–91(in Arabic)

EL-GUINDI, FADWA, 'Veiled Activism: Egyptian Women in the Contemporary Islamic Movement', *Peuples Méditerranéens*, 22/23, 1983: 79–80

ELSHTAIN, J.B., 'Moral Woman and Immoral Man: A Consideration of the Public-Private Split and its Political Ramifications', *Politics and Society*, 4, 1974: 453–73

EL-SOLH, CAMILIA, 'Migration and the Selectivity of Change: Egyptian Peasant Women in Iraq', *Peuples Méditerranéens*, 31/32, 1985: 243–58

EVERS, HANS-DIETER, WOLFGANG CLAUSS AND DIANA WONG, 'Subsistence Reproduction: A Framework for Analysis', in Joan Smith *et al.* (eds), *Households and the World Economy*, Beverly Hills: Sage Publications, 1984: 23–36

FEDERATION OF EGYPTIAN INDUSTRIES, *1978 Year Book*, Cairo, ARE, 1981 (in Arabic)

FERCHIOU, SOPHIE, *Les femmes dans l'agriculture tunisienne*, Aix-en-Provence: Editions du Sud, 1985

FERNEA, ELIZABETH, 'Women and Family in Development Plans in the Arab East', *Journal of Asian and African Studies*, XXI, 1986: 1–2

FERNEA, W.W., *Women and the Family in the Middle East: New Voices of Change*, Austin: University of Texas Press, 1985

FLORY, V., 'Women and Culture in Islam', *Muslim World*, 30, 1940: 17

FRIEDMAN, H., 'Household Production and the National Economy: Concepts for the Analysis of Agrarian Formations', *Journal of Peasant Studies*, 7, 1980: 158–84

FRIEDMAN, KATHY, 'Households as Income Pooling Units', in Joan Smith *et al.* (eds), *Households and the World Economy*, Beverly Hills: Sage Publications, 1984: 37–55

GABALLAH, KAMAL, 'Social Obstacles to Egyptian Labour Migration', *Al-Ahram al-Iqtisadi*, 745, 1983: 12–17 (in Arabic)

GADANT, MONIQUE (ed.), *Women in the Mediterranean*, London: Zed Press, 1986

GALLIN, RITA, 'Women and Work in Rural Taiwan: Building a Contextual Model Linking Employment and Health', paper presented at the Annual Meeting of the National Women's Studies Association, Urbana-Champaign, 11–15 June 1986

GERNER, DEBBIE, 'Roles in Transition: The Evolving Position of Women in Arab Islamic Countries', in F. Hussein (ed.), *Muslim Women*, London: Croom Helm, 1984: 71–99

GINAT, J., *Women in Muslim Rural Society*, New Brunswick: Rutgers University Press, 1981

GLAVANIS, K. AND P. GLAVANIS, 'The Sociology of Agrarian Relations in the Middle East. The Persistence of Household Production, *Current Sociology*, 31(2), 1983: 1–109

GLAVANIS, KATHY, 'Aspects of Non-Capitalist Social Relations in Rural Egypt: The Small Peasant Household in an Egyptian Delta Village', in N. Long (ed.), *Family and Work in Rural Societies*, London: Tavistock, 1984: 30–60

GOODE, W., 'Industrialization and Family Change', in B.F. Hoselitz and W.E. Moore (eds), *Industrialization and Society*, The Hague: Mouton, 1970: 237–59

GOUELI, A., 'National Food Security Program in Egypt', paper presented at the IFRI – Cimmyt Conference on Food Security, Mexico, 1978: 23–30

GRAN, J., 'The Impact of the World Market on Egyptian Women', *MERIP Reports*, 58, 1977: 3–7

GRAN, PETER, *Islamic Roots of Capitalism*, Austin: University of Texas Press, 1979

HALE, SONDRA, 'History, Development and Liberation: Northern Sudanese Women', paper presented at the African Studies Association Annual Meeting, Los Angeles, Calif., November 1981

HAMED, OSAMA, 'Egypt's Open Door Economic Policy: An Attempt at Economic Integration in the Middle East', *International Journal of Middle East Studies*, 13, 1981: 1–9

HAMMAM, MONA, 'Women Workers and the Practice of Freedom as Education: The Egyptian Experience', unpublished PhD Dissertation, University of Kansas, 1977

——, 'Egypt's Working Women: Textile Workers of Chubra al-Kheima', *MERIP Reports*, 82, 1979: 3–13

——, 'The Continuum of Economic Activities in Middle Eastern Social Formations, Family Division of Labour and Migration', paper presented at the Burg Wartenstein Symposium on 'The Sex Division of Labor, Development and Women's Status', 2–10 August 1980, New York: Wenner-Gren Foundation for Anthropological Research, 1980

——, 'Labour Migration and the Sexual Division of Labour', *MERIP Reports*, 95, 1979: 3–11, 31

HAMONT, *L'Egypte sous Mehmet Ali*, Paris, (n.p.), 1843

HARIK, I., *The Political Mobilization of Peasants: A Study of an Egyptian Community*, Bloomingdale, Indiana: Indiana University Press, 1974

——, *Distribution of Land, Employment and Income in Rural Egypt*, Cornell University: Rural Development Committee, 1979

HARRIS, MARVIN, *The Rise of Anthropological Theory*, New York: Thomas Y. Crowell, 1968

HARRIS, OLIVIA AND KATE YOUNG, 'Engendered Structures: Some Problems in the Analysis of Reproduction', in J. Khan and J. Lobera (eds), *The Anthropology of Pre-Capitalist Societies*, London: Macmillan, 1984: 109–47

HATEM, MERVAT, 'Women and Work in the Middle East: The Regional Impact of Migration to the Oil Producing States', paper presented at the Conference on Women and Work in the Third World, University of California, Berkeley, 10–14 April 1983

——, 'Class and Patriarchy as Competing Paradigms for the Study of Middle Eastern Women', *Comparative Studies in Society and History*, 29(4), 1987: 811–18

HOFFMAN-LADD, VALERIE, 'Polemics on the Modesty and Segregation of Women in Contemporary Egypt', *International Journal of Middle East Studies*, 19(1), 1987: 23–50

HOPKINS, NICHOLAS AND SOHEIR MEHANNA, 'Egyptian Village Studies', Economics Working Paper No. 42, Agricultural Development Systems Project, Arab Republic of Egypt–University of California, Giza, Egypt, 1981

HOPKINS, NICHOLAS, *Agrarian Transformation in Egypt*, Boulder, Colorado: Westview Press, 1987

HUSSEIN, ADEL, *The Egyptian Economy from Independence to Dependency, 1974–1979*, Beirut: Dar al-Kalimah lil Nashr, 1981 (in Arabic)

HUSSEIN, FREDA, *Muslim Women*, London: Croom Helm, 1984

HUSSEIN, MAHMOUD, *Class Conflict in Egypt: 1945–1971*, New York: Monthly Review Press, 1973

IBRAHIM, SADD EDDIN, 'Oil, Migration and the New Arab Social Order', in M.H. Kerr and S. Yassin (eds), *Rich and Poor States in the Middle East*, Boulder, Colorado: Westview Press, 1982: 17–70

IMAM, MUSTAFA AND GAMAL ZAYDA, 'Egyptians Working in the Arab Countries: Future Uncertainties', *Al-Ahram al-Iqtisadi*, 747, 1983: 8–18 (in Arabic)

JOSEPH, SUAD, 'Urban Poor Women in Lebanon: Does Poverty Have Public and Private Domains?', paper presented at the Annual Meeting of the Association of the Arab-American University Graduates, Chicago, 1975

——, 'Women and Politics in the Middle East', *MERIP Reports*, 138, 1986: 3–8

JULES-ROSETTE, BENNETTA, 'Women's Work in the Informal Sector: A Zambian Case Study', Women in International Development, Working Paper No. 3, Michigan State University, East Lansing, Mich., 1982

KAPTEIJINS, LIDWIEN, 'Islamic Rationales for the Changing Social Roles of Women in the Western Sudan', unpublished MS, 1985

KEDDIE, NIKKI, 'Problems in the Study of Middle Eastern Women', *International Journal of Middle Eastern Studies*, 10, 1979: 225–40

KEYDER, C., 'Paths of Rural Transformation in Turkey', *Journal of Peasant Studies*, 11 (1), 1983: 34–49

KHAFAGY, FATMA, 'Women and Labor Migration', *MERIP Reports*, 124, 1984: 17–21

——, 'Impact of Oil and Migration on Arab Women's Work Patterns', paper presented at the Conference on Women and Arab Society: Old Boundaries, New Frontiers, Eleventh Annual Symposium, 10–11 April 1986, Georgetown University, Center for Contemporary Arab Studies, Washington DC

KHATTAB, H. AND SYADA EL DAEIF, *The Impact of Male Migration on the Structure of the Family and Roles of Women in Egypt*, Giza, ARE: The Population Council, 1982

KOPTIUCH, KRISTIN, 'Fieldwork in the Post-Modern World: Notes on Ethnography in an Expanded Field', paper presented at the 84th Annual Meeting of the American Anthropological Association, Washington DC, 1985

KORAYEM, KARIMA, 'Women and the New International Economic Order in the Arab World', *Cairo Papers in Social Science* 4 (4), 1981a: 45–79

——, 'The Rural–Urban Income Gap in Egypt and Biased Agricultural Pricing Policy', *Social Problems*, 28 (4), 1981b: 417–29

——, 'The Rural–Urban Income Gap and Biased Agricultural Pricing Policy', in G. Abdel Khalek and R. Tignor (eds), *The Political Economy of Income Distribution in Egypt*, New York: Holms and Meier, 1982

——, *The Impact of the Economic Adjustment Policies on the Vulnerable Families and Children in Egypt*, Cairo, ARE: Third World Forum and UNICEF, 1987

KUPPINGER, PETRA, 'Recent Trends in the Study of Arab Women', Student Paper, Department of Sociology-Anthropology, American University in Cairo, 1988

LARSON, BARBARA, 'The Status of Women in a Tunisian Village: Limits to Autonomy, Influence and Power', *Signs*, 9 (3), 1984: 417–33

LEACOCK, E., 'Class, Community and Status of Women', in Ruby Rohrlich-Leavitt (ed.), *Women Cross-Culturally: Change and Challenge*, The Hague: Mouton, 1975: 601–16

LEACOCK, E. AND H. SAFA (eds), *Women's Work: Development and the Division of Labor by Gender*, South Hadley, Massachusetts; Bergin and Garvey, 1986

LESCH, ANN M. AND EARL L. SULLIVAN, 'Women in Egypt: New Roles and Realities', Universities Field Staff International, Africa, Report No. 22, 1986

LEWIN, ELLEN, 'Feminist Ideology and the Meaning of Work: The Case of Nursing', *Catalyst*, 10/11, 1977: 78–103

LONG, NORMAN (ed.), *Family and Work in Rural Societies: Perspectives on*

Non-Wage Labour, London: Tavistock, 1984

LYNCH, P. AND H. FAHMY, *The Craftswomen of Kerdassa Egypt: Household Production and Reproduction*, Geneva: ILO, 1984

MAFEJE, ARCHIE, 'The Problem of Anthropology in Historical Perspective: An Inquiry into the Growth of the Social Sciences', unpublished MS, 1976

MAHER, VANESSA, *Women and Property in Morocco*, Cambridge: Cambridge University Press, 1974

MARCH, K. AND R.L. TAQQU, *Women's Informal Associations in Developing Countries*, Boulder, Colorado: Westview Press, 1986

MARSOT, AFAF LUTFI AL-SAYYID, 'The Revolutionary Gentlewomen in Egypt', in L. Beck and N. Keddie (eds), *Women in the Muslim World*, Cambridge, Massachussetts: Harvard University Press, 1978: 261–76

MARTELLA, MAUREEN, 'The Rise of Industrial Homework in the Third World: An Analysis of its International Context and Conceptual Issues', in *Women Creating Health*, 1985

MAYFIELD, J.B., *Local Institutions and Egyptian Rural Development*, Ithaca: Center for International Studies, Cornell University, 1974

MAYO (newspaper) Cairo, ARE, 11 May 1985

MERNISSI, FATIMA, *Beyond the Veil: Male/Female Dynamics in a Modern Muslim Society*, New York: Schenkman, 1975

——, 'Capitalist Development and Perceptions of Women in Arab Muslim Society: An Illustration of Peasant Women in Gharb, Morocco', in Fatima Mernissi, *Rural Development and Women in Africa*, Geneva: ILO, 1984: 123–28

MIES, MARIA, *The Lace Makers of Narsapur: Indian Housewives Produce for the World Market*, London: Zed Press, 1982

MINCES, J., *The House of Obedience: Women in Arab Society*, London: Zed Press, 1982

MINISTRY OF AGRICULTURE, *Agriculture Policies*, Cairo, 1980 (in Arabic)

MOHAMED, SHYKHOUN E., 'An Economic Analysis of the Expansion of Production and Marketing of Aromatic Crops and their Products in ARE', MA Thesis, Faculty of Agriculture, University of al-Azhar, Cairo, ARE, 1980 (in Arabic)

MOHIEDDIN, MOHAMED, 'Peasant Migration from an Egyptian Village to the Oil Producing Countries: its Causes and Consequences'. PhD Dissertation, Department of Sociology, University of North Carolina at Chapel Hill, Chapel Hill, 1987

MOHSEN, S., 'The Egyptian Woman: Between Modernity and Tradition', in C. Mathiasson (ed.), *Many Sisters: Women in Cross-Cultural Perspective*, New York: The Free Press, 1974

MORSY, SOHEIR, 'Sex Differences in the Incidence of the Folk Illness of Uzr in an Egyptian Village', in Lois Beck and Nikki Keddie (eds), *Women in the Muslim World*, Cambridge, Massachusetts: Harvard University Press, 1978a

——, 'Gender, Power and Illness in an Egyptian Village', *American Ethnologist*, 5(1), 1978b: 137–50

MORSY, SOHEIR AND ASHRAF EL-BAYOUMI, 'The "Brain Drain" and Dependent Development', *Al-Mustaqbal al-Arabi*, 26–32, 1980 (in Arabic)

MORSY, SOHEIR, 'Reorientation in Capitalist Development: A Note on Sadat's Infitah', paper presented at the Central States Meetings of the American Anthropological Association, Ann Arbor, Mich., 9–11 April 1980

——, 'Paths of Rural Transformation: An Egyptian Case Study', a Report of Research in Progress presented at the Population Council Study Group Meeting on 'Worker Migration and Rural Transformation', Cairo, ARE, 10–11 May 1981

——, 'Familial Adaptations to the Internationalization of Egyptian Labour', Women in International Development, Working Paper No. 94, Michigan State University, East Lansing, Mich., 1985

——, 'Islamic Clinics in Egypt: The Cultural Elaboration of Biomedical Hegemony', paper presented at the Annual Meeting of the American Anthropological Association, Chicago, Illinois, 18–22 November 1987

——, 'Spirit Possession in Egyptian Ethnomedicine: Origins, Comparison and Historical Specificity', paper presented at the Workshop on 'Contributions of the Zar Cult in African Traditional Medicine', Institute of African and Asian Studies, Khartoum, Sudan, 11–13 January 1988

MURSI, FUAD, 'This Economic Opening', *Dar al-Thaqafa al-Jadida*, Cairo, ARE 1976 (in Arabic)

——, *The Arab Challenge to the International Economic Crisis*, Cairo, ARE: Arab Studies and Publishing, 1985 (in Arabic)

MURSI, NADIA, 'Women's Work during the Petroleum Era', paper presented at the Conference on the Impact of Petro-Economy on the Conditions of Arab Women, Cairo, ARE: Egyptian Committee for Afro-Asian Peoples Solidarity, March 1988 (in Arabic)

MYNTTI, CYNTHIA, *The Effects of Breastfeeding, Temporary Migration and Contraceptive Use on the Fertility of the Yemeni Arabic Republic*, Cairo, ARE: The Population Council, 1978

——, 'Yemeni Workers Abroad: The Impact on Women', *MERIP Reports*, 15 (4), 1984: 11–16

NAIM, SAMIR, 'Towards a Demystification of Arab Social Reality: A Critique of Anthropological and Political Writings on Arab Society', *Review of Middle East Studies*, 3, 1978: 48–62

NASH, JUNE, 'Ethnographic Aspects of the World Capitalist System', *Annual Review of Anthropology*, 10, 1981: 393–423

——, 'Implications of Technological Change for Household Levels and Rural Development', Women in International Development, Working Paper No. 37, Michigan State University, East Lansing, Mich., 1983

NASH, JUNE AND M.P. FERNANDEZ-KELLY (eds), *Women, Men and the International Division of Labour*, Albany: State University of New York, 1983

NELSON, CYNTHIA, 'Women and Power in Nomadic Societies in the Middle East', in C. Nelson (ed.), *The Desert and the Sown*, Berkeley: Institute of International Studies, 1973: 43–60

——, 'Public and Private Politics: Women in the Middle Eastern World', *American Ethnologist*, 1, 1975: 551–64

——, 'Old Wine, New Bottles: Reflection and Projections concerning Research on Women in the Middle East', paper presented at the Conference on the State of the Art of Middle Eastern Studies. University of Calgary, Canada, 1–4 August 1986

NELSON, C. AND LUCIE SAUNDERS, 'An Explanatory Analysis of Income-Generating Strategies in Contemporary Rural Egypt', Women in International Development, Working Paper No. 122, Michigan State University, East Lansing, Mich., 1986

NEWCOMER, P., 'Toward a Scientific Treatment of "Exploitation": A Response to Dalton', *American Anthropologist*, 79, 1977: 115–18

OBERMAYER, CARLA M., 'Some Notes on Women's Economic Participation in North Yemen', in *The Measurement of Women's Economic Participation: Report of a Study Group*, Giza, ARE: The Population Council, 1979

PAPANEK, H., 'The "Work" and "Non-Work" of Women', *Signs*, 4, 1979: 475–781

PATAI, R., *Golden River to Golden Road*, Philadelphia: University of Pennsylvania Press, 1969

POEWE, KARLA O., 'Universal Male Dominance: An Ethnological Illusion', *Dialectical Anthropology*, 5, 1980: 111–12

RADWAN, SAMIR, 'Towards a Political Economy of Egypt: A Critical Note on Writing on the Egyptian Economy', *Review of Middle Eastern Studies*, I, 1975: 93–100

——, *Agrarian Reform and Rural Poverty*, Geneva: ILO, 1977

RASSAM, AMAL, 'Towards a Theoretical Framework for the Study of Women in the Arab World', in Unesco (ed.), *Social Science Research and Women in the Arab World*, London, Dover, NH and Paris: Unesco and Frances Pinter, 1984

REDCLIFT, N., 'The Contested Domain: Gender, Accumulation and the Labour Process', in N. Redclift and E. Mingione (eds), *Beyond Employment: Household, Gender and Subsistence*, Oxford: Basil Blackwell, 1985: 92–125

REITER, R., 'Introduction', in R. Reiter (ed.), *Toward an Anthropology of Women*, New York: Monthly Review Press, 1975

REMY, D., 'Underdevelopment and the Experience of Women: A Nigerian Case Study', in R. Reiter (ed.), *Toward an Anthropology of Women*, New York: Monthly Review Press, 1975: 358–71

RICHARDS, ALLEN, 'Egypt's Agriculture in Trouble', *MERIP Reports*, 84, 1980: 3–13

——, *Egypt's Agricultural Development 1800–1980*, Boulder, Colorado: Westview Press, 1982

RICHARDS, ALLEN AND P.L. MARTIN (eds), *Migration, Mechanization and Agricultural Labour Markets in Egypt*, Boulder, Colorado: Westview Press, 1983

ROSALDO, M. AND L. LAMPHERE (eds), *Women, Culture and Society*, Stanford: Stanford University Press, 1974

ROSALDO, M., 'The Use and Abuse of Anthropology: Reflections on Feminism and Cross-Cultural Understanding', *Signs*, 5 (3), 1980: 389–417

ROSENBURY, A., 'Rent, Differentiation, and the Development of Capitalism Among Peasants', *American Anthropologist*, 78, 1976: 45–58

RUBBO, A., 'The Spread of Capitalism in Rural Columbia: Effects on Poor Women', in R. Reiter (ed.), *Toward an Anthropology of Women*, New York: Monthly Review Press, 1975: 333–57

RUGH, ANDREA, 'Coping with Poverty in a Cairo Community', *Cairo Papers in Social Science*, 1(2), Cairo: AUC Press, 1979

SAAD, R.L. MIKHAIL, 'Social History of an Agrarian Reform Community', MA Thesis, Department of Sociology-Anthropology, American University in Cairo, 1987

SABEA, HANAN, 'Paths of Rural Transformation: Stratification and Differentiation Processes in a New Lands Village', MA Thesis, Department of Sociology-Anthropology, American University in Cairo, 1987

SAID, EDWARD, *Orientalism*, New York: Pantheon Books, 1978

ST JOHN, *Egypt and Mohamed Ali*, London, 1841

SAYIGH, R., 'Roles and Functions of Arab Women: A Reappraisal', *Arab Studies Quarterly*, 3 (3), 1981: 258–74

SEDGHI, H., 'Women in Iran', in L. Iglitzin and R. Ross (eds), *Women in the World: A Comparative Study*, Santa Barbara: Clio Books, 1976: 219–28

SELL, RALPH, 'Gone for Good?', *Cairo Papers in Social Science*, 10 (2), Cairo: AUC Press, 1987

SHAFIQ, AMINA, 'Impact of Petro-Economy on Arab Women: the Present and the Future', paper presented at the Conference on the Impact of the Petro-Economy on the Conditions of Arab Women, Cairo, ARE: Egyptian Committee for Afro-Asian Peoples Solidarity, March 1988 (in Arabic)

SHILLING, NANCY ADAMS, 'The Social and Political Roles of Arab Women: A Study in Conflict', in J. Smith (ed.), *Women in Contemporary Muslim Societies*, London: Bucknell University Press, 1981: 100–45

SMARAKKODY, AMARA, 'The Impact of European Laws on the Status of Women in Sri Lanka', *Occasional Papers in Anthropology*, 1, 1979: 133–42

SMELSER, NEIL, 'Mechanisms of Change and Adjustment to Change', in

B.F. Hoselitz and W.E. Moore (eds), *Industrialization and Society*, The Hague: Mouton, 1970: 32–54

SMITH, J., *et al.* (eds), *Households and the World Economy*, Beverly Hills: Sage Publications, 1984

SMOCK, A. HAPMAN AND N.H. YOUSSEF, 'Egypt: From Seclusion to Limited Participation', in J. Giele and A. Smock (eds), *Women's Roles and Status in Eight Countries*, New York: John Wiley and Sons, 1977: 35–79

SUKKARY-STOLBA, SOHEIR, 'Changing Roles of Women in Egypt's Newly Reclaimed Lands', *Anthropological Quarterly*, 58 (4), 1985: 182–9

SULEIMAN, MUHAMAD, 'All Work and No Play', *Newsweek*, 24 January 1983: 20–5

SULLIVAN, EARL L., 'Women and Work in Egypt', in *Women and Work in the Arab World. Cairo Papers in Social Science*, 4 (4), 1981: 1–43

——, *Women in Egyptian Public Life*, Syracuse: Syracuse University Press, 1986

SUTTON, C., *et al.*, 'Women, Knowledge and Power', in Ruby Rohrlich-Leavitt (ed.), *Women Cross-Culturally: Change and Challenge*, The Hague: Mouton, 1975: 581–600

SWANSON, JON C., *Immigration and Economic Development: The Case of the Yemen Arab Republic*, Boulder, Colorado: Westview Press, 1979

TADESSE, Z., 'The Impact of Land Reform on Women: The Case of Ethiopia', in L. Beneria (ed.), *Women and Development: The Sexual Division of Labour in Rural Societies*, New York: Praeger, 1982: 203–22

TIANO, SUZAN, 'The Separation of Women's Remunerated and Household Work: Theoretical Perspectives on "Women in Development"', Women in International Development, Working Paper No. 2, Michigan State University, East Lansing, Mich., 1981

TOMICHE, N., 'Egyptian Women in the First Half of the Nineteenth Century', in W.R. Polk and R.L. Chambers (eds), *Beginnings of Modernization in the Middle East*, Chicago: University of Chicago Press, 1968

TUCKER, JUDITH, 'Egyptian Women in the Work Force', *MERIP Reports*, 50, 1976: 3–9

——, 'Problems in the Historiography of Women in the Middle East: The Case of Nineteenth-Century Egypt', *International Journal of Middle East Studies*, 15, 1983: 321–6

——, *Women in Nineteenth Century Egypt*, Cairo: American University in Cairo Press, 1986

UNITED NATIONS, *International Migration Policies and Programmes: A World Survey*, United Nations Department of International Economic and Social Affairs, Population Studies No. 80, 1982

VALOARAS, V.G., *Population Analysis of Egypt*, Cairo: Demographic Center, 1972

WAHBA, MOURAD, 'The Egyptian Village and Pharaonic Civilization', in Mourad Wahba (ed.), *Proceedings of the International Seminar on Rural*

Women and Development, Cairo: Ain Shams University, Middle East Research Center, 1980: 177–80

WALLERSTEIN, I., *et al.*, 'Household Structure and Production Processes. Preliminary Theses and Findings', *Review*, V (3), 1982: 437–58

WARRINER, D., *Land Reform and Development in the Middle East*, Oxford: Oxford University Press, 1962

WATERBURY, JOHN, *Egypt of Nasser and Sadat: The Political Economy of Two Regimes*, Princeton: Princeton University Press, 1983

WIKAN, U., *Behind the Veil in Arabia: Women in Oman*, Baltimore and Lanson: Johns Hopkins University Press, 1982

WILLIAMS, J.A., 'Veiling in Egypt as a Political and Social Phenomenon', in J. Esposito (ed.), *Islam and Development*, Syracuse: University of Syracuse Press, 1980: 71–85

WOJNO, MARK, 'Countrymen Return: Colonial Migration and Rural Economy in Northern Portugal', PhD Dissertation, Michigan State University, 1982

YOUSSEF, NADIA, *Women and Work in Developing Societies*, Westport, Connecticut: Greenwood Press, 1974

——, 'Women in the Muslim World', in L. Igliztin and R. Ross (eds), *Women in the World: A Comparative Study*, Santa Barbara: Clio Books, 1976: 203–18

——, 'The Status and Fertility Patterns of Muslim Women', in L. Beck and N. Keddie (eds), *Women in the Muslim World*, Cambridge, Massachusetts: Harvard University Press, 1978: 69–99

YOUSSEF, NADIA, *et al.*, *Women in Migration: Third World Focus*, Washington, DC: International Center for Research on Women, 1979

ZAKARIYA, FUAD, *Reality and Illusion in the Contemporary Islamic Movement*, Cairo: Dar al-Fikr Lil Dirasat wal Nashr wal Tawzi'a, 1986 (in Arabic)

ZIMMERMAN, S., *The Women of Kafr el Bahr*, Leiden: Research Centre for Women and Development, University of Leiden, 1982

ZURAYK, H., *Women's Economic Participation'*, in Frederick Shorter and H. Zurayk (eds), *Population Factors in Development Planning in the Middle East*, New York and Cairo: The Population Council, 1985: 3–58

3

Women's participation in economic, social and political life in Sudanese urban and rural communities: The case of Saganna in Khartoum and Wad al-'Asha Village in the Gezira area

Zeinab B. El Bakri
El-Wathig M. Kameir

I. Introductory Remarks

Despite interest in development, the distribution of its fruits and obstacles in its path, it is only recently that the issue of gender and its involvement in the development process has received due consideration. Understanding the role of gender in development, however, requires a detailed and serious scientific study of the position of women in specific societies, with the understanding that women's roles are flexible and rapidly changing. This task has yet to be undertaken by development planners in Sudan (who are almost invariably male), and this has reflected negatively on women's potential gains from development plans and/or projects.

Bearing in mind the above, the aim of the present study has been to compare the situation of women in two Sudanese communities, one urban and one rural. The study examines differences in status, roles in the community, and more specifically analyses modes of economic, social and political participation in order to assess women's principal patterns of decision-making and obstacles to participation.

The authors extend their thanks to Nabawiyza Mohamed Majjoub and Amal Hassan for their fieldwork and data collection in, respectively, the village of Wad al-'Asha and the Saganna area. This study was prepared in 1986/87.

Such a study helps to fill a gap in basic research on women in Sudan, that is, research which tries to gather broad information on women and their daily activities. This research can serve as a framework for policy-making based on women's perceptions of those daily activities and problems relating to them.

The two areas chosen for the study are firstly the neighbourhood of Saganna in Khartoum (the capital) and secondly the village of Wad al-'Asha, lying in the central Gezira area of Sudan.

A. Women's studies in Sudan

Women's studies in Sudan have gone through two basic stages. The early stage, characterized by the neglect of women as a research priority, must be related to development conceptions in the post-independence period, from 1956 until the 1970s. Women and women-related issues were seldom given their deserved research attention and when studied were dealt with in a cursory and superficial manner that neglected some of their fundamental dimensions.

The neglect of these issues when recognized was rationalized by the argument that they were of secondary importance in a country such as Sudan, where the basic concern for the past twenty-five years has been the pursuit of that illusory aim – 'development'. Research was thus focused on such matters as economic development, economic growth and technological advance. Studies related to women were considered less important because it was assumed that they were not crucial to the generation of 'development'.

The rationale for giving minimum research attention to women was related to another point, namely the conception of development as a basically technical process to be achieved by planning from above, involving the building of more factories, the setting up of more ambitious development schemes and the like. Seldom was development seen as a process fundamentally relating to the behaviour and lives of men and women in society and oriented towards improving the position of the underprivileged among them.

Such views tended to overlook the fact that women play crucial roles in production, especially in agricultural areas. In Africa, for instance, it is estimated that women undertake over 60 per cent of agricultural work in addition to carrying out the domestic chores of cooking, cleaning, washing, fetching water, childcare, etc. Despite this, women in the Third World are ignored in development planning, their economic contribution devalued and their positions primarily viewed in respect of stereotypes relating to their domestic roles (El Bakri *et al.*, 1985).

The second stage (starting with the declaration of the United Nations Decade for Women in 1975) was characterized by a reversal of the above trends and a new interest in research on women. However, this research aimed at using the funds pouring in from international agencies to set up 'women's projects' rather than actually seeking to improve the welfare of the women themselves. The resulting research has therefore been of a rather poor quality and of questionable scientific validity.

B. *Methodological considerations*

The investigative framework was based on the following theoretical assumptions: the majority of women are adversely affected by current development policies leading to their marginalization and disenfranchisement, while at the same time increasing their workload and responsibilities. Thus the methods aimed at examining women's roles and position at the micro-level and situating this within an historical macro-system in order to understand and fight the marginalization of the majority of women and the deterioration of their status (Steady, 1983: 17).

Specific research questions considered included the following:

(1) What is the general contemporary position of women and how has it changed over time?
(2) What role do women play outside the domestic sphere? Specifically, what role, if any, do they have in production outside the home? How does this affect their position within the domestic sphere and decision-making?
(3) In what kind of social activities do women engage?
(4) How can we characterize women's involvement in political life? What hindrances exist, and how can their participation be enhanced?
(5) However, the major question was: how have national policies in urban and rural societies in Sudan differentially affected the situation of women and their forms of participation in the lives of their communities?

The research took into account the following theoretical considerations:

(1) That the position of women cannot be understood without

an adequate understanding of the dynamics of Sudan's political economy and developments within it during past years.

(2) It follows from the above that the interaction of two major factors can be said to influence the situation of Sudanese women and to account for the variety of social, economic and political experiences which characterize their life styles.

(a) Firstly there is the factor of social class, which is crucial in determining the type of life-style women lead, their role in production, reproduction, etc. Consequently, it would be difficult to overlook the basic differences between urban middle-class women and their ideologies and rural working women and their needs and aspirations.

(b) The second factor is the degree of influence of Arab/Islamic culture in the various regions of the Sudan. Women's status seems generally to have been higher (for example, they have a larger role in production, are socially freer, have more say in public affairs, etc.) in areas with least Arab/Islamic influence (specifically western and southern Sudan). In the context of the present study, it will be clear that the first factor (that of social class) is more important in both areas studied, since both can be seen to exist in regions where Arab/Islamic culture is relatively dominant.

C. *Sudanese political economy: The dynamics of urban and rural society*

The Sudanese social formation has assumed its present structure as a result of incorporation into the world capitalist market through direct colonization at the turn of the twentieth century. With the final establishment of the colonial state under British rule, policy was largely dictated by:

(1) a concern to provide privileged access to cheap raw materials;
(2) the aim to develop and protect markets for commodities produced in Britain.

In pursuit of these objectives the colonial state embarked on a plan of capital accumulation mainly through:

(1) the reorientation of productive activity to serve export–

import purposes by creating a peasant economy directly linked through trade to the requirements of the world market (e.g. the development of irrigated agriculture in the Gezira Scheme of which the rural community chosen as part of this study is part);

(2) the penetration of capitalist activities into pre-colonial structures through the imposition of the money market to derive profits primarily by extraction of surpluses from the peoples of Sudan (taxation, consumer cash goods, etc.).

The processes of capital accumulation during the colonial period disrupted the former, essentially pre-capitalist subsistence economies, distorting them into petty-commodity producing structures to serve as suppliers of cheap labour for capitalist enterprises.

Those who remained in the villages became increasingly dependent on cash earnings to help cover their daily needs. In some parts of northern and western Sudan it was possible for farmers to turn themselves into export-producing cultivators. However, those who failed to meet their needs in this way were forced to seek wage-labour in agricultural schemes or in urban centres as the only viable alternative (El Bakri and Kameir, 1987). Colonial policies thus radically changed the structure of urban and rural society in Sudan.

The above policies did not change very radically during the post-colonial period (after 1956) but have continued to be followed by various national governments.

1. Dynamics of urban society The pattern of urbanization in the Sudan has evolved in close correspondence with the main objectives of the British colonial state and its modes of capital accumulation. The perceived role of urban areas (and especially the capital, Khartoum), namely to facilitate the export of raw materials (especially cotton) to satisfy the needs of British industry, began to be reflected in their very spatial structure.

The replanning of Khartoum after the British invasion in 1895 was confined to the area within the ramparts which had been built by Gordon[1] around the old town. This area was not, however, great enough to accommodate the labourers who had come to rebuild Khartoum and to seek general employment there. Areas of wasteland outside the town proper, called the *deims*, were therefore

---

1. Charles G. Gordon (an Englishman) was recruited in the mid-1860s by I. Pahsa, Viceroy of Egypt, as Governor-General to destroy the slave trade on the Nile and thereby obtain European assistance for Egypt's ambitions to incorporate the Sudan into a state encompassing the entire Nile basin.

set apart for them. Migrant labourers were being recruited by government departments for the construction of large and permanent office buildings, warehouses and other extensive public works such as roads, transportation and the Khartoum river wall built in 1905.

This earlier labour migration was, however, primarily characterized by its temporary nature. The migrants tended to oscillate between urban wage-employment and their home areas, and many were engaged in seasonal movement to agricultural areas, particularly the Gezira. However, during the post-Second World War period, the nature of urban migration began to change and most migrants became increasingly dependent on wage-employment. This proletarianization became reflected in the increasingly permanent residence of migrant workers in the town, which of course resulted in an increased pressure on existent urban land, especially when migrants began to bring their families with them.

In the post-independence period (after 1956), little change occurred. In fact the limited development of industry, confined to urban centres in north and western Sudan, further attracted labour to urban areas, which came to witness extreme concentrations of both labour and capital. Surpluses from rural areas were reinvested, in particular in Khartoum, leading to marked disparities between rural and urban areas, as will be described later.

The first development of squatter areas began to appear in the 1960s and indicated the development of a category of urban poor. This group is to be distinguished from earlier migrants who participated in the building of Khartoum and later settled in working-class areas in the centre of the town (e.g. Saganna, the urban area under study).

Despite the increasing flow of migrants during the 1970s, their participation in the labour force in regular employment did not rise commensurately. This was partly due to increased dependence on capital intensive technology. However, the underlying reason was that surpluses appropriated from extractive agriculture were not reinvested in productive projects but rather were directed to urban areas in 'real-estate, conspicuous consumption, etc. All this has resulted in widespread unemployment, underemployment and casual employment in urban areas (El Bakri and Kameir, 1987).

There are very strong indications that the Sudan, like most other developing countries, is experiencing a shift in the incidence of poverty. Although at the moment about two-thirds of the poorest population groups reside in rural areas, with the present high rate of migration to urban areas more than half the poor will be living in the urban areas by the end of the twentieth century. It should be remembered that the high rate of urban growth is occurring simultaneously with high rates of population growth in rural areas.

2. Dynamics of rural society   The two main forms of economic activity in Sudanese rural areas are agriculture and pastoralism. Agriculture in the Sudan is the main mode of economic activity, in which 85 per cent of the labour force is engaged, contributing about 40 per cent of GDP, providing more than 90 per cent of the country's hard currency earnings and 90 per cent of exports (Taisier, 1982: 9–10). Also, except in periods of rapid social change, agricultural policies in Sudan have invariably reflected the interests of the dominant socio-economic forces in Sudan. Central to the ethos of agricultural strategies in the Sudan have been the twin objectives of expansion of state-owned irrigation schemes and massive state support for the private sector (Taisier, 1983: 9–10).

Agriculture in the Sudan can generally be said to conform to two broad types. The first is generally labelled the traditional sector, where agriculture follows traditional rather than capitalist modes of production and is primarily for use-value. The household constitutes the main unit of production and consumption.

The second, usually referred to as the modern sector, is that characterized by the large, government, irrigated schemes (e.g. the Gezira Scheme) and private, rainfed, mechanized schemes. Here production is based on capitalist relations.

Consistently, since colonial times, agricultural policies have favoured the modern sector, producing cash crops, notably cotton, for export markets. Thus government schemes saw a relative concentration of services for scheme tenants, in addition to opportunities for raising productivity, through the use of pesticides and fertilizers, credit schemes, etc.

The private, mechanized schemes have meanwhile been based on a philosophy of making as much profit as possible at the least possible cost, with no attention being paid to proper rotation and the deteriorating effect on the environment. In fact the unplanned expansion of these schemes has been a major cause of desertification. Furthermore, the enormous returns from these enterprises were never reinvested in the areas of production, but were invariably transferred to urban areas to be reinvested in non-productive endeavours such as transport and real-estate.

Also, since the 1970s the Sudan has followed a development programme commonly known as the 'bread-basket strategy' after its intention to make the country the chief food supplier to the Arab

166

world. The strategy is characterized by the overwhelming goal of maximizing agricultural exports regardless of the consequences for the local population and the economy at large.

Generally at least 87 per cent of Sudan's female labour force is concentrated in agriculture. Of these, 78–90 per cent are involved in the traditional subsistence sector, whereas only 10 per cent are involved in the modern sector (A. Farah, 1984: 11).

However, due to the type of agricultural policies followed by the state (emphasizing exports, private investment and the bread-basket strategy), the continued viability of this agricultural-subsistence sector is steadily decreasing, more specifically due to the following reasons:

(1) the continued low-level of production forces;
(2) the encroachment of private, mechanized schemes on land previously allotted to subsistence farmers;
(3) the problems of desertification and drought and their effect on the availability of food;
(4) the absence of credit schemes, agricultural extension services, etc., and general lack of state support.

As stated above, this traditional sector is where the vast majority of women producers work, and it is clear that it is they who suffer most from these agricultural policies and the deterioration they cause. Survival options open to them are:

(1) to remain in increasingly unviable subsistence farming and undertake other vital use-value tasks, including care of children and the elderly while men seek employment on commercial agricultural schemes;
(2) at a later stage, and especially after the drought, to become agricultural labourers themselves on large commercial schemes (as we shall see in an analysis of women's situation in Wad al-'Asha);
(3) finally to migrate to urban areas (primarily Khartoum), where women resort overwhelmingly to informal economic activities (especially begging, petty trade, prostitution, etc.).

3. Rural–urban disparities Surpluses siphoned off from rural areas have consistently been invested in urban areas. This has led to wide rural–urban disparities which can be seen in unemployment, income distribution, levels of consumption and the misallocation of services and infrastructure.

Unemployment currently running at an average rate of 2.9 per cent ranges from 1.5 per cent in rural areas to 7.5 per cent in semi-urban areas and 9.6 per cent in urban areas. Although it may appear from these figures that urban areas suffer more from unemployment, in actual fact the rural unemployed attracted to towns constitute the bulk of the urban unemployed.

A sharp disparity can also be noticed as regards income distribution, with the rural areas receiving far less than urban areas. Whereas 34.5 per cent of the rural population receive the lowest income in the country, only 3.8 per cent of the urban population fall within this category. Of the urban population, 22.2 per cent are among the highest income group, while only 3.1 per cent of the rural population fall within this category.

Government expenditure figures also reveal that the country's revenue is spent in favour of the urban population and the state apparatus itself. According to the 1973/4 statistical survey, only 1.1 million Sudanese pounds (£s) were allocated for the Ministry of Co-operation and Rural Water Supplies. £s.11.3 million were allocated to health services for the country as a whole and education received a budget of £s.20.4 million. However, these amounts are mainly spent on the administration of existing services – unavailable in many rural and semi-rural areas (Mahmoud, 1984: 28–30).

In the above background section on political economy and the dynamics of urban and rural societies in Sudan the following points were emphasized:

(1) The specific structure of Sudanese society is the result of a combination of factors including the aims of the colonial state and aspects of indigenous Sudanese society.

(2) Production became geared to the export of cotton as the main cash crop threatening the viability of subsistence modes of life.

(3) Both rural and urban areas became affected as wide disparities developed between them. The growth of urban areas must be seen as an outcome of the concentration of services within them. Surplus from rural areas was siphoned off in the form of migrant labour and profits, reinvested in urban areas.

(4) State policies favouring exports continued to reduce the viability of traditional agriculture and encourage migration to agricultural schemes and urban areas.

D. A note on the study of participation

Since the present study has concentrated on the aspect of participation, we need to ascertain whether the participation of women in the economic, political and social spheres has increased or decreased, in response to which societal factors, and what has been the impact of 'modernization' and development on women.

Regarding economic participation, we must recognize that this is conditioned by women's class status (and all that this entails in terms of access to education and other resources), women's primary identification as wives and mothers, and the occupations available to them within the confines of a developing economy. Economic participation is used in a broad sense to include both formal jobs in the modern sector of the economy and non-wage-paying occupations.

As regards political participation, there are two possible approaches to an analysis of female political behaviour. The first can be called the 'institutional' approach. Here political participation relates to voting, working for political parties, campaigns, etc. The problems with such an approach, according to Jacquette, are that much

politics occur outside conventional political institutions. While female suffrage in many of the countries for which we have data has coincided with recent periods of relatively open 'democratic' politics, the military coups in the 1960s serve to remind us that democratic government is not a permanent pattern. Indeed many political scientists have taken the position that electoral politics when they occur, are only one element of a much broader spectrum of more or less legitimate political activity, including strikes, coups, demonstrations, and behind-the-scenes bargaining between the Government, however constituted, and key groups (Jacquette, 1980: 235).

The second approach, by contrast, concentrates on extra-institutional activity. We have been obliged in this present study to rely more on the first approach due to the almost total lack of measures or indicators of participation in these extra-institutional spheres (ibid.).

As regards social participation, we have been primarily interested in the social activities of women, their participation in social networks and generally the way in which they spend their social time in a segregated society.

Before ending this brief section it is necessary to emphasize that the boundaries between these three types of participation are pri-

Table 3.1 Population of Saganna

	No. of Families	Male	Female	Total
Saganna West	678	2,966	2,227	5,193
Saganna East	445	1,504	1,366	2,870
Total	1,123	4,470	3,593	8,063

Source: Dept. of Statistics, 1983 National Census.

marily used for analytical purposes and are not strictly maintained in the real life of the women concerned, for clearly what is 'economic' can also be 'political' and vice versa. The three spheres are also directly related to each other and are mutually influential.

II. Lives of women and their families in Saganna, Khartoum

Saganna is relatively close to the centre of Khartoum. Its boundary is marked to the north by the police barracks of Khartoum North, to the south by the area of Maygoma, to the west by Hurriya Street and to the east by Khartoum South. Administratively it is divided into two areas, Saganna East and Saganna West. Table 3.1 shows the number of families and total population.

The area was established in August 1927 when the first house, that of Sheikh Mohamed Dahab, the *umda* (headman) of the area, was built. Before occupying its present site, Saganna lay east of the present Council of Ministers, until the colonial officials demolished it as it was too close to the military prison. The name Saganna in fact comes from the Arabic root *sign*, meaning 'prison', and it stuck even after Saganna moved to its present site. At the time, it was surrounded by military barracks of the Egyptian armed forces and the *deims*, or workers' houses.

Ten mud houses were initially built. Running water was not available until 1936, and electricity was only laid on in the early 1950s. Saganna market was established in 1936.

The population is a mixture of several northern Sudanese ethnic groups, notably Kunuz, Mahas, Shaygiyya, Danagla and Jaaliyiyin. Most of the inhabitants of the original site were employees of the British colonial government or workers; the population has remained essentially unchanged. This is corroborated by a survey of Khartoum[2] including Saganna, according to which 64 per cent of the population were found to belong to the above-mentioned ethnic groups.

The same survey contained information on male educational levels. Only 12 per cent of men surveyed were illiterate, while 44 per cent of household heads had completed secondary education. The same survey revealed that 48 per cent of the latter were government employees and 52 per cent of their fathers had also been government employees. The study furthermore indicated that 60 per cent of heads of household were born in Khartoum and that 72.2 per cent owned their houses.[3]

Most of the population of Saganna are not recent migrants. They clearly have a relatively high level of education and mostly belong to fixed income-groups of government employees. The significance of the latter fact is that they are among the groups most hit by the current economic crisis. The present study provides a necessary complement to this survey as it addresses the specific situation of women and how they perceive their realities and those of their families and community.

Being mostly working class and lower middle class in composition, two political trends have tended to dominate the area: the activities of the National Unionists and the Communist Party. Historically the area has been characterized by a relatively high rate of political consciousness (related to education), and as such played an important role in the nationalist movement and subsequent political movements such as the October 1964 and April 1985 uprisings. The area was especially active in the movement for spreading education by opening schools through self-help (*al-ta'lim al-ahli*).

The main development of recent years is the usurpation of increasing quantities of residential land by the market area. The nature of Saganna market itself is changing from that of a local market catering to the daily needs of the area's inhabitants to that of a market for building materials. This is in turn is leading to a rise in the value of land in the area. In the face of economic difficulties many inhabitants are selling their land and moving elsewhere in the town's new extensions.

2. A two-year research project on urban poverty in Khartoum carried out between 1982 and 1984 by Zeinab El Bakri and El-Wathig M. Kameir and other researchers under the auspices of the Economic and Social Research Council, Khartoum.
3. Head of household is defined in the context of the survey as 'male'.

A. Women in Saganna

In Saganna, as in other urban areas since the early decades of the century, women lived completely segregated lives, their only roles being those of wife and mother. They were to a large extent economically dependent and were not allowed to go out at all unless chaperoned and then only within the confines of the extended family and neighbourhood. They were not even permitted to go to the market to buy items for themselves or provisions for their houses. This was the task of men (although some older women, ex-slave women or women of disrepute did frequent markets).

Women were unable to choose their husbands and marriages were to a large extent arranged within the extended family, at an early age, to paternal or maternal cousins. Polygamy was widespread, but divorce less so, being considered shameful. Children were highly valued and generally the number of children was a measure of a woman's power over her husband, a childless woman being usually powerless.

The main activities of women were domestic, involving the rearing of children, cleaning, washing and preparation of food. The latter was time-consuming since most people lived in large compounds where men and women were separated and where guests could be expected at any time. Women received help in these activities from children but also from servants, if the family had any.

Other activities included visiting female neighbours and family especially at rites of passage, such as deaths, births, marriages and circumcisions. On these occasions women would gather in large numbers and pool their labour in order to feed the large numbers of people who would attend these occasions and expect a family's hospitality. This pooling also involved economic resources (utensils, money, consumer goods) for the benefit of the woman in whose house the occasion was held and it was generally expected that she would reciprocate on other occasions. Such networks also provided an opportunity for women to display their clothes, cosmetic treatments, etc., and were generally the only outlet for women outside the confines of the family compound.

Apart from the few from selected families who attended religious schools (*khalwas*), women in Saganna during the early decades of the century, like other women in Sudan, were by and large illiterate. Some women in Saganna attended *bayt-al-khiyatta* (literally meaning the sewing house). This was a uniquely female, specifically urban and more middle-class institution. It specialized in teaching young girls the arts of sewing, needlework, cooking, etc., in addition to general household duties. Its principal aim was essentially preparing urban women from certain families of the middle and lower-middle class for their future roles of housewife and mother.

During this period the only area of work open to women was that of petty trade. Older women worked as petty traders of traditional handicrafts produced by young girls in the home. Tradition forbade these young girls from appearing at the market.

Women's appearance in the wage-labour market, dependent as it was on education and economic need, came rather late. The first professions to attract women were nursing and midwifery. However, women who entered these professions were primarily of former slave origin, since this was a category in economic need.

Teaching as a profession also attracted women, once education began to spread. During the 1940s, teachers came to play an important role in trade unions and the nationalist movement at large. Their education was an important factor in this regard. They came primarily from the ranks of the urban middle and lower classes. They have also played important leadership roles in women's organizations. With the further spread of education, women came to be incorporated into clerical posts in various government ministries, especially during the 1950s and 1960s.

In terms of political participation, women's role has by and large been non-institutional. They played a supportive role to men during the 1920s and 1930s, preceding the crystallization of the nationalist movement. With the growth of that movement their role became more active, especially with the development of women's organizations. The 1960s were characterized by further increase in women's education and formal employment, meaning a reduction in women's former economic dependence. The granting of suffrage rights to women in 1968 meant that they obtained the right of institutional political participation.

The main changes to the above situation came during the 1970s when the consequences of state policies, notably the increased involvement of foreign capital, failure of development projects, the successive devaluation of Sudanese currency, reduced production and severe shortages in basic consumer goods, all worked to effect and reproduce a severe process of impoverishment for vast sections of Sudanese society, especially those belonging to fixed-income groups.

The dire economic situation has forced large numbers of women, especially from the lower and lower-middle classes to engage in various forms of income-generating activities. Being generally unskilled, and in the face of a widespread employment crisis, these women have been practically barred from the formal job market.

The enormous burden of continuing to feed the family, of maintaining some form of stability and more or less normal social life in the face of such a situation has invariably fallen on the women (Kenyon, 1987b: 57).

B. Women's organizations in Saganna

The main organization in Saganna is the Women's Union, the first branch of which was started in 1964 by a group of students, who relied on the existing consciousness and importance of organizational activities in the area (notably with regard to trade unions). At that time the branch had about fifty to sixty members, most of whom were young and educated. The older women were not interested, still being under the influence of sectarianism and religion. The main activities of this organization in the 1960s were to raise women's consciousness regarding education, political rights and some social customs which the union regarded as socially harmful (e.g. certain practices associated with death and marriage ceremonies). This branch was able to set up a sewing class, a literacy class, a day-care centre and used regularly to celebrate national occasions such as independence day and the like.

After the suspension of the Women's Union in 1971, it was forced to go underground and its activities became severely curtailed. With the return to democracy in April 1985, the Saganna branch of the Women's Union was reactivated, its membership rising to seventy-seven members, with an executive committee of ten, most of them government employees.

Since 1985, the role of the union has been the political mobilization of women to vote during elections. The union also participates in activities such as the national child immunization campaign, to raise consciousness of mothers regarding health issues, etc.

Besides the Women's Union, some women participate in the activities of the Sudanese Youth Union (thirty-three women) and in the Democratic Alliance of the area (thirty-one women). It should be noted that women who actively participate in all these organizations tend to be young, educated and with reduced family responsibilities.

The Women's Union has been instrumental, since 1983, in setting up what has been termed the Housewives' Organization (*Jamiyat Rabat al-Biyut*). The principal aim of this organization is to facilitate access of housewives to scarce consumer goods at reasonable wholesale prices. The underlying idea is to combat the domination of the black market over basic consumer goods in the context of the present economic crisis (including such items as soap, cooking oil, eggs, flour, etc.).

This organization has been fairly successful and has met with the enthusiasm of women in Saganna. It is run by a committee who undertake to transfer the goods from where they are produced to the women. The main problem they face is that of raising enough capital to enable women to obtain large quantities of the goods in question. Another problem is that of overcoming all the bureaucratic obstacles in order to obtain the permits to allow the women to receive the goods. In this they have to contend with blackmarketeers who have easy access to the required permits through corruption.

Another 'informal' organization, but one which is very prevalent in Saganna, is that of the rotating credit associations or *sandugs* (literally 'boxes'). This institution is not a recent phenomenon. Some estimates reckon that it has existed since the 1940s, when it was used by women to obtain scarce consumer goods, such as sugar, tea, etc., which were rationed during the Second World War. Each member made a fixed contribution of goods or money and each member in turn would take the entire contribution either weekly or monthly. The order in which members received the contribution was determined according to their individual needs, so that if one of the women had a family occasion coming up (e.g. birth of a child, circumcision, etc.) she would have priority of access to the goods and/or money (Rehfish, 1989: 680–703).

Sandugs are usually composed of family members, neighbours and friends who are trusted and whose participation is considered to be reliable. Several women may agree to organize a *sandug* because one of them finds herself in need of money to meet an unexpected expense. Founder members will then contact others whom they trust, inviting them to join. Anyone introducing a new member will normally then be responsible for bringing the latter's contribution to the organization (ibid.).

Sandugs differ according to the number of members, the amount of the contribution, whether these are made in cash or in kind, and the length of time involved. The value of contributions clearly depends on the social class of the members and will thus be found to vary widely.

It is pertinent at this point to ask what functions *sandugs* serve for women, and what they mean for different groups of women.

Their main function is that they are a means of forced savings. In recent times the need to save has been much greater and yet much more difficult given the prevailing economic circumstances. The *sandug* has allowed a more formalized saving process.

Sandugs have also provided accumulation of cash at particular moments which enable women to buy household utensils, furniture, make house repairs, etc., all of which would otherwise have been impossible. According to a study by Kenyon in El-Gal'a, Sennar, another Sudanese urban area:

> Without the box there would be no development in El-Gal'a, I was told several times by different women. It is the accumulation of ready cash in this way whether it be from their husbands or from their own hard won incomes, which enable a family to rebuild its fences, install a toilet or build a new room as well as meet major social expenses such as the birth of a new baby or a child's circumcision (Kenyon, 1987a: 23).

The meaning of this institution for women has therefore to be related to its role in furthering their economic independence in the context of difficult economic circumstances.

At the end of this section on women's organizations in Saganna two points can be made: firstly, there certainly exists what may be labelled an organizational awareness, that is, a consciousness of the importance of organizing, evident in the fact that the first branch of the Women's Union was established as far back as 1964; secondly, that organizations which have diverse, but more 'political', aims, e.g. Women's Union and the Democratic Alliance, attract young educated women, and generally have a restricted membership, while organizations with specific economic aims have wider membership and attract a wider range of women.

C. Interviewing women in Saganna

To gain detailed information on women in Saganna, a sample of thirty of them were interviewed. The questions asked related to basic demographic information (age, education, marital status, etc.) but also to such areas as social and political participation and perception of the main problems faced by women in the area.

Table 3.2 reveals a relatively young population although the over-50 age-group is adequately represented.

Despite the relatively young age of the sample Table 3.3 shows that a majority are married, illustrating the importance of marriage as a goal for families. The low rate of divorce can certainly also be

Table 3.2 Age structure of interviewees

Age	Number
20–30	10
31–40	11
41–50	4
Over 50	5
Total	30

Table 3.3 Marital status of interviewees

Marital status	Number
Married	22
Divorced	2
Widowed	4
Single	2
Total	30

Table 3.4 Educational level of interviewees

Education	Number
Illiterate	7
Primary	6
Secondary	15
University	2
Total	30

related to this fact.

Table 3.4 reveals a relatively high educational standard. A clear majority are literate, those who are illiterate belonging mostly to the over-50 age-group. This must be related to specific features of the area including its role in promoting non-governmental education (referred to earlier), the emphasis on education as a demand of the nationalist movement and Saganna's role in that movement, in addition to the fact that some of the population has worked as government employees, which requires a minimum standard of education.

A majority of women work in informal economic activities (see Table 3.5). Interviews revealed the profile and opinions of these

Table 3.5 Occupations of interviewees

Occupation	Number
'Housewife' only	8
'Housewives' involved in informal economic activities	11
Teacher	2
Government official	7
Unemployed	2
Total	30

women: (a) They engage in activities ranging from dress-making in their homes to selling prepared food, utensils and clothes on credit. These are women with relatively low levels of education who would therefore find it rather difficult to become formally employed. At the same time they need to supplement the incomes of their husbands and families (two are actually widowed). These activities are part-time and characterized by the fact that women do not have to be outside their domestic spheres for prolonged periods of time, thus reducing problems of child care. Income is not fixed, thus assuring the women a certain amount of security since they do not have to reveal to family members exactly how much they are earning. They can adjust the activity to suit their domestic schedule. They can easily drop in or out according to daily or long-term needs. (b) Most women view these informal economic activities as providing a supplementary rather than primary income. (c) Unless the need of women was very great, it was generally found that economic activities were less important than social and/or domestic demands. A sick child, presence of guests, certain social ceremonies such as death or marriage could all cause a woman to stop working temporarily (Kenyon, 1987: 59). (d) Despite the time, effort and often capital involved, the returns are not always large. This must be related to women's lack of expertise especially in marketing activities. Often, however, even a small income will be considered satisfactory for an immediate need and therefore acceptable (ibid: 60). (e) The decision to undertake such activities was invariably taken by the women themselves. On the other hand those who are 'housewives' only are those married to persons who can afford to allow them to remain economically dependent, although that is an increasingly rare option for women in Saganna.

In addition, in order to further ascertain women's status, we asked them about the occupations of their husbands, or fathers in

Table 3.6 Occupations of husbands/fathers of interviewees

Occupation	Number
Government official	10
Worker	6
Self-employed	14
Total	30

Table 3.7 Type of family of interviewees

Type	Number
Extended	19
Nuclear	11
Total	30

Table 3.8 Size of family of interviewees

Size	Number
Less than 5	3
6–10	20
Over 10	7
Total	30

the case of single women.

Table 3.6 indicates that the greatest number of husbands/fathers are self-employed, ranging from being a taxi-driver, to owning a neighbourhood shop, to being a carpenter, etc. The number of government officials and workers was likewise large, again confirming our earlier description of Saganna as being primarily working and lower-middle class in nature. The large number of self-employed must be related to the problems of unemployment arising out of the current economic crisis in the country. It should be added that most women who were informally employed were married to workers.

Tables 3.7 and 3.8 above show that most families are of the extended type and further that they mostly fall in the six to ten size-range. The fact that most families are extended must be related to two points which in turn affect women's position in the area: first, that due to the serious housing crisis and the economic crisis

Table 3.9 Income of interviewees per month

Income (Sudanese pounds)	Number
Less than 500	9
500–1,000	18
Over 1,000	3
Total	30

Table 3.10 Interviewees' membership in organizations

Membership	Number
Rotating credit associations (*sandug*)	17
Women's Union	8
Housewives' Organization	10
Co-operative	4

more generally, it is rather difficult for couples to set up an independent nuclear family household; and second, that the family remains the main locus of support for women. Widowed, divorced or single women will almost invariably reside with their original families. The above facts must be taken into account when attempting to explain the large family size in Saganna.

From Table 3.9 it is seen that most families' income falls in the range of between 500 and 1,000 Sudanese pounds monthly. This is a relatively medium income, not high when compared with the current rate of inflation and large family size in the area.

From Table 3.10, it is clear that most women interviewed were members of rotating credit associations. This large number must be related to our earlier discussion of the type of organization and its nature. Specifically, membership is not time-consuming and gives immediate benefits to women in terms of their economic standing. The same can be said of the Housewives' Organization. In fact both these organizations together with the co-operative must be seen as means which solve some of women's immediate economic problems without demanding too much of their time.

As for membership in the Women's Union, this is dominated by young, educated women, primarily government officials and teachers, who perceive women's problems in the area as being of a more political nature.

D. *The division of labour between the sexes*

In all situations there is a clear division of labour between the sexes unmitigated even by the exigencies of age, education and formal employment. Household chores are the responsibility of women, including cooking, cleaning and taking care of children. Full-time servants are increasingly difficult to hire, given the economic situation, and those who can afford it resort to hiring part-time help to undertake certain specific tasks (such as cleaning or washing, for instance). In general children, especially female children, are expected to help in housework. Men are considered the main 'breadwinners' of the household and might help with shopping for food if it involves travelling long distances. In most cases this division of labour was viewed as a hindrance to women's public participation.

E. *Social participation*

Social participation, seen to include taking part in ceremonies, visiting neighbours and relatives at certain times, or generally what is called *mujamalat*, is clearly perceived by society to be a woman's duty and that perception is accepted by women. The importance of such activities is attested by the fact mentioned earlier that these social activities are quite often given priority over economic activities. Most decision-making concerning such activity has historically been in the hands of women and continues to be so. It is they who decide whom they will visit, which ceremonies to attend, etc. All the women in Saganna said they took part in *mujamalat*, but again all stated that there was a marked reduction in the amount of such activity due to the increased difficulty of combining formal employment with domestic responsibilities and especially child care, which signified a severe restriction on women's time. This fact was stated strongly by women working in government offices where they were restricted by fixed office hours.

The system of *wajib* (small money gifts from guests at certain social occasions such as births) constitutes an important part of women's social and economic participation. It is part of a system of reciprocal giving/delayed investment in which women engage, which helps support the specific pattern of social participation in the area. When close family members and immediate neighbours are celebrating an important social occasion, a woman is expected to help by providing labour, especially cooking, cleaning and sharing her utensils. For occasions involving more distant relationships, however, a woman is invited to attend as a guest, and after sharing a meal is expected to contribute financially. Once a woman has entered into such a *wajib* relationship, she expects the other to return the sum with interest later when she herself is celebrating. If the same amount of *wajib* is returned, it implies the debt is repaid and no further *wajib* relationship is anticipated. A woman may continue the relationship with services rather than with money if she is without funds, but it is generally preferable to keep as many *wajib* relationships open as possible since this is an interest-bearing system (Kenyon, 1987: 62–3).

As Kenyon observes in her study on El-Gal'a:

> In the context of poor urban society the *wajib* system is an important means of promoting one's own or one's family's social welfare, or investment for future occasions and an insurance against hard times. A *wajib* relationship implies some obligations (duties) on both parts, and, although these are not as great as kin, they certainly are regarded as some form of investment (ibid.: 63).

The above discussion demonstrates two important points: firstly, the importance of social participation for women especially in terms of the support it provides for them; secondly, the intricate relationship between economic and social participation. Women often engage in informal economic activities in order to be able to support their specific pattern of social participation (*mujamalat*); yet increased employment (especially formal employment) is dealing a death blow to this.

F. Political participation

Despite the obvious shortcomings of an 'institutional' approach to political participation as pointed out earlier, we have primarily considered whether women have specific political affiliations, whether they participate in elections, campaign for certain issues, etc. We also looked into the specific obstacles hindering political participation.

Most women exhibited clear political affiliations, as illustrated in Table 3.11. The interview showed that the political affiliation of women usually matched that of their husband, except in two cases where there was a marked difference. A relationship was also found to exist between education and membership of the Communist Party. The large affiliation to the Democratic Unionist Party is in line with the history of this party in the area since the beginnings of the nationalist movement.

Table 3.11 Political affiliation of interviewees

Political Affiliation	Number
Communist Party	8
Democratic Unionist Party	9
National Islamic Front	3
Umma Party	1
No affiliation	9
Total	30

Note: Both the Democratic Unionist Party (DUP) and the Umma Party developed in the 1940s during the nationalist struggle. They both rely on their sectarian influence (the Khatmiya and Ansar sects) and are representative of traditional forces in Sudanese society, especially the traditional urban and rural bourgeoisie.

Table 3.12 Political affiliation of husbands/fathers of interviewees

Political Affiliation	Number
Communist Party	5
Democratic Unionist Party	12
National Islamic Front	3
Umma Party	2
No affiliation	8
Total	30

As regards voting, most women in Saganna participated in the April 1986 elections and a high overall urban rate for women was generally noticed.

As far as more informal political activity is concerned, the following facts are pertinent. From 1969 to 1985, the Sudan Women's Union (the government women's organization) was not able to set up a branch in Saganna due to women's resistance. This was an example of informal political activity. Meanwhile, in local council elections it proved difficult to find enough women to stand for office, despite the reservation of 25 per cent of local council seats for women.

The general attitude concerning the main obstacles to political participation was that formal political participation as such was low in the neighbourhood and it was generally perceived to be a male phenomenon. Besides, once again the principal obstacle cited was that of domestic responsibilities invariably shouldered by women.

From the above, the following points emerge:

(1) That most women have clear political affiliations but this is mostly affected by male decision-making.

(2) Due to domestic responsibilities and the way the sexual division of labour is structured, women shy away from more permanent formal political participation, which would be demanding on their time. Thus, women shied away from running for the local council elections and no woman from the area ran for the national elections. When it came to more temporary informal political activity women were involved. The silent resistance to establishing a branch of an organization in which they did not believe is a case in point. Here decision-making was clearly in their hands, but more important still, their domestic lives were not affected.

Another question posed during the interviews concerned perception of the most important problem facing them in the area of Saganna. All thirty said that daily living had become more difficult due to the economic situation and the ensuing sharp rise in prices, inflation and other effects. Products were much more expensive and not readily available, except on the black market. This response illustrates two crucial points: that a) it is women who are bearing the brunt of the economic crisis; and that, b) their responsibilities in facing the crisis are causing a drastic change in their life-style.

For an area such as Saganna the time of the economically dependent woman is clearly over. The development of housewives' organizations, and membership in rotating credit associations must be seen within such a context as furthering women's economic independence.

We have considered above aspects of the position of women in Saganna as a clue to the position of women in Sudanese urban areas. In the coming section, we shall examine another community to determine whether the dynamics of rural society work to affect women differently as regards their economic, social and political participation?

III. Lives of women and their families in the village of Wad al-'Asha

The village of Wad al-'Asha lies in central Sudan, south of Wad Medani, which is the capital of the region, and four miles south of

Barakat, the headquarters of the Gezira Scheme. This Scheme is one of the oldest irrigated agricultural schemes in the country, growing cotton, the Sudan's main cash crop.

The village is adjacent to farmland and has a population of about 4,000 people. The village houses appear intertwined since there are usually no surrounding walls, although some houses are separated by very small bushes. The roads are winding, narrow alleys reflecting the lack of planning of the village site.

The houses differ in their structure and the number of rooms. Most, however, are built of red brick and only a minority are made of mud. The average house is made up of one large room and another with a veranda-like structure (*rakooba*) used as a kitchen. They may often include more rooms with attached verandas for extended families. The furniture in this room is usually similar, including several beds (wooden or metal) and a set of tables, together with additional mattresses to be used for lodging guests during important family ceremonies. Men and women do not usually have separate courtyards although a kind of reception room may be set aside for men at the level of the extended, rather than of the nuclear family. New more 'modern' buildings made up of a bedroom, living room, sitting room, etc., usually built by the migrant sons of the village are now being built on the outskirts.

The village has both water and electricity services and many of the villagers own electrical appliances such as tape-recorders, radios, TVs, refrigerators and a few video-cassette recorders. This is a direct result of the influence of migrants working in the oil-rich Arab countries. Prior to the phenomenon of out-migration, however, the social services of the Gezira Scheme contributed to providing such items as refrigerators and TV sets on credit.

There is a village medical centre, with a medical assistant, a health visitor and a nurse. One co-educational primary school was built in 1968. Before that villagers sent their children to neighbouring villages, which is still the case for those continuing education in secondary school. Finally, there is one cultural/sports club with membership restricted to males.

A. *The Gezira Scheme*

The Gezira Scheme, within which the village of Wad al-'Asha is located, lies in the triangle of land south of Khartoum. Two sides of the triangle are formed by two rivers, to the east the Blue Nile and to the west the White Nile. The southern boundary can be taken to be the railway line which runs from Sennar in the east to Kosti in the west. The total area of the Gezira Region is about 5 million acres, but the Scheme itself occupies around 2 million acres.

The government corporation which today runs the Scheme is called the Sudan Gezira Board, employing directly about 10,000 people. Agricultural operations are carried out by 70,000 tenants, their families and various types of hired labour. The whole Scheme provides employment for around a quarter of a million people.

* Although different crops are cultivated, the main crop is long-staple cotton. The production of the Gezira Scheme contributes a major part of the total Sudanese exports of cotton, which in turn forms a considerable part of overall national exports. The cultivation of cotton on this scale in the Gezira is facilitated by a complex irrigation system, which relies on two dams on the Blue Nile at Sennar and al-Roseiris.

The Scheme was originally set up as a combination of government, commercial and local involvement. Thus the British government was responsible for construction and maintenance of all irrigation works. The management of the scheme was in the hands of a British company, the Sudan Plantation Syndicate. Labour was to be supplied by the inhabitants of the area. Each tenant was allocated an area of land on which he and his family was supposed to grow cotton, *dura* (sorghum) and perhaps a fodder crop.

Whereas prior to setting up the scheme production had been organized according to a variety of multiple social relations, in the situation created by the scheme the tenant was related to the new means of production only as an economic actor, in other words he ceased producing for subsistence purposes. Previously, his product had little or no exchange-value and neither had his labour. Now he was almost totally concerned with producing a commodity which for him only had an exchange-value and his labour was now turned into a commodity (Barnett, 1975: 186–95).

B. *Social composition of the village population*

Most of the people of the village of Wad al-'Asha are farmers and workers in the Gezira Scheme, irrigation works and cotton ginning factories, and several are government officials. Some families own tenancies; most own nothing.

Generally no wide differences were noticed in the standard of living of the village's population. However, two crucial qualifications need to be made:

(1) Some families have made an effort to educate their sons,

despite the absence of schools in the village, enabling them to enter the civil service.

(2) The price of cotton as a cash crop has considerably decreased in recent years, commensurately with a sharp rise in the cost of living. This has meant that agricultural work has ceased to interest male youth, including those who have not had a chance to complete their education. Some have been attracted by work in factories (especially textile factories), others have opted for the lucrative chance of migrating to oil-rich Arab countries.

Two important consequences have resulted from the above facts:

(1) the educated and the migrants have begun to create a new life-style which is causing wide divergences within the village social structure;
(2) women have come to play crucial roles in agriculture.

Both these points will be elaborated upon later.

C. Women in Wad al-'Asha

There is a clear discrepancy in educational opportunity for men and women. Men have a better educational standard and some have even seized the opportunity of entering higher education. Only in 1986/7 were two women able to join the College of Hygiene and the Higher Nursing College, and in 1988 one woman was able to enter the Higher Nursing College and one the university. This is in addition to twelve women who have completed secondary school and are currently looking for employment.

1. Forms of women's economic participation It is important here to compare the situation of women before and after the setting up of the Scheme. Before the Scheme, agriculture functioned for subsistence. The peasant household was an important unit of production where women had considerable influence over production activities and decisions concerning them. Women in rural areas were not generally isolated from production as they were in urban areas. Due to the Islamic inheritance laws, they were also able to own land.

With the setting up of the Scheme, however, the entire situation changed. The household ceased to be a viable unit of production

187

and was now turned into production for exchange. Women were not allocated land on the Scheme which included all arable land in the villages.

Although women can legally own tenancies, no effort was made to build a role for them into the Scheme. Rather they were incorporated as dependents of male tenants or as unpaid family agricultural labour. As non-tenants, women had no legal status on the Scheme. Tenancies were allotted to individuals not to families. However, tenancies obviously require much more than one man's labour and tenants were expected to use their families in production (Bernal, 1988: 3). As family members of tenants rather than being tenants as such themselves, women had no direct access to the limited benefits offered by the Scheme such as profit, payments and cash advances for cotton production, regardless of whether or not the tenants farmed.

The household became less important as a unit of production and this weakened women's influence over production processes and decisions. Resources and decisions came to be concentrated in the hands of male Scheme owners, employees and the tenants themselves.

The most important change has been the decline of agriculture as a source of subsistence or accumulation for villagers. Furthermore, since the 1960s, cotton productivity and profits have witnessed a decline. At present it is no longer possible to sustain a household by farming alone. Villages have diverse household economies that combine some farming on the scheme with wage employment and/or commercial activities. Villagers frequently migrate and remittances have become an important source of income. While these changes are not solely due to the Scheme, it contributed greatly to the increased dependence of villagers on the market and labour migration because it undermined the agricultural-subsistence base of the village.

2. Towards an increasing feminization of agricultural work Until the 1960s, the tenant used to depend for agricultural labour on himself, his male children and paternal and maternal cousins. However, with the spread of education and the increased need of families for a fixed income leading to migration and labour shortage, tenants began to depend on seasonal agricultural labourers mostly from Western Sudan or the Eastern Blue Nile area (al-Butana). He would usually cover their living expenses and house them on the outskirts of the village.

However, in recent years, especially in the late 1970s, the former dependence on seasonal agricultural labour has decreased due to the following reasons:

(1) the development of agricultural schemes close to the home areas of these labourers, e.g. the Rahad Agricultural Scheme east of the Blue Nile;
(2) drought and famine which has forced people from Western Sudan, the hardest hit area, to leave their homes altogether and seek more permanent employment in urban areas;
(3) the rise in the price of *dura* (sorghum), the staple food, has meant that the living expenses of these agricultural labourers has risen tremendously, thus reducing the viability of hiring seasonal agricultural labourers.

It is the women who have by and large replaced the seasonal labourers in agricultural operations. They are either considered as family labour (and therefore do not receive a wage), or they have turned into agricultural labourers for other tenants.

The specific reasons for increased entry of women into this type of agricultural work include the following:

(1) the phenomenal rise in the cost of living has forced many women to work to increase family income;
(2) the occurrence of specific family circumstances, e.g. unemployment or death of a husband, etc.;
(3) the desire to fulfil certain personal needs (e.g. buying gold ornaments or clothes), or other non–basic household needs such as fancy crockery, sheets, etc.;
(4) providing an independent income which will enable women to contribute to certain social occasions (i.e. *wajib*);
(5) for those women whose families own tenancies, taking part in agricultural work is almost a matter of honour.

Agricultural work is seasonal and includes work on cotton tenancies and on vegetable farms.

Wheat is the only crop in the cultivation of which women do not participate, due to the mechanization of all agricultural operations.

The cotton growing involves four stages covering eight to nine months of the year. The first stage begins in August with the sowing of seeds, which involves some children and women. The growth of the cotton plant is usually accompanied by the growth of some weeds, which necessitates weeding the fields, an operation which is also carried out by women. Then follows the third operation called *shalkh*, which involves thinning the plants. This operation is also carried out by women and begins in December or January. The fourth and most important operation is the cotton-picking process which requires a great deal of labour and is once again dominated by women. Cotton-picking continues until the month of April.

The work of village men in cotton cultivation is practically restricted to controlling irrigation, weighing the cotton once it is picked, supervising its packing into jute bags and making sure it reaches the ginning factories.

Women leave for the fields around 6 a.m. after they have completed certain household chores such as making *kisra* (the staple bread). They generally have to walk long distances to reach the fields, the nearest tenancy lying a kilometre from the village. They carry their breakfast with them, a meal usually made up of *kisra*, eaten after the addition of water, salt, chillies and/or tomatoes if in season. An alternative would be bread and *tahniyya* (a sweet paste made of ground sesame seeds and sugar). Drinking-water is also carried to the fields. Work continues until 2 p.m., or even 4 p.m. during the cotton-picking season, with a break for breakfast.

The height of the cotton plant differs according to the strain of cotton grown, as does its roughness. This means that moving between the cotton plants is rather a tough process and obliges the women to wear special clothes to protect their bodies from the plants and from the heat of the sun. This is usually a long sleeved dress, trousers and a long piece of cloth around the waist and forming a kind of basket for collecting the cotton picked. At the end of the working day, each woman carries what she has picked to be weighed.

Wages are different for each agricultural operation. For cotton-picking, the most important operation, a certain price is placed for each *guffa* (basket) picked. This *guffa* usually weighs approximately 35 lbs.

The productivity of women differs according to the type of cotton grown. For instance in 1980–1987 for the Shambat type of cotton, the productivity of the most skilled female cotton-pickers never exceeded three *guffas* (i.e. $35 \times 3 = 105$ lbs. of cotton) after a whole day's work (6 a.m. – 4 p.m.). The price paid per *guffa* was £s.3.5. For other cotton types, productivity was much higher, often reaching nine *guffas* per day; the price per *guffa* was however only £s.2.

For other agricultural operations, wages are often set according to the time of day that the work is done, so that a particular wage is given for work accomplished during the morning (i.e. 6 a.m. – 10 a.m.), called *dahayiyya*, and another wage for the afternoon period called *duhriyya* extending from 3 p.m. – 5 p.m. It is noticed that wages for the morning period are higher than the afternoon period since it is longer.

From the above, therefore, it is clear that a marked sexual division of labour exists and that it has changed over time. Previously agriculture was the principal source of subsistence in which the household carried out agricultural operations regarding which decision-making was a household matter.

Presently, it is obvious that women in Wad al-'Asha, by and large legally regarded as non-tenants on the Scheme, undertake the bulk of cultivation, in combination with some subsistence agriculture. This is in addition to shouldering domestic labour of cooking, cleaning and caring for children. Men's roles in agriculture must meanwhile be seen in relation to their legal status as tenants on the Scheme. They take the decisions concerning agricultural operations (although these are shaped by the overall Scheme objectives), supervise irrigation works, make sure cotton is properly packed, etc.

The main reasons behind the above is that in the context of the current economic crisis, the viability of agriculture as a livelihood has decreased. Men are seeking new sources of income beyond the confines of the village, leaving cultivation to women. However, due to their non-tenant status on the scheme, women are being marginalized from the potential benefits of such a process, despite the additional burdens they are taking on.

In order to gain additional information, interviews were conducted with a sample of ten women in Wad al-'Asha. From these interviews the following points arose:

(1) The extent of participation in agricultural production clearly depends on the degree of need for an additional income. Although the decision to participate (especially as an agricultural labourer) is taken by the women, the work is viewed as arduous and unpleasant. Those whose parents or husband own a tenancy are practically forced to engage in agricultural work.

(2) The level of education is generally low; none of those interviewed had ever progressed beyond primary school.

(3) Almost none of the males (fathers, brothers, husbands) were fully engaged in agriculture. Their role remained supervisory or they had formal employment elsewhere. Lacking skills, women have no option if they wish to raise their income but to remain in agriculture.

191

(4) The arduousness of agricultural work and the length of the working day are curtailing women's participation in other spheres.

(5) There is a clear lack of services catering especially for women's needs. The lack of a girls' school, childcare facilities, mother and child health services are all felt by women.

(6) An awareness exists of the importance of developing skills. Several of the women interviewed had acquired some skills in dressmaking and viewed this as a way out of complete dependence on agricultural work.

3. Women's social participation   Due to the arduous nature of agricultural work, most of the time women return home extremely fatigued and drained. After dinner they undertake other necessary household duties such as washing clothes, cleaning and preparing things for the next day. Such activities place a limit on the time and energy women may devote to social participation.

Generally, however, the village is characterized by close social relations and women place great importance on fulfilling social obligations which might extend beyond the confines of the village to neighbouring villages and often to the nearby town of Wad Medani if someone from the village has to be hospitalized.

These social occasions go beyond being mere social visits to pass the time and usually imply a material contribution (*wajib*). Women might forego going to the fields for a day or two to attend an important social occasion or ceremony, such as a death or marriage.

At present there are no formal women's groups or organizations in the village. Recently, some women in Wad al-'Asha started a group with the aim of buying a quantity of cooking utensils, beds, sheets, mattresses etc. These items are then loaned to individual women for their social occasions. The establishment of this group is seen as the beginning of a developing consciousness by women of their needs.

It was also noticed that an interest in organizational activity existed among young women who had some education. Recently when a representative of a voluntary health organization called for a meeting in the village to set up a free one-day service to care for village children, this was met with enthusiasm from the young women.

As in urban areas, decisions concerning social participation are taken by women, although this form of participation is affected by the heavy workload of women in the village.

4. Political participation in Wad al-'Asha   As tenants, men are directly linked to extra-communal and national institutions. Tenants furthermore belong to various organizations including a union established since the late 1940s. Through this union and their shared conditions with tenants on other irrigated schemes, local men have become actors in national politics. Women have not had the same opportunity to develop a broader social/political consciousness or organization. Even though working on the scheme, they have non-tenant status and therefore are excluded from union activities and other contacts. Generally, no organized politics exist within the village and none of the large political parties have branches there.

The above statements need some qualification, however, since some interest in politics was noticed among young educated women. Some wore 'Islamic' garb (*hejab*) to indicate their support for the National Islamic Front.

IV. Comparing women in both communities

Several factors were mentioned in the introduction as being crucial to the analysis of women's status within any given society. The first was that of social class, the second was the degree of influence of Arab/Islamic culture, and the third was the general political economy of the Sudanese social formation.

Regarding the first factor, women in Wad al-'Asha and Saganna can be seen to belong to different social classes. The former belong to the class of rural agricultural labourers while the latter belong to the urban lower-middle or working classes. Both groups live in an area where Arab/Islamic culture dominates, so this factor must not be seen as exerting any crucial differences between the groups.

Women in both regions exist within the boundaries of a specific political economy which has developed historically in such a way that certain aspects of it have exerted similar influences on both rural and urban society and therefore on both groups of women. Perhaps the most important of these common trends is the current economic crisis which has historically resulted from the situation of economic dependency of Sudanese society as regards the world capitalist system and all this has entailed in terms of development problems, severe economic deterioration and widespread poverty.

The principal effect on women has been a rise in rates of women's economic participation in order to raise family income, together with a decrease in their social participation and a change in the latter's nature due to the constraints on women's time and energy.

In the urban area, the main trend has been an increase in the numbers of women deciding to leave the domestic sphere to enter all sectors of the urban economy. However, due to the specific structure of the urban economy itself and its inability to provide formal employment for all, this increase has primarily been in what have been called informal economic activities. In all cases this trend has resulted in the increased economic independence of women but not necessarily in an improvement in their overall well-being, as they continue to shoulder the burden of domestic labour. However, it has given women the opportunity for decision-making in the activity of their choice. Petty selling remains the most important of these activities.

In the rural area studied, the trend has been toward the practical feminization of the agricultural labour force in the village. Men have removed themselves from the realm of most agricultural operations, retaining a supervisory role and their legal status as tenants, while at the same time seeking formal employment primarily through labour migration. Again this has meant greater economic independence for village women but at the expense of combining this with almost equally arduous domestic responsibilities.

Urban women tend to have more choice of economic activity. For instance they can choose to sell cooked food, or provide beauty treatments and other services. This is a function of the wider market for services in a metropolitan area such as Khartoum with all its concentration of wealth and its housing of the country's middle and upper classes, who need such services. In the village, meanwhile, given the limitations of the local market, of skills and of capital, agriculture is virtually the only option for women seeking work.

As regards some of the characteristics of the two groups of women studied, the following points can be noted:

(1) Generally women in the urban area have a higher standard of education; the illiteracy rate is low, contrary to the situation in the village. This is due to the fact that historically formal education for women began and developed in urban areas and that any training opportunities available are concentrated there. Greater opportunity for women to develop skills in urban areas gives them more employment opportunities than rural women.

(2) The same can be said about health services. Access to both public, but especially private services is clearly easier in urban areas, which is a further indication of the enormity of rural–urban disparities.

(3) The main similarity between both groups is that women's responsibilities within the home are unchanged. They remain responsible for domestic labour and rearing of children. Alternative child care facilities are usually sought within the confines of the extended family. The nature of domestic labour is clearly different, related to differences in diet and availability of technology, but remains in any case in women's hands.

It follows from the above that women's dual responsibilities, especially in a context of severe economic crisis, where infrastructures to mitigate this duality are generally lacking, have come to constitute the main obstacle to women's public participation. This is clearly felt more in the rural than in the urban area.

(4) Income levels are clearly higher in the urban area. Despite the fact that agricultural work is certainly more arduous, a lower value is attributed to it. This lower value is in turn reflected in women's status in the form of reduced wages for agricultural work.

(5) Social participation is viewed primarily as the women's realm as is decision-making regarding it. In both areas women thought that the increase in their economic participation was affecting the level of social participation. Social occasions were, however, still rated as being important and involved an interchange of economic resources between women, in the form of money (*wajib*), utensils, labour, etc. The scale of such occasions is different in urban and rural areas.

(6) The existence of formal women's organizations remains an urban phenomenon. Women's organizations have not yet reached rural women or dealt with their pressing problems. As regards informal networks/organizations, these were much more developed in the urban areas especially in the form of rotating credit associations. In the rural area, we saw the beginnings of such an organization.

(7) More generally, the political participation of women in the urban area was seen to be higher. This is due to a generally higher level of education among women in urban areas and in particular in Saganna, which has had a history of political involvement since the nationalist movement. The fact that Khartoum is the seat of the national government where most national politics take place should likewise not be forgotten.

Regarding trade-union activity, an important form of political participation, the following can be said:

(a) Since there is an increased chance for urban women to be formally employed (as compared with rural women), this signifies that they may have a greater chance of joining trade unions. Urban women involved in informal economic activities, constituting the majority, have not until now had a similar opportunity.

(b) Rural women working as family labour do not by and large have the status of tenants and are therefore barred from tenants' organizations.

(c) Rural women working as agricultural labourers have not yet formed any organization and it is unlikely that they will do so in the near future.

V. Conclusions

The case-studies show that despite wide divergences in women's positions, certain elements in the political economy of the country, especially the current economic crisis, are exerting a levelling influence on the situation of women. The main result of this has been significant rises in levels of women's participation in the economy but not necessarily resulting in commensurate improvements in their overall well-being.

The specific dynamics of urban as contrasted with rural society have shaped women's responses to this situation of crisis.

We feel that this means that certain general recommendations can be made which, if executed, will help in ameliorating the situation of women. These recommendations should be publicized and brought to the attention of national machinery, of non-governmental organizations, women's groups and other institutions. However, the crucial understanding should remain that any radical changes in the situation of women are dependent on radical changes in the structure and processes of society as a whole. These recommendations include the following:

(1) The urgent need for carrying out studies in different parts of the country to find out what women are doing and how their roles are changing. Only thus can an adequate data base be provided on women in the country and adequate planning for women become a reality.

(2) It follows then that more attention must be given to women in the process of development planning. The current gender-biased ideology of development planners must be changed.

(3) It is imperative that women themselves should organize and should be encouraged to do so by government (both local and

national) through provision of venues for meetings, publicity and general support. Women in informal economic activities would benefit most from such organization, since they are not covered by government legislation which is limited to formal employment in the modern sector of employment, which excludes most women.

(4) The main problem of women in both urban and rural areas remains the fact that besides economic production outside the home, they have to shoulder domestic responsibilities including child care. Alternative child care facilities would therefore have the effect of enhancing women's overall participation roles. Such alternatives however can only be viable with state support.

(5) The issue of education, training and skill acquisition is crucial. Women can broaden opportunities only by acquiring varied skills. This again requires both state and NGO support.

(6) Above all the deterioration in the situation of women can only be dealt with if turned into a political issue. This can only be done by women themselves.

References

BARNETT, TONY, 'The Gezira Scheme: Production of Cotton and the Reproduction of Underdevelopment', in Ivar Oxaal *et al.* (eds), *Beyond the Sociology of Development: Economy and Society in Latin America and Africa*, London: Routledge and Kegan Paul, 1975: 186–95

BERNAL, VICTORIA, 'Land, Income and Power: Gender Issues in Agricultural Development', paper presented to Conference on Sudanese Studies: Past, Present and Future, Khartoum, 1983

EL BAKRI, ZEINAB AND EL-WATHIG M. KAMEIR, 'Aspects of Women's Political Participation in Sudan', *International Social Sciences Journal*, Special issue on 'Women in Power Spheres', Vol. XXXV, No. 4, Paris: Unesco, 1983: 605–24

EL BAKRI, ZEINAB *et al.*, 'The State of Women's Studies in the Sudan', *Development Studies and Research Centre, Monograph Series*, No. 25, 1985

EL BAKRI, ZEINAB AND EL-WATHIG M. KAMEIR, 'Corruption and Capital Accumulation: The Case of Urban Land in Khartoum', *Development Studies and Research Centre, Monograph Series*, No. 29, 1987

EL-SAYED, MAHASIN KHIDIR, 'Women's Work Participation Patterns in Sudanese Agriculture', unpublished PhD thesis, University of Khartoum, 1980

FARAH, AMNA, 'Enhancing Women's Participation in Agriculture and Rural Development', paper presented to Development Studies and Research Centre Seminar on the Contribution of Women to Development, Khartoum, 1984

FARAH, FIRYAL AL-SAYYID, 'The Development of Social Welfare and its Role', paper presented to Development Studies and Research Centre Seminar on the Contribution of Women to Development (in Arabic), Khartoum, 1984

JACQUETTE, JANE, 'Female Political Participation in Latin America', in J. Nash and H.I. Safa (eds), *Sex and Class in Latin America: Women's Perspectives on Politics, Economics and the Family in the Third World*, London: Routledge and Kegan Paul, 1976

KENYON, SUSAN, 'Women and the Urban Process: A Case Study from el-Gal'a, Sennar', in A. Saghoyroun (ed.), *Population and Women in Development* (n.p.), 1987a

——, 'Sudan's Shadow Economy: Working Women in Poor Urban Sudan', in A. Saghoyroun (ed.), *Population and Women in Development* (n.p.), 1987b

MAHMOUD, FATIMA BABIKER, *The Sudanese Bourgeoisie: Vanguard of Development?*, London: Zed Books, 1984

REHFISH, F., 'Rotating Credit Associations in Greater Khartoum', in V.G. Pons (ed.), *Urbanization and Urban Life in the Sudan* (n.p.), 1989: 680–703

STEADY, FILOMINA, C., 'Research Methodology, an Investigative Framework for Social Change: The Case for African Women', paper presented to AAWORD Seminar on African Women: What Type of Methodology?, Dakar, 1983

TAISIER, MOHAMED ALI, 'Towards the Political Economy of Agricultural Development in the Sudan 1956–1964', unpublished PhD thesis, University of Toronto, 1982

——, 'The Road to Jouda', *Review of African Political Economy*, No. 26, Special Issue on Sudan, 1983

UNICEF, *Development Programmes for and with Women in Sudan: An Annotated Inventory*, Khartoum: UNICEF, 1984

Appendix: Report of the Unesco Regional Working Group on Women's Participation in Public Life in the Arab States Region, organized in co-operation with the Institute of Archaeology and Anthropology, University of Yarmouk (Irbid, Jordan, 13 to 16 December 1986)

I. Introduction

This regional working group of experts on women's participation in public life in the Arab States region was organized by the Division of Human Rights and Peace, Sector for Social and Human Sciences of Unesco in co-operation with the Institute of Archaeology and Anthropology, University of Yarmouk and took place in Irbid, Jordan, from 13 to 16 December 1986. The host country had also arranged for the patronage of the regional working group by Her Majesty Queen Noor of Jordan.

This regional working group comprised part of Unesco's programme of research in the social sciences concerning the status of women and their participation in economic, social and political life.

The regional working group brought together eleven specialists in the social sciences in their personal capacity of experts from different countries in the Arab States region to discuss the broad theme of women's participation in public life with reference to social sciences research trends and needs in this area. In addition, observers from the Union of Arab Lawyers, the International Federation of Business and Professional Women, the Palestine Liberation Organization (PLO), as well as national observers from Jordan attended the meeting.

The agenda items discussed were as follows:

(1) State of research in the social sciences on the various forms of women's participation in community and public life.

(2) The ways and means by which women are involved in organizing and running economic, social and community life at local levels, through informal as well as formal structures.

(3) The process of the formalization and institutionalization of public life and how women have been able to participate therein and contribute to public policy at local and national levels:

(a) opportunities opened up for women's participation in public administration;

(b) women's participation in political parties, access to legislative bodies, contribution to legal professions and the judicial process, participation in ministerial and other appointed posts;

(c) women's relationships with local councils and other social, economic and public institutions at local levels.

(4) Changing patterns of women's participation in the salaried labour force and their entry into professional life, taking into account economic and social changes in the region.

(5) The role of women's organizations and other voluntary and nongovernmental organizations in encouraging women to involve themselves in public issues.

(6) Discussion of priority themes for future study and elaboration of proposed research framework.

The Head of the Section of Anthropology, Institute of Archaeology and Anthropology, University of Yarmouk, warmly welcomed participants, observers and other invited guests to the regional working group. The working group would deal with the state of social sciences research and future priorities as regards women's participation in public and political life.

The representative of Unesco then warmly welcomed, on behalf of the Director-General of Unesco, the representative of Her Majesty Queen Noor of Jordan, the President of Yarmouk University, participants and observers to the regional working group. This regional working group was organized as part of Unesco's programme in the social sciences for the advancement of women. It brought together specialists in various social science disciplines (anthropology, sociology, law, economics and mass communication), in their personal capacity, from universities and research institutions in the Arab states region. The theme of women in public life had been identified as a priority theme for study in different countries and regional contexts in the Unesco Approved Programme and Budget adopted by its General Conference. Research on this theme had already been undertaken in selected countries of Latin America, Europe and Asia and an international meeting of experts (Dubrovnik, Yugoslavia, December 1984) had examined this theme and in particular factors influencing women's roles in decision-making in political, economic and scientific life.

This was the second meeting in the region of social scientists convened by Unesco concerning social sciences research on women, the first having been a regional experts meeting on 'multi-disciplinary research on women in the Arab world' which took place in Tunis, Tunisia from 18 to 21 May 1982. This meeting, which resulted in the publication of the book *Social Sciences Research and Women in the Arab World* (Unesco, 1984), assessed the general state of social sciences research on women in the region, examined issues of theory and methodology and pinpointed some research priorities.

Since 1982, there had been a growth of concern and research undertaken by local researchers on their societies, and women's economic and social situation therein, and the working group would assess trends in research with particular reference to the theme of women in public life.

As seen from the agenda, 'public participation' would be looked at in a broad sense and cover various areas of concern including the ways and means by which women organized themselves and contributed to economic, social and political life at local levels not only in formal but also in informal ways – the latter having been less apparent to the public eye.

Public participation likewise meant patterns of women's participation in the salaried labour force and in various aspects of professional life. In this respect the meeting would look at the effects of social and economic changes in the region, including the impact of the discovery of oil and of the oil economy on the region, for both oil-producing countries and those exporting labour. What were the relationships of women's participation in the formal labour force with labour migration or the use of a substantial expatriate labour force? What was the value attributed to the various forms of women's economic participation in different countries of the region?

Opportunities were opened up for women's involvement in professional life in public administration after independence. Some women had become employed as professors and social scientists within universities and research institutes and had entered professions formerly closed to them. Finally, the meeting would examine the extent to which women had been able to play a role in formal political life, and the various ways (including through women's organizations and voluntary associations) that women were able to contribute to public issues. Factors favouring and constraining women's public participation would be analysed.

Increasing evidence had revealed that the process of development as it occurred in different local and national contexts was not always automatically beneficial for all women, especially for many rural women and the urban poor. To understand the complexity of social reality and women therein, due account should be taken of the diversity of rural and urban contexts, of different ecological conditions and production systems, of social class variables and of cultural variations of different communities and regions, in addition to the question of gender. A historical perspective likewise would help to deepen understanding of the questions being examined.

A major objective of the working group was to identify priority issues for future research on women's public participation in the Arab states region, and to elaborate a framework for a research project that could be undertaken in several countries of the region during 1987.

The President of Yarmouk University welcomed the representative of Her Majesty the Queen and all the social science specialists present at the regional working group which was an example of co-operation between the University of Yarmouk, the Institute of Archaeology and Anthropology and Unesco. He thanked the Secretary-General of the Jordanian National Commission for the valuable contribution of the Commission to the preparation of the meeting. The significance of this seminar arose from the fact that Arab women had become active participants in all social, economic and political fields, and an element to be reckoned with in various governmental and private institutions and voluntary work. Female involvement in different activities was not confined to urban women only; in fact rural young women had also become engaged in active walks of life, joining universities, community colleges, polytechnics, etc., side by side with their urban sisters, competing for the highest qualifications and realizing that their role in national development and progress could not be inferior to that of the city people.

The working group provided an occasion to examine studies and research underway on the position Arab women occupy in public life, some of the obstacles faced, and priorities for future research.

The representative of Her Majesty Queen Noor of Jordan welcomed all those in attendance at the seminar on a subject which was of much more than academic interest to an Arab nation trying to identify and address the challenges of national development in a coherent manner. The past decade of brisk and often haphazard growth in the Arab world had given way to a new, more demanding era of restraint. The role of Arab women in public life was directly related to this new socio-economic context.

The fact that over one-third of all Jordanians under the age of twenty-five were in school and more than half of the university students in the country were women, suggested that there was a need to look inside one's own communities, countries and nations to tap the human talent that had always been the catalyst and cornerstone of national development.

Arab women remained the single largest under-utilized factor in the social and economic development process despite the emergence of more educated women. During the accelerated growth and high inflation years between 1974 and 1983, Jordan's social structure encouraged women to work because the family often needed the additional income that a working daughter or mother could bring in.

Now that slower economic growth has lowered inflation rates and increased unemployment, would social pressures and traditional male prerogatives force educated young women to forego the professional opportunities that many of them had looked forward to during their long years of study?

The particular challenge in the Arab world was more complex than simply to offer men and women equal opportunities of education, employment, advancement and social benefits. It was the challenge of fusing the contemporary quest for equality of opportunity with the powerful instincts of an ancient social heritage that had traditionally defined a woman's public role in a highly restricted manner, in favour of her domestic role as wife and mother. While it was clear that an educated woman's domestic role contributed substantively to the human development of her family and the socio-economic development of her community, it was important now that the Arab world matched its emphasis on education with an equal emphasis on the manner in which all its men and women could make use of their education and talents.

The representative of the Queen of Jordan concluded her speech by wishing the working group success in its deliberations and declaring the meeting open.

II. State of research in the social sciences on the various forms of women's participation in community and public life

Soheir Morsy introduced the agenda item on this theme. She noted that the concept of public and political life and women's participation therein were being examined, and questioned whether the use of these terms would not tend to lead to a dichotomous view of women in public versus private life. This was a framework of reference imposed from the outside by those unfamiliar with the realities of Arab women's situation.

When referring to women's participation, what were the objectives that should be kept in mind? Women's public participation should be analysed in relationship to the economic and social changes within given societies and the region as a whole, and taking into account the international context.

Soheir Morsy invited participants to give a presentation on the status of research on women in public life based on their own research and the experience of their particular countries.

Studies assessing research trends in the Maghreb countries had been prepared for the Unesco regional meeting of experts on 'multidisciplinary research on women in the Arab world' which was organized by Unesco in Tunis in 1982. Since that time considerable research has been carried out in the Maghreb countries. In Tunisia, in particular, a series of studies was completed under the Ministry of Women but was never published. In general, Tunisia is distinguished by relatively high proportions of women working in the formal labour force, a large percentage in the factories established by multinationals. In spite of all constraints, this entry of women into the formal labour force has given some women a margin of economic independence. However, this economic role has not been translated into the political sphere be it in the unions or in the government. Likewise, women's legal rights in Tunisia are considerable, but women have not been able to take advantage of them in practice.

International support of funding during the Women's Decade 1975–1985 was considered essential in stimulating studies related to women in Syria. The speaker noted that his major concern had been with sociology, development issues and social structures and that his interest in research on women had begun through co-operation with the Arab League, including preparation of a sociological map of Arab women and a study on laws pertaining to women. Two M.A. theses had been prepared, on woman as a mother and as a teacher. The Syrian League of Women had likewise supported some studies which, although not academic, gave an indication of the situation of women. These studies concerned women and development and the impact of women working outside the home on the family.

The depth and quality of studies concerning women in society in Egypt compared to those in other parts of the Arab states region was noted. Over the last ten years there occurred a shift of emphasis from studies focusing on women in the family and on the law of personal status in isolation to studies dealing with women in the wider society, particularly the labouring classes. There is a data bank concerned with information on women in the Arab region and Egypt in particular, in the National Centre for Sociological and Criminological Studies. The existence of such a data bank in a national institution appeared unique in the countries where research was reviewed.

A number of studies had been undertaken on women's situation in Lebanon, but were not co-ordinated or adequately known. Published work on women and various aspects of law were discussed. The speaker stressed the isolation of researchers from each other and above all from the mass of women. The work of the internationally funded Institute for Women's Studies in the Arab World was noted.

The assessment of the status of research on women in Saudi Arabia required a fairly good acquaintance with such studies in order to categorize and evaluate them. Such studies are mostly found in PhD dissertations, where various areas of women's lives are studied. In addition, Saudi social scientists (women and men) as well as students majoring in the social sciences are conducting research on women's role and problems within the context of the socio-economic changes that have taken place in Saudi society. The women's voluntary associations are addressing themselves as well to integrating women within the national development programmes. It is important to mention in this context that Western conceptualization of women's roles in society and their participation in public life is found to be limited theoretically and inadequate methodologically when applied to the reality of Saudi women.

Some studies on women had been undertaken in Kuwait, but had so far been mainly impressionistic and descriptive. Further analytical work was therefore required. The speaker mentioned her research at the Department of Sociology, University of Kuwait on women's participation in the labour force, specifically on job mobility and promotion. She had looked at specific problems engendered by their dual roles of work within the family and outside it in the professional world. The question of what were considered suitable jobs for women was analysed through questionnaires to a sample of women and men. This revealed that women conformed to social expectations and considered teaching and secretarial jobs as the most suitable professions for them. Those considered most unsuitable were job situations where women and men interacted, such as, for example, business and sales work as well as engineering and architecture when this involved on-site activities. More in-depth studies were required to understand the problems faced by women and to help solve them.

The observer of the Jordanian Women's Federation noted a few studies carried out in university departments (mainly BA and MA theses). She laid emphasis upon the importance of studies concerning women's integration in development. The nature of legal and institutional structures governing development policies in Jordan and how they affect women was a subject of debate among observers from Jordan.

The PLO observer focused upon research prepared for a long series of Arab and international conferences. In the context of national liberation, the studies were seen as tools to change reality, and not as purely academic studies. Studies on Palestinian women supported by the Society of the Factories of the Children of Palestine Martyrs (SAMED), the United Nations Economic and Social Commission for Western Asia (ESCWA), and the Arab Thought Forum were also mentioned.

The observer from the Arab Lawyers' Union spoke of the establishment of a commission on women within the organization. This commission held a meeting in Cairo in February 1985. A study has been prepared on various aspects of women's legal status in Jordan and comparing this with other countries in the Arab states region. The Union plans to continue research in this area and is interested in co-operating with Unesco and other organizations in undertaking work in this field.

There were a number of points that were common to the different presentations:

1. Problematic of research

The importance of placing the study of any aspect of women's life within the wider social, political and economic context was stressed. The need to compare women's experience between classes and between regions and to assess critically the importance of economic changes on political participation of women was stressed. Although the same economic forces affect the Arab region as a whole, social and political formations reflect a particular historical legacy. Therefore, in spite of common economic forces, the situation of women differs markedly in different societies and countries.

The study of women has to take into account two levels of analysis: characteristics that are common to the Arab region and those that are particular to certain societies of the region. Thus, the experience of Arab women should be studied in the context of the particular social structure in which they live.

The *anthropologists and sociologists* in the gathering sought to deepen understanding through field research and comparative studies between countries and classes yet were clearly struggling to achieve some measure of autonomy for academic institutions and academic researchers in defining priorities of research. In addition to the statistical and descriptive work that had been produced, analytical studies were urgently required. Some of the sociologists had worked with international or government bodies and had reached different forms of accommodation with these sources of funding.

The *lawyers* were particularly concerned with documenting legal patterns, with disseminating the knowledge in a popularized form and with carrying out joint research with social scientists on legal institutions in practice and in society. Opinions differed as to whether the problem lay in the law being well ahead of practice in the guarantee of human rights or whether problems lay in the texts and institutions of law as well.

The *education activists* hoped that research would provide a tool for policy-makers or a tool for social movements seeking social change.

2. Research methodology

Studies so far had been mainly descriptive and needed to be made analytical, comprehensive and in-depth. Comparative research both within countries and in different countries on common themes was considered important. The need for multidisciplinary research was stressed by one speaker and the need to take into account the variable of gender when conducting social sciences research. It was considered necessary by participants to re-evaluate theoretical frameworks and concepts and develop alternative ones when necessary in order to understand women's situation within their societies.

Several participants mentioned quantities of unprocessed statistical data in university departments. Many sought to go beyond purely statistical measures and data (such as that gathered by state agencies) and to carry out detailed field projects. The categories according to which statistical data are gathered are problematic and produce misleading results.

3. Institutional framework for research

The institutional framework of research appeared the major obstacle to many of the speakers. Much of the research had been financed by international or foreign government funds. This direct expression of outside dependence was coupled with limited state funding and at the same time considerable demands on the part of policy-makers for research results serviceable for development as planned by the state. The difficult position of national academic institutions and those who work within them represented a brake upon sustained and integrated research. There were several sides to this problem: (i) constraints upon intellectual exchange in many areas arising from social and political structures; and (ii) the limited institutional autonomy of science (this was somewhat less true in Egypt and the Maghreb than in the Moshreg and the Arabian Peninsular); (iii) an absence of university support for research, as opposed to teaching.

In conclusion, it appears that multiple contrary demands were placed at the same time upon academic social scientists: to carry out primary research, to provide data for government directed research, and to popularize their findings to a wider society. These difficulties may be general to the academic social sciences but they appeared here in a particularly acute form.

In spite of these institutional problems, considerable research is being carried out. However, even when results are published, distribution is sporadic at best between Arab countries.

III. The process of the formalization and institutionalization of public life and how women have been able to participate therein and contribute to public policy at local and national levels

Laure Moghaizel introduced the discussions on this agenda item. She began by offering a broad definition of public and political life as the administration of a country's affairs, distinguishing between the formal and informal institutions of this administration. Of the formal institutions she mentioned the government and local government agencies – including judicial structures, public sector employment and the security apparatus as well as formal legislative and executive bodies; on the informal side she mentioned political parties, unions and other popular groupings.

With regard to women's participation in these institutions, she asked those present to focus upon the obstacles peculiar to women in their participation in these institutions and on whether the few women who were in positions of authority were in fact in any manner representative of women's interests at large or, in fact, merely hostages to the dominant power of men. Lastly, she asked participants to consider whether the allocation of places for women on legislative bodies, the establishment of separate ministries for women's affairs, or the entry of women into political parties represented an effective contribution to women's participation.

The interpenetration of the formal political and the less obvious but often more basic structures determining the political was stressed by several speakers. Thus, more traditional societies have to be examined as they exist on the ground and as they have changed over time and not in terms of a definition of the political sphere, suitable perhaps for Western parliamentary systems but without any descriptive or analytical value in the analysis of political phenomena in more traditional societies.

Several contributions addressed the link between women's work and political participation. It was suggested that the terms of analysis adopted must start from the global patterns of labour – both in the wage-labour sector and in the unwaged sector – and not overlook the way in which political structures rest upon the enormous economic contribution of women (and children). In some cases this would indicate great gaps between various forms of women's economic contribution and their weight in public leadership at many levels of society. The participants noted in this regard the danger of confusing women's entry into the wage-labour market with women's accession to any powers of decision-making: what was at issue was simply the provision of a cheap labour force. Equally, historical analysis of the changing division of labour between the sexes – particularly in the older centres of development such as Syria – was judged important where this could indicate how women moved into professions only as these professions became less socially and politically central.

Important problems in the existing legislation were noted by several speakers. Most Arab legal systems are of a plural nature – aspects of civil, labour and criminal law are in good part derived from European codes. Laws of personal status, by contrast, derive from religious laws on the whole, while national constitutions were often written in the wake of progressive movements of national liberation. The very text of these laws are, in two countries at least, in open contradiction with each other in the rights they give to women.

Building upon the remarks of Laure Moghaizel's presentation, several participants re-emphasized that the presence of a few women in positions of formal authority meant little or nothing concerning women's participation (or representation) in decision-making as a whole. Attention to the type of women who are in power and the type of laws which control accession of women to positions of power was again emphasized.

IV. Changing patterns of women's participation in the salaried labour force and their entry into professional life taking into account economic and social changes in the region

Soraya Altorki introduced this agenda item, noting that the concept and definition of work and notably women's work has been a subject of debate. Today's discussions were concerned with women's paid labour. Salaried labour was valued in society, and was a right that should be shared between women and men. There were a number of socio-economic factors, as well as ideological factors that affected how and in which types of work women participated in different countries. These included varying approaches and policies to development (e.g. favouring agriculture or an intensive industrialization policy, emphasis on the service sector). Labour migration, especially to oil-producing countries, likewise affected women's labour participation, pushing them at times in labour exporting countries to fill men's former work roles. What would happen to these women when men returned under the impact of the decline in oil prices? Paid labour for women should also lead to women's control of the output of their labour.

These points raised were further developed in the discussions that followed. One speaker observed that all labour was paid in one way or another (so-called 'paid and unpaid' work), whether in cash, kind, or in reciprocal services. It was just a question of the manner in which it was paid.

Women's move from labour within the home, in addition to work in salaried labour tended to follow certain patterns. Women were, for instance, more present in salaried agricultural labour and the services sector rather than in productive and decision-making jobs. The expansion of the service sector had in fact opened up various jobs for women, including teaching, nursing, secretarial jobs and, more recently, in medicine. However, women's opportunities for paid work remained limited to culturally acceptable areas.

Conflicts that may arise for working women between this role and their domestic responsibilities were discussed, as well as changes arising from the socialization of the young into new roles and new values (independence, co-operation and equality between the sexes).

V. The role of women's organizations and other voluntary and non-governmental organizations in encouraging women to involve themselves in public issues

Assessing the historical development of the movement

It was observed that the experience of each Arab country with regard to the women's organization movement could vary across the following dimensions:

(1) the length of existence;
(2) the major objectives;
(3) the historical context and motivation;
(4) the degree of association with women's needs;
(5) the degree of connection with the political and economic ideology of the country concerned;
(6) the question of autonomy versus control by governmental agencies; and
(7) the type of membership: coming from the grass roots or from the top.

Evaluation of its role

As to the subject of evaluation, a number of questions were suggested as a frame of reference. These are:

(1) To what extent did the women's organizations reach women on the grass roots level?
(2) To what extent have they integrated women into national programmes on development?
(3) To what extent have they created social networks for women that could be made effective in serving women's issues?
(4) To what extent have they affected public opinion favourably on women's issues?

Existing studies

Studies on women's voluntary organizations tend to be either superficial or critical of the main motivation for their existence in the first place.

Discussions

Participants proceeded, in presenting their evaluation, by first going over the historical development of the movement in some Arab countries. From this overview, a number of similarities were highlighted:

(1) Most of the women's organizations started with the intention of upgrading the socio-economic situation of needy women either through welfare aid or training in some skills.
(2) The thrust of the movement came as voluntary activities initiated from the top by a 'bourgeois' group of women.
(3) Most of the individual organizations are integrated into national feder-

ations in order to strengthen their objectives and resources (wih the exception of a few cases). Also, creating one pan-Arab federation of women's organizations is seen as a necessary goal to be achieved in a lasting form.

(4) Governmental support and control have been essential features or conditions for the existence of the women's organizations in most countries.

Exception

One exception of the proceeding pattern is the case of the Palestinian women's organizations. They were established as a grass root movement, with definite political objectives. These objectives turned over the years to concentrate around the matter of survival, touching therefore upon every aspect of daily needs.

Issues to be considered

The following issues were drawn from the discussions for further studies, evaluation and re-initiation of new programmes:

(1) The issue of financial support. Resources are scarce because of the increasing causes and needs which create growing competition over diminishing resources.

(2) The issue of training without: (a) guaranteeing a follow-up programme to ensure the effective use of such training, and (b) taking into consideration the suitability of such training to the social environment concerned.

(3) The issue of co-ordination between the women's organizations and other agencies concerned with programmes on development.

The call for a new type of association

From the preceding context it was seen of utmost significance to create an association for Arab women researchers concerned with research on women in the Arab world. This would permit continued communication between women specialists in the region and an exchange of research results.

VI. Discussions of priority themes for future study and elaboration of proposed research framework

Samraa Anbar Moustafa introduced the discussions on this agenda item. Participants were asked to give their suggestions on topics for possible future research. In addition, some details were worked out for a research project that could involve studies in several countries of the region.

A. Suggested topics for future research

Women and Work

Discussion called for study of the situation of women in the labour force analysed within the framework of recent social and political changes within the region. The studies should employ a comparative framework across regions and classes and should tie more in-depth research on specific cases to the general context of recent social and political change. The following aspects of this broad problem were stressed:

(1) Studies comparing the official statistics and the actual extent of women's participation in productive labour so as to expose the extensive under-registration of female labour, be it wage labour or non-wage labour.

(2) Studies analysing the problematic relationship between women's participation in the formal labour force and the exploitation or liberation of women.

(3) Historical analyses of the division of labour between the sexes and the effect of women's participation in the waged and salaried labour force upon that division of labour.

(4) Studies of the effect of wage labour on women's economic power within the domestic sphere.

(5) Study of the various factors determining women's entry and exit from different sectors of the paid labour force, including economic, legal, political, social and cultural factors, bearing in mind the problems of comparison across regions and across classes in a given society.

(6) Studies of the effects of investment by the multinational corporations on women's involvement in the salaried labour force.

(7) Studies of women's entry and participation in the labour force under adverse political conditions such as foreign occupation, war, etc. with a special case study of Palestinian women under occupation.

Women and Law

(1) Survey of legal texts that pertain to women's participation in public and political life and the contradictions between different sets of texts such as constitutions, laws of personal status and labour laws.

(2) Study of the mechanisms utilized in implementing laws that pertain to

women's participation in public and political life.

(3) Studies dealing with the migration of women for work, and especially low-income women, and the measure to which they have legal protection both in importing and exporting countries.

Women and Public Policy
(1) Studies to determine the actual content of policies to 'integrate women into development'.
(2) Development of a popular guide to women's legal and political rights written in simple language and comprising chapters prepared by lawyers and sociologists from different Arab countries.
(3) Studies on opportunities available to women in public administration.
(4) Studies to assess various strategies ensuring sufficient employment for women.
(5) Studies that identify problems and obstacles that limit the productivity of working women.
(6) Studies on the efficacy of training programmes and the educational system in enabling women to secure employment and achieve advancement.
(7) Studies that examine contradictions in expectations concerning child-bearing, child care and wage labour.
(8) Examination of public health policy, particularly as it relates to the control of female fertility taking into account the international dimensions.
(9) The study of official mass communications policies and programmes aimed at women, assessing the content of these programmes, the extent to which they disseminate accurate information on basic legal rights, as well as the study of the relationship between the messages transmitted and actual economic conditions.

Gender, Culture and Communication
(1) The relationship between informal networks created by women and the efficacy of these networks in influencing decision-making in formal structures or in women gaining actual power within them.
(2) Studies on the changing patterns of female mental illness and the ways in which it is expressed and treated.
(3) The problems women writers face before male domination of publication and the press.
(4) Study of the social backgrounds and personal profiles of the rare women who succeed to high positions of formal authority and decision-making.
(5) Study of the major currents of thought, especially the positions they adopt concerning women's participation in work and public life, and the relationship of these currents to changing economic conditions.
(6) The technology of communication and its social impact especially in terms of developing women's possibilities for social networks, communication and work.

(7) Traditional and changing sex roles and their impact upon women's participation in public life.

(8) The contradictions between ideal values and actual individual behaviour and between religious beliefs and actual practices.

Women's Organizations

(1) Studies on the history of women's organizations comparatively and within each region.

(2) The role of women's organizations in enabling women from different social strata of participate in public and 'political' life.

(3) The changing concept of the functions and aims of women's organizations.

Conceptual and Methodological Themes

During the discussions a number of conceptual and methodological problems were addressed. These could form research themes in their own right.

(1) Problems with statistical measures and survey methods: replacement of measures that necessarily exclude women from analysis.

(2) Comparative studies of what forms the political sphere in different societies and social groups.

(3) Problems in the definition of comparable social and economic units in studies of the region.

(4) The employment of non-traditional sources in the writing of social history on women such as oral history, letters, life histories, etc.

(5) Development of a framework for the analysis of women's labour. One such framework was presented which highlighted four main areas:

    (a) the definition of women's work
    (b) women in the labour force
    (c) distribution of women in various sectors of the economy
    (d) the effect of women's work on the relations of women and men.

B. *Proposed research topic on the changing pattern of the petroleum economy and the effect of that on women's participation in the labour force*

An important question that needs to be dealt with is: What are the periods that are considered an oil boom period or an oil recession period? Here, we can note that the 1970s will be considered the oil boom period and the 1980s will be considered the oil recession period, with 1985 presenting definite indications of that recession.

There must have been changes in the terminologies used before and after the boom period. Changes must also have occurred in the motivations of people toward education and toward work. The oil boom would not only instigate changes in various terminologies and the motivations toward

Appendix

Figure: Suggested research model*

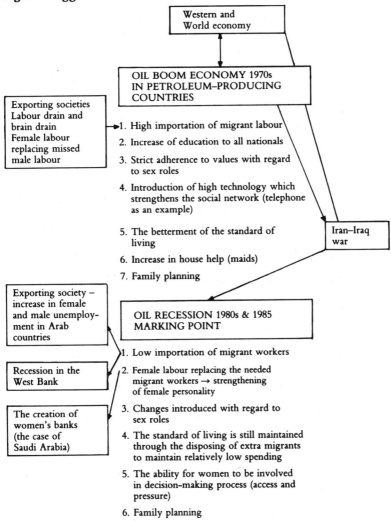

* presented by Samraa Anbar Moustafa

work, but it would introduce changes in the value system itself.

This topic was selected for discussion as it represented a specific illustration of the effects of rapid social and economic changes in the region, and their impact on changing patterns of women's participation in the salaried labour force. This means that in addition to the impact of oil, other significant socio-economic changes affecting specific countries and the region as a whole could be included in such a research project.

List of participants and observers

Participants

SORAYA ALTORKI, Department of Anthropology, American University in Cairo, EGYPT

SAMRAA ANBAR MOUSTAFA, Department of Sociology, University of Kuwait, KUWAIT

SIMA BAHOUS, Department of Journalism and Mass Communication, University of Yarmouk, Irbid, JORDAN

SOPHIE FERCHIOU, Centre de recherches économiques et sociales, Tunis, TUNISIA

LAYLA JABRI, Lawyer, Damascus, SYRIA

LAURE MOGHAIZEL, Lawyer, Beirut, LEBANON

SOHEIR MORSY, Anthropologist, Cairo, EGYPT

MARTHA MUNDY, Institute of Archaeology and Anthropology, University of Yarmouk, Irbid, JORDAN

FATINA SHAKER, Sociologist, SAUDI ARABIA

SETENEY SHAMI, Head, Department of Anthropology, Institute of Archaeology and Anthropology, University of Yarmouk, Irbid, JORDAN

KHADER ZAKARIA, Sociologist, Damascus, SYRIA

Observers

Arab Lawyers' Union: ASMA KHADR

International Federation of Business and Professional Women: NAELA RASHDAN and AIDA MUTLAQ (the latter also representing Jordan Women's Federation)

Journalist, Jordan: ZALIKHA ABU RISHEH

Ministry of Planning, Women's Department, Jordan: D. MANAWER KUNDI

Palestine Liberation Organization (PLO): ISSAM ABDEL-HADI, SUHA EID

Appendix

Representative of the Queen

MRS INA'AM MUFTI, Representative of Her Majesty Queen Noor and Director-General, Noor Al-Hussein Foundation

Yarmouk University

MOAWIYAH IBRAHIM, Director, Institute of Archaeology and Anthropology
MAJEED GHANMA, Director, Public Relations
AMAL HARAKEH, Centre for Jordanian Studies

Unesco

Sector of Social and Human Sciences: CARRIE MARIAS, ROSEMARY CASTELINO